MADE IN CHINA

JASPER BECKER

Made in China

*Wuhan, Covid and the Quest for
Biotech Supremacy*

HURST & COMPANY, LONDON

First published in the United Kingdom in 2021 by
C. Hurst & Co. (Publishers) Ltd.,
83 Torbay Road, London NW6 7DT
© Jasper Becker, 2021
All rights reserved.
Printed and bound in Great Britain by Bell & Bain Ltd, Glasgow

The right of Jasper Becker to be identified as the author of
this publication is asserted by him in accordance with the
Copyright, Designs and Patents Act, 1988.

Distributed in the United States, Canada and Latin
America by Oxford University Press, 198 Madison Avenue,
New York, NY 10016, United States of America

A Cataloguing-in-Publication data record for this book is
available from the British Library.

ISBN: 9781787384675

This book is printed using paper from registered
sustainable and managed sources.

www.hurstpublishers.com

CONTENTS

CONTENTS

1

INTRODUCTION

The pandemic began in Wuhan around mid-November 2019. Unusually large numbers of people began turning up at all the main hospitals, seeking help. They felt sick as if they had the usual winter flu—only it seemed worse. They couldn't breathe. They lost their sense of smell and taste. Rumours began to circulate that there was a new and dangerous disease spreading. A virus that is both new and lethal is a rare thing. When it was identified a few months later, people started to ask where it came from and why it started in Wuhan. This book attempts to answer those questions by looking at what happened during those first months in Wuhan in order to understand who might be responsible.

People in central China are used to getting a new winter bug each year. A new influenza virus strikes with predictable regularity in the autumn and it's usually gone sometime after Spring Festival, when the weather gets warmer. So for a lot of people to go to the trouble of seeking help was not necessarily a cause for alarm, but it was the first indication that something unusual was happening.

Winter flu viruses seem to emerge from the marshes of the Yangtze Valley with its many lakes and rice paddies as if its cold dank winter climate encourages fresh mutations every year. South of the Yangtze, houses and offices are traditionally built, without heating, and people put on their woollen underwear or padded cotton pants (sometimes both) and stay indoors more. This may also be a factor.

Much about influenza viruses remains a mystery, even though they have been studied for nearly a century. In China the family of influenza viruses only began to be seriously monitored and investigated after the year 2000. There is a lot still to be discovered. We don't really know much about what sort of influenza viruses circulated in the population of China before then, or how many people they killed each year, because no one ever kept any records.

It's much easier to grasp why the COVID-19 virus might spread quickly from Wuhan. The city is located at the crossroads of China, where the Han Jiang (Han River) enters the mighty Yangtze. From Wuhan you can head upstream to Sichuan and the mountains of Tibet, or downstream to Nanjing and Shanghai. Or you can travel north up the Han River.

China is very mountainous, so it has always been easier to move goods and people from east to west along these rivers. The Ming Dynasty built an extraordinary canal (the Grand Canal) to take goods from the Yangtze Delta north to supply its capital, Beijing, and the troops manning the Great Wall. The railways made the canal redundant, and the trains heading north from Canton (now Guangzhou) terminated in Wuhan. The trains from Beijing going south, too, terminated in Wuhan. And so did the new lines running west from Shanghai and Nanjing.

A lot of people had to change trains or steamships in Wuhan, but there was nothing much to keep anyone. No charming temples, hutongs or palaces, nor shopping boulevards. Just a few warehouses and Western buildings dating from its days as a Treaty Port. It was prosperous enough, and a grand university campus had been established. All Wuhan's hospitals were built, often by foreign missionaries, with funds raised by charity donations.

When I visited it in the late 1980s, Wuhan was struggling to find a new role after the delinquencies of the Mao era. It struck me as such a dismal place that I vowed never to return. For one thing, it is unbearably hot and humid in the summer—it is one of the so-called Three Furnaces of China—and in those days no one had air conditioning. For another, it does not really have a centre or a soul. It is actually three distinct towns separated by the two wide rivers. Mao Zedong had tried to empty all the main cities and disperse the urban population to the countryside, and by the early 1960s, the state had lost interest in investing in the infrastructure of cities. In Wuhan this meant that there weren't nearly enough bridges, so I spent most of my trip stuck in traffic jams just trying to get from one meeting to another.

At that time, the three parts of the city probably did not have more than a combined population of two million. Wuhan is now described as a mighty metropolis of eight million, and sometimes is even said to have eleven million, but this gives a misleading picture. Urban residents used to be described as anyone who got state rations. These days China's modern urban planning policy tries to prevent the key cities from growing into sprawling third-world mega cities, so instead, the fast-growing new urban population is being housed in lots of small satellite cities. So what used to be rural towns has been re-designated as part of the Wuhan metropolitan area, and this is where most of the new housing is built. And it's all clusters of high-rise blocks for the masses and villa compounds for the new rich.

Almost all the residents work in the many new industrial and science parks that have been built around Wuhan. To make up for the lost years when China was preparing to survive a nuclear war, it had now lavished vast sums on new infrastructure to tie all these scattered towns and industrial parks together with new bridges, high-speed railways, airports, harbours, motorways and light railway metro systems. Everything has the shiny new look of something that has just been unwrapped.

Wuhan is not only a commercial-industrial centre, but also a defence and aerospace hub. It is home to 350 research centres and industrial institutes, as well as 1,700 companies working in the aerospace, shipbuilding and biotechnology sectors. It is here where satellites, missiles and space launchers are built.

In the 1980s, Deng Xiaoping's price reforms had benefited the rural areas first. The peasants got rich selling their extra produce. For the first time in decades, they were allowed to move outside their villages without permits, if only to take their goods to sell in newly re-opened markets in the cities. Even then, they were stopped and inspected at the city boundaries as they transported their chickens or vegetables on donkey carts and bicycles. It was the first step in a gradual process by which travel became normalised.

For decades, free travel had been impossible in China, but by the time the Wuhan virus appeared, China was a nation of enthusiastic travellers and tourists. Indeed, the Chinese are the biggest single group of international travellers. Added to this, hundreds of millions travel regularly inside the country for work or pleasure. Not content with being restricted to public transport, the Chinese have been buying cars in vast numbers. China is the world's biggest car market.

The ease and frequency of travel inside and outside the country—and Wuhan was once again becoming a major transport hub—meant that any infectious disease originating in Wuhan was able easily to spread across China or across the globe in a way that had been impossible twenty years before. This added a new dimension to China's health challenges.

In the past, China pushed public sanitation and clean water. It targeted the vectors of certain diseases by trying to wipe out pests such as rats, flies, mosquitoes and snails. There were mass vaccination campaigns against smallpox and other diseases. Public information campaigns urged people to boil their water, to stop spitting on the street, and to stop smoking. By 2000, China was largely free of the plague, smallpox, cholera, polio, typhoid and paratyphoid, which had brought misery for thousands of years. The exceptions were influenza and pneumonia. The top priority of health experts both abroad and in China was to prevent a repeat of the 1918 Spanish flu pandemic, which had killed between 50 and 100 million people around the world. The virus had appeared out of nowhere in 1918 and then mysteriously disappeared several years later. Many of its victims did not die directly of the flu virus, but of secondary infections such as pneumonia caused by bacteria. These can now be defeated with antibiotics.

Flu pandemics were a big threat. The 1957 Asian flu, which caused 1 to 4 million deaths worldwide, was first reported in Hong Kong. The 1968 pandemic, also called the Hong Kong flu, was only a little less severe. Another pandemic, in 1977, may also have come out of China. We deal with this later in the text. More recently, there have been other scares from bird flu, swine flu and SARS. Most of these are now thought to have started in mainland China, though no one is very sure why or how. It might be connected to the fact that people in China and South East Asia live in close proximity to each other, as well as with pigs, chickens and ducks. This situation means a virus that has mutated has plenty of opportunities to move to a new host.

Preventing and preparing for another deadly flu virus became a top priority for Western governments. Enormous efforts go into monitoring the annual flu outbreaks around the world, preparing and delivering flu vaccines and stocking up on all kinds of supplies in case disaster should strike again.

China began to cooperate with the World Health Organisation (WHO) around 2000, which brought it into the worldwide monitoring and tracking system. Its experts advised it on how to set up monitoring and warning systems. Beijing drew up a new plan to set up a nationwide network of laboratories to test for and to investigate infectious diseases, especially influenza. The Wuhan Institute of Virology was chosen to be the first top biosecurity lab in the country equipped to deal with highly contagious microbes. Inevitably, many believe that there is a connection between its presence in Wuhan and the mysterious outbreak of COVID-19, but there are quite a few other laboratories and biotech factories in Wuhan that deal with microbes.

A turning point came after 2002 when the first SARS virus appeared. It is also a coronavirus and quite different from the influenza virus. Its sudden emergence and disappearance took everyone by surprise, because it was able to spread rapidly across China and the outside world. Many feared it could be as deadly as the HIV/Aids virus, the cause of another major twentieth-century pandemic. It was a shocking reminder of how quickly a new deadly virus could spread around the globe, and how powerless governments could be if it wasn't quickly contained.

The new strains of winter flu that appear each year in China are quite exceptionally nasty. They hit me every one of the eighteen years that I lived in Beijing. Each year it was different. Sometimes, a dry hacking cough that didn't go away for months. Other years, a thick greenish phlegm that had to be constantly coughed up from deep within the lungs. Other times it was high fevers, a running nose or fatigue. After moving back to England, I barely had one bad winter flu in ten years.

Beijing is not far from the Gobi Desert, and there was a commonly held notion that the soft dust which filters through all windows and doors, clogging people's lungs, carries the infections. If so, it was understandable that there was no way to protect oneself, yet many people still tried, by wearing face masks. Under Mao, the state deliberately built factories and coal-fired power stations in the middle of big cities such as Beijing. Many people also heated their homes with little stoves using coal briquettes. The result was a level of air pollution that was Dickensian. The smog was sometimes so thick that for weeks on end it was hard to see from one end of my street to the other.

After the turn of the century, the state started relocating the factories to the small towns in the countryside or to industrial parks. Natural gas replaced coal. But cars, trucks and buses became a new source of smog as so many more people and goods were being moved around. A study published in the *Lancet* by Tulane University in 2018 reports that the Chinese, above all urban male Chinese who tend to smoke, suffer from more chronic obstructive pulmonary lung disease—100 million adults—and more lung cancer and tuberculosis than almost anyone else in the world (though India is becoming a close rival). For the sufferer, and probably quite a few doctors, many of the symptoms of the severe winter flus are not so different from various lung diseases. A cough and a fever could mean anything. It is safe to assume that for long periods no one in China was able to work out the incidence and death rate from winter flus. There was little testing, and few reliable records were kept.[1]

Against this background, it is not surprising that with a new coronavirus, such as SARS or COVID-19, with symptoms like a winter flu or a lung disease, many incidences would easily be overlooked. Indeed, it might mean that such a new virus could be circulating for a long time without anyone noticing or trying to investigate, at least until it affected the strata of society that have access to large urban hospitals.

It must be remembered that only a small part of the Chinese population—such as Communist Party members and those directly employed by the state or in state-owned factories—benefit from a reasonable level of health care insurance with easy access to doctors and hospitals. Everyone else has to pay out of their own pocket. Covering the medical bills of a sick person is often a crippling burden, and can lead to debt or bankruptcy. Many opt for traditional Chinese medical doctors or local quacks.

Another factor to consider is the change in diet that came with the rise of Chinese living standards. In the 1980s few people in China ate meat as a regular part of their diet. Peasants were allowed to keep a few chickens, maybe a pig or two, in their front yard, or they could graze a cow or a few sheep on rough ground. Thirty years later, the Chinese are eating a lot of meat, and much of it comes from animals reared using intensive factory farming methods. Consequently, vast numbers of pigs, chickens, ducks and cows are being raised in closely packed sheds and treated with all kinds of antibiotics, the sort of circumstances that raise the risk of epidemics and viruses crossing over from animals to humans and causing epidemics. By 2019, China was home to half the world's 800 million pigs. With 5 billion chickens, China has far more than any other country in the world. This may be the reason why many new strains of influenza viruses infecting poultry, swine and other mammals originate in China. Hundreds of millions of pigs and birds have been culled for fear that these viruses could mutate and start a new pandemic.

Viruses have been around for billions of years and are extraordinarily numerous, but only a handful of entirely new viruses that threaten humans have been found in modern times. So, to understand where COVID-19 comes from, it is vital to pinpoint when it started.

One of the new early warning tools for diseases that have become popular with the WHO and its experts is the data collected from internet searches or from satellite imagery. It is a quick and cheap way to learn what is going on. So naturally, after the COVID-19 virus struck, some people began trying to trace its origin by looking at satellite imagery of hospital parking lots, as well as at internet searches. A rise in the number of searches for cough, fever or diarrhoea is an extremely useful early warning sign.

A group of researchers at Harvard University studied data from the Chinese Baidu internet search engine for key words, as well as satellite images of the parking spaces occupied in the main hospitals, and compared what was happening in 2019 to the same period in 2018. There is a slight uptick in October 2019, which gets stronger in early November and December and rises steeply in January 2020. This may indicate that a new virus was circulating in October.

A report that the American television news networks obtained in May 2020, from undisclosed private experts, claims there was no mobile phone activity in a high-security part of the Wuhan Institute of Virology between 7 and 24 October, but that hitherto there had been consistent use of mobile phones. Analysis of mobile phone data from the area surrounding the institute also suggested that roadblocks were in place between 14 and 19 October. The twenty-four-page report suggested that this 'supports the release of COVID-19 at the Wuhan Institute of Virology'. This report was subsequently investigated by American intelligence agencies, but nothing has been made public to confirm or reject this story.

Wuhan hosted the Military World Games between 18 and 27 October, a sports festival attended by 10,000 athletes from over 100 countries. It kicked off with an impressive light show and torch procession. The various sports competitions took place at venues all around Wuhan. The Chinese orienteering team was accused of cheating.

On returning home many athletes, including some from France, reported falling ill with a flu-like virus. It is possible that they just came down with an unfamiliar Chinese winter flu: since no testing was done, it is not clear if they had the COVID-19 virus. Nearly 300 members of the US military attended, and news reports later claimed that COVID-19 cases at military bases were linked to those who had returned from Wuhan. The US team used chartered flights that stopped at Seattle, where some of the earliest cases appeared.

The Chinese Foreign Ministry spokesman Zhao Lijian released a tweet suggesting that it could have been the Americans who brought the virus to Wuhan. 'It might be U.S. Army who brought the epidemic to Wuhan. Be transparent. Make public your data. The U.S. owes us an explanation', he said. 'Certain media say this coronavirus is the China virus. This is extremely irresponsible, and we firmly oppose that. We are still tracing the origin of the virus and there is no conclusion yet.'

If the virus was spread around the world by those returning from this sports event, then it would make sense that in late November or early December some countries would have begun noticing cases. A French patient attending a hospital in Paris was likely infected in mid-December. The virus may have been in Italy around the same time. A study done by Italy's Higher Health Institute (ISS) examined forty sewage samples collected from water treatment plants in northern Italy between October and February.[2] Waters of two of the largest cities in the hard-hit northern regions—Milan and Turin—contained genetic traces of the virus on 18 December, but samples from October and November were negative. Waters from the city of Bologna—in the northern Emilia Romagna region—started showing traces of the coronavirus in late January. Italian researchers suspect that a higher than usual number of cases of severe pneumonia and influenza in Lombardy in the last quarter of 2019 shows that the virus arrived earlier than previously thought.

Italy may have seeded the European outbreak, because there are over 300,000 ethnic Chinese living in Italy, many of whom live in Milan and other towns in Lombardy. The Chinese workforce naturally travels backwards and forwards, especially over Christmas and then Chinese New Year in February.

The outbreaks in the United States may have been seeded both by travellers arriving from Europe or from China. The US first identified cases among travellers who had flown to Seattle from Wuhan on 15 January, but some others have reported having the symptoms as early as December.

A picture emerges of the virus appearing in early October or possibly even September. A team of researchers at the University of Cambridge tried to trace the source of the virus by mapping its genetic history and identifying the first person infected. Geneticist Dr Peter Forster and his team also concluded that it probably emerged at some point between 13 September and 7 December.

In the state-run media account, made public five months later, fifty-four-year-old Dr Zhang Jixian, head of the respiratory department at Hubei Provincial Hospital, reported the existence of a novel coronavirus to health officials in China on 27 December. In her account, it started when an elderly couple living near the hospital went to see her complaining of a cough and a high temperature. She ordered CT scans and found their lungs showing signs similar to those she had seen while working during the 2002/3 SARS outbreak. Investigating the state of their son's lungs, she grew alarmed. She reported everything to the head of the hospital, who passed it on to the local centre for disease control. She also cordoned off an area in the department's ward to hospitalize four patients. More patients were brought in, and she set up a nine-bed isolation ward.

In another version of events, it was Ai Fen, the director of the emergency department (the walk-in A & E department) of the same hospital who first came across the disease. On 18 December 2019, Ai met a porter from the fishmonger's market whose lung scan showed 'multiple patchy blurry shadows scattered in lungs'. On 27 December, a second patient walked in with similar symptoms and was ordered to have a scan. On the afternoon of

30 December, the test results of the second patient showed infection with a coronavirus. Ai Fen reported this to Dr Zhang. She also took an image of the report, circled the word 'SARS' and forwarded it to a doctor at another hospital. Soon it reached Li Wenliang, an ophthalmologist at the Wuhan General Hospital, who immediately forwarded it to his WeChat friends and colleagues, warning them of a SARS type virus. From then on news spread quickly on WeChat.

It made sense that Ai Fen, the head of the walk-in emergency department, would have been the first to have found out about the disease, and would have ordered the scans in the first place. But it is also possible that people infected with the virus might have been turning up at hospitals from October onwards and no doctor thought their symptoms were suspicious enough to order further investigations.

It is noteworthy that neither Ai Fen nor Li Wenliang were really acting as whistleblowers attempting to warn the public in defiance of the authorities. They were merely warning their fellow doctors, presumably out of concern for their colleagues' wellbeing. However, they may have known that they were breaching the stringent post-SARS epidemic regulations on disease control, which forbade 'spreading rumours'.

On 31 December, the Wuhan Central Hospital reprimanded Ai Fen for spreading rumours. On 1 January 2020, an official at the Hubei Provincial Health Commission ordered at least one private genomics testing company to cease testing samples of a SARS-like virus from Wuhan and to destroy all existing samples of the virus. A Guangzhou-based genomics company sequenced most of the virus. Soon other genome companies came to the same conclusion

A few days later, the Wuhan police (called the Public Security Bureau in China) detained Li Wenliang and seven other doctors and forced them to sign a letter confessing they had made 'false statements' which 'severely disturbed social order'. On the same day, the National Health Commission ordered all research institutes to stop publishing any information on the new virus, and to destroy existing samples of the virus or transfer them to approved testing sites.

The Chinese authorities first publicly confirmed the existence of COVID-19 on 9 January 2020, and two days later notified the WHO of an outbreak of a suspicious virus. By 12 January, China shared the genetic sequence of a new coronavirus with the outside world.

Two things stand out from these accounts. It took nearly half a year for China's official media to release their version of events, which centres on the main state-run hospital in Wuhan. This suggests that China has not made bigger efforts to find the source of the outbreak by tracing back all those with whom the original patients had been in contact. The original story reported by the Chinese, and which was repeated by Western experts, claimed that the outbreak came from people who had contact with animals such as bats or pangolins kept at the Huanan fishmonger hall, but this theory was later abandoned.

Another possibility is that the authorities have done more tracing work but, for unknown reasons, have not released the results of these investigations. One Hong Kong paper, the *South China Morning Post*, reported in March seeing internal documents which said that China identified the first COVID-19 case as a man in Hubei Province (i.e. somewhere near Wuhan) on 17 November, and that after that about one to five new cases were reported every day until, by 15 December, the number of total infections reached twenty-seven. Some of the cases were likely backdated after health authorities had tested specimens taken from suspected patients.[3]

So now that we know when the pandemic started, it is time to look where the new virus might have come from and why it appeared in Wuhan of all places. To understand it better, we must start with the history of plagues in China.

2

BUBONIC PLAGUE

The bubonic plague—the black death—is perhaps the most dev-astating human disease of all time, and it was in China that the bacillus that causes it was first identified. In 1894, it was spreading through southern China like wildfire. The epidemic broke out in Guangzhou (Canton) in March 1894, and within a few weeks the bacillus had killed 80,000.

At the British colony of Hong Kong, panic was rising. From Canton people set out for Hong Kong on river boats, trying to outrun the plague. The authorities summoned James Lowson, a twenty-eight-year-old Scottish doctor, who arrived in May to take charge, but it was too late. The disease had preceded him and was spreading rapidly. The hospital and the governor had been too slow to stop boats reaching Hong Kong and Kowloon. The authorities belatedly started house-to-house searches, disinfected buildings, burned corpses and isolated suspected cases on a quarantine ship. By October 1894, the plague in Hong Kong had killed more than 6,000 people. A third of the population fled Hong Kong. After that outbreak the plague occurred in Hong Kong almost every year, and in the twentieth century took more than 20,000 lives.

At the time no one knew what caused the plague or how it spread. For many years, European doctors thought it was bad air, also called *mal aria* or *miasma*. They believed it was inhaled through the nose, so doctors wore beaky masks stuffed with herbs to protect themselves. By 1894, everyone knew that small-pox, another deadly disease, was preventable. Back in 1801, Edward Jenner had discovered that milkmaids, once infected by cowpox, acquired immunity. He went on to trial and launch a method of inoculation that was adopted around the world. Even so, it would be a long time in the future before the variolas virus that causes smallpox was identified, and indeed even in 1894 no one knew that there was such a thing as a virus, as they are too small to be seen with a conventional microscope.

By the time the plague had arrived in Hong Kong, the idea that animals could be the host of dangerous diseases was becoming a popular concept. In 1882, the German microbiologist Robert Koch was the first to prove that the cause of an infectious disease was a microorganism. He identified bovine TB, *Mycobacterium bovis*, a respiratory disease in cattle and other animals such as badgers, and showed that it was also a threat to humans. The bacteria can be transmitted to humans even if they have no direct contact with a sick animal—for example by drinking milk or consuming other dairy products. The French scientist Louis Pasteur discovered that heating milk rendered it safe. By 1925, what became known as the pasteurization of milk was accepted as a reliable method of preventing the spread of the disease.

Koch would also go on to discover the bacillus that causes cholera. Around this time, there were many ambitious scientists eager to become the first to identify a new microbe that caused dangerous diseases. So when news of the plague epidemic spread, the microbe hunter Baron Kitasato Shibasaburō, who had studied in Berlin with Robert Koch, left Japan and in June 1894 arrived in Hong Kong. Hard on his heels was Alexandre Yersin, a young Franco-Swiss scientist who had studied with both Pasteur and Koch, and who arrived from French Indochina.

The older Japanese scientist had already won scientific glory by discovering the role of *Clostridium tetani*, the bacterium that causes tetanus, then better known as lockjaw. Kitasato almost immediately looked and found a bacillus growing in the body of those who had died from the plague. He inoculated a mouse and, at autopsy, found a bacillus similar to that seen in the blood of another patient. Lowson was certain that Kitasato had discovered the plague bacillus. On 15 June he wired the *Lancet*.

However, while the celebrated Japanese scientist grew his bacteria in an incubator at 37 C, Yersin cultured his samples at room temperature on a bench top in a straw hut. We now know that the plague bacillus grows best at 30 C, the mean temperature of June in Hong Kong. At 37 C other bacteria take over and contaminate the sample. In Kitasato's case he had mistakenly identified bacteria responsible for pneumonia, not plague.

Yersin had not been given access to the cadavers of plague victims. He tried examining the blood of some patients and then bribed two English sailors in order to get into the morgue. There, he stuck a pipette into the swollen lymph node of a fresh corpse and then examined the results under a microscope. He could see the bacilli and injected them into some mice and guinea pigs. The animals quickly died, and he was able to observe the same bacilli in their lymph nodes. Yersin named the bacillus *Pasteurella pestis*, after his mentor, Louis Pasteur, but, as he was ultimately credited with being the first to link the bacillus to the plague, it was named in his honour—*Yersinia pestis*.

The outbreak of the plague in Canton and Hong Kong is part of the third great plague pandemic. The first started around 541 CE in the Byzantine Empire. Known as the Plague of Justinian, it may have killed half of Europe's population. The second, the

Black Death, started in 1346 and carried off a third of the population of Europe. The third pandemic was truly global, as it reached every corner of the world. Ships from Hong Kong brought it to India where, some say, 10 million perished.

The plague is a terrifying disease. It kills 40 to 80 per cent of victims within about seven days. Pneumonic plague spreads like wildfire because it is transmitted directly from person to person via coughs and sneezes. The mortality rate is 100 per cent and death comes quickly, in one to three days. The third and rarest form is septicemic plague, which occurs if the bacillus enters the bloodstream. It is so deadly that the victim can die even before symptoms appear.

Once *Yersinia pestis* was identified it took only a few more years to develop a successful vaccination. As it is a bacterium, not a virus, scientists would later be able to treat it with antibiotics. Yet despite the new work of Yersin and Kitasato, governments around the world struggled to contain the pandemic. As they did, however, they created a methodology that is still deployed today.

The legacy on the mentality of government officials and the public is so substantial that it is worth unravelling in order to understand how China reacted to the COVID-19 virus in 2019:

1. A pre-occupation with zoonotic transmission.
2. State eradication campaigns against animal hosts.
3. The invention of cloth face masks.
4. Severe and compulsory quarantining and isolation policies enforced by the police.
5. Multi-national cross-border task forces and legislation.
6. The formation of a central health and epidemic prevention organization.
7. China considered a breeding ground of epidemics.
8. Highly secret state biological (and counter biological warfare programmes) in Japan, the USSR and China using *Yersinia pestis*.

9. The actual use of bioweapons by the Japanese against Chinese civilians in wartime.
10. The alleged use of bioweapons by the United States against China during the Korean War.

The first consequence of the third plague is that China gained a reputation as the origin locus of the plague and other diseases. In the case of *Yersinia pestis*, we are now sure that this is true, that it originated in China, or rather the steppe lands of central Asia, around 3,000 years ago.

The next discovery about the plague came about after an outbreak in Manchuria. This may have been a separate outbreak from the third pandemic. Russian (and French) researchers travelling in Mongolia around 1895 began to suspect that fur trappers and herdsmen had caught it by eating marmots, which the Mongols call *tarbagan* or *tarabagan*. These large rodents live in burrows on the grassland and are shot for their fur. They are curious animals and easy to shoot: a hunter waving a stick with feathers and fur will cause them to pop out of their burrows to take a look. Their flesh makes for a tasty meal. Hot stones are stuffed in the gutted animal and the skin is tied. It is left to cook until it is done. When I tasted it in Mongolia, it had been cooked as a stew and had a dark, chewy, gamey taste.

Then in 1910 there was a serious plague outbreak in Manchuria, the homeland of the Manchu Emperors (the Qing Dynasty). The Court asked Wu Liande (Wu Lien-teh in the earlier spelling system), born in Penang, a Cambridge graduate who had also studied at the Pasteur Institute, to take charge. He brought the outbreak under control with measures that were little short of martial law and achieved success within four months. He quickly organised disease population surveys and put whole towns under lockdown. Those suspected of being sick were immediately brought to a hospital and isolated. The dead were no longer allowed to be buried (in fact the ground was frozen too hard) but had to be cremated immediately, along with their clothes and bedding, a change in Chinese custom for which he sought permission from the Forbidden City.

The disease spread along the railway line, but Wu used his authority to stop both people and trains from moving. He was the first to design and promote the wearing of masks made of layers of gauze and cotton. These were thicker than those used in the West, where their use was generally confined to surgeons. As the disease was pneumonic, the masks sharply cut the fatality rate. According to Dr Christos Lynteris, a medical anthropologist at the University of St Andrews, there was a famous incident when Dr Wu was challenged by a French doctor, Gérald Mesny, who was a famous old hand in the region. Wu explained his belief that the plague was pneumonic and airborne, but the French doctor put him down, saying 'What can we expect from a Chinaman?' To show he was right, he went to attend the sick at a plague hospital without wearing Wu's mask, and two days later was dead from the plague.[1]

As the mask was so effective, it left a great impression on the public. Masks became popular all over China, Hong Kong, Taiwan, Japan and South Korea. People began wearing face masks whenever there was a threat of an epidemic. It was also the cheapest and simplest measure that any government could take. Further, the Chinese now began to embrace the notion that a centralised authority with sweeping powers of compulsion should be empowered with the task of eradicating not just the plague but other diseases such as smallpox, diphtheria, typhoid, malaria and so on.

In the year following the containment of the outbreak, Dr Wu helped convene the First International Plague Conference to debate the epidemiological and public health aspects of the disease. The historic event was attended by scientists from the United States of America, the United Kingdom, France,

Germany, Italy, Austria-Hungary, the Netherlands, Russia, Mexico and China. It lasted over three weeks and featured various demonstrations and experiments. At the conference, the Russian scientists Danylo Zabolotny and Anna Tchourilinia announced that they had traced the initial cause of the outbreak to hunters who had contracted the disease from marmots.

Wu raised the question of why traditional marmot hunters had not experienced deadly epidemics before. It is likely that Mongol hunters killed, skinned and ate the animals. The Chinese immigrants, mostly from Shandong, who poured into Manchuria when the empire finally permitted Han Chinese to migrate there, around 1910, captured the marmots to sell as exotic delicacies in wet markets. That meant they had been around live marmots for much longer.

After the conference Dr Wu set up the North Manchurian Plague Prevention Service, which continued operating until 1931. Another plague outbreak struck in 1920 and again in 1928, but the death toll in each case was lower. As scientists continued studying the marmot, they suspected that, even though the marmot might be a reservoir of the bacteria, it was actually the fleas living in the marmot's fur that spread the plague. The fleas fed off its blood and they became active when the animals emerged out of hibernation in the spring.

Much later it became clear that fleas too are harmed by the bacterial infection. The midgut and the proventriculus—a valve-like area that keeps ingested mammalian blood from escaping—gets blocked by the microbe. The flea starts to bite more aggressively in order to feed itself and this hastens the spread of the bacteria. Eventually the rodent will die, so the flea tries to jump to another host, such as a human, whom they will bite. They live in clothing, especially the furs and skins worn by people in Manchuria. They can also jump onto rats, gerbils and other animals, especially after the marmots are dead.

The next step was for the state to take on the responsibility of eradicating marmots, rats, gerbils and any other 'vermin' that may house the fleas. The plague reached San Francisco in 1900, and suspicion fell on the residents of Chinatown, which consequently was put under quarantine. Eventually, and after some hesitation, the city set about disinfecting every street, beginning with Chinatown. Earthen basements were concreted, concrete ones flooded with carbolic acid, walls washed with lye, streets asphalted, cesspools filled in and decrepit dwellings demolished. The city organised a ferocious rat eradication campaign. After the 1906 San Francisco earthquake the state mobilised an army of rat catchers who killed as many as 13,000 rats a week. After corpses were autopsied, it was found that around 1.5 per cent were infected. Another, similar, rat eradication campaign was launched in Los Angeles in 1924, but by this time it was discovered that squirrels and other animals could host the fleas and help infect humans. They too began to be hunted down.

Around the world governments took similar measures, none more so than Russia after 1917 when the new Communist regime took power. In the late 1920s, Moscow started extermination campaigns against the marmots. The Soviet anti-plague programme was extremely ambitious. It mobilised tens of thousands of people. They put poison outside the marmot burrows and also targeted other rodents such as gerbils, which were gassed, snared or shot. The civilian population was also ordered to plough over burrows and to set grasslands on fire. Later, the state used aeroplanes to spray vast areas with DDT. The programme seemed to work, at least according to Soviet data, which showed that the incidents of plague had dwindled away to nothing by 1942.

Historians looking back at European history now think that the great plague of Justinian and the Black Death must have originated in China, or at least the central Asian steppes. It was perhaps brought from the East by nomadic horsemen, such as Huns or Mongols, to the Black Sea and from there spread by rats carried on ships.

Yet this theory does have some holes in it. The fleas that live on marmots are not the same as those that flourish on humans. Nor are all rats and rodents natural reservoirs of the bacillus. Plus, the theory doesn't quite explain why a disease like the plague can suddenly disappear and then re-emerge decades or even many centuries later.

In the 1950s, for example, the grassland rodents returned in the USSR and there were fresh outbreaks of the plague. The Soviet Union hid these outbreaks from the World Health Organisation in breach of its obligations and insisted that the plague had been wiped out. Eventually, the Soviets gave up the eradication programmes and instead concentrated on managing the rodent population and doing further research.

While the plague pandemic left a huge imprint on the Chinese consciousness, the Spanish flu pandemic of 1918 left almost no impression. It killed 50 or even 100 million people around the world, yet the outbreaks in China seemed to have been minor. Perhaps the deaths were not recorded properly, but in cities like Shanghai, where official records were certainly kept, the death rates were low. The mortality rate was around 1.9 per cent for those infected, compared to 9 per cent in San Francisco. In Hong Kong, only a few hundred deaths were attributed to the flu.

To some, this is evidence that the virus originated in China, and the Chinese therefore had developed some immunity to it. The Chinese Labour Corps might have then brought it to America and France. These were 94,000 Chinese labourers recruited in northern China during the latter part of the war, to help dig trenches and perform other kinds of tasks. They were brought by ship to Vancouver and then travelled by train across Canada to Halifax, from where they were shipped across the

Atlantic to ports in England and France. So that might explain how the disease arrived in America and spread to troops arriving in the same ports.

At the time, people thought that the Chinese didn't get the flu because they treated themselves with traditional Chinese medicine remedies. In Hebei province, the local government recommended that villagers drink a soup prepared with powdered mung bean and rock sugar several times a day.

It is certainly interesting—as this book will describe in more detail later—that the same disease can be observed to affect different countries and ethnic groups in different ways.

Meanwhile in China, the Republican government and the various humanitarian and missionary societies, often funded by Westerners, worked hard to build on Dr Wu's pioneering efforts. In 1919, the new Republican government set up a National Epidemic Prevention Bureau. Its task was to develop vaccines and sera against smallpox, the plague and other infectious diseases. It gathered epidemiological data, started vaccinations (at least in the big cities), and supported microbiological research. It also tried to produce vaccines against anthrax in cattle and sheep as well as rinderpest. The Bureau's staff travelled around villages explaining how people can catch diseases from sick animals. The staff worked hard to train nurses and doctors and to create a public health system to combat smallpox, tuberculosis, typhoid, tetanus, scarlet fever, diphtheria, cholera etc.

The Nationalist government exerted very little real authority over most areas of China, since this was the era of the warlords. In 1931, the Japanese seized Manchuria from one of these warlords and then tried to conquer or subdue the whole of China. The fighting between warlords and the Anti-Japanese War meant that huge numbers of poorly equipped and badly supplied soldiers moved around the country and confiscated the peasants' food supplies. Millions had to flee their homes in search of safety and food. Then at one stage, the Nationalist government tried to stop the Japanese by breaching the Yellow River dikes and flooding a huge area. All these events triggered numerous outbreaks of many infectious diseases.

To counter the epidemics, the KMT government, when and where it could, ordered the police, soldiers and neighbourhood or clan associations to force people to comply with campaigns for everything from street cleaning to vaccination programmes. These 'medical police' could and did impose *cordons sanitaires*, isolate the sick and, in some cases, march into people's homes and seize their property.

The evident ability of Western medicine to defeat perennial diseases in China persuaded some people of its superiority over traditional Chinese medicine. It was a new way of understanding things, pitting modernity against tradition, science against superstition.

These days, visitors to Beijing or any major Chinese city will struggle to find the Temple to the Five Plague Gods, even though there used to be one in every city. In Taiwan there are still hundreds of them. The Taoist or folk tradition held that the Ministry sent plagues and pestilence as a punishment for the misdeeds of humanity. On the fifth day of the fifth month, the whole community performed a ceremony to apologise with prayers and offerings.

In typical Chinese fashion, the plague gods were not envisaged as the terrifying hooded apocalyptic horsemen, but as members of a divine bureaucracy. They were painted as dressed in the robes of a mandarin from some bygone dynasty who held their audience tablets, necessary when attending court functions, in front of them. They were officially the Five Commissioners of Pestilence (Wen Shen), who governed Heaven's Ministry of Epidemics. Each had the head of a different animal—tiger, ox, rooster, horse and goat—but in this divine bureaucratic hierarchy, they had well-defined duties, each responsible for managing epidemics of a different season.

On mainland China, people no longer worship at the Wen Shen temples, and they have been torn down. Still, many Chinese continue to hold a mixture of beliefs drawing on both Western and Chinese traditions. Chairman Mao's personal doctor reported that Mao never took a bath nor brushed his teeth. His second in command, Marshal Lin Biao, had numerous medical phobias and spent a lot of his time consulting Chinese medical tracts seeking cures. While the Nationalist leaders generally referred to traditional Chinese medicine as fraudulent quackery, Mao talked of it as a national treasure.

Meanwhile, outside China, the scientific world continued to find evidence to support the theory that zoonotic diseases, those transmitted via animals, are the most common and the deadliest. They included the plague, rinderpest, smallpox, malaria, tetanus, rabies, yellow fever and tuberculosis. Yet this new knowledge would shortly be turned into a new instrument of modern war.

3

GERM WARFARE

A less well-known consequence of the third bubonic plague pandemic and the outbreaks in Manchuria was a growing military fascination with germ warfare, in particular with weaponizing the most virulent form of *Yersina pestis*.

The first country to engage in biological warfare research was the Soviet Union. In 1928, by secret decree, the USSR Revolutionary Military Council ordered the beginning of an offensive biological warfare research and development programme. It signed a decree about the weaponization of typhus. The Leningrad Military Academy began a trial cultivating typhus in chicken embryos. The secret police carried out experiments on political prisoners held at the Solovetsky Camp, a former monastery in the distant White Sea near the Arctic Circle, involving typhus, glanders and melioidosis. Another laboratory was set up near Moscow, which became the Red Army's Research Institute of Microbiology.

The Military Chemical Agency, controlled by the Soviet People's Commissariat of Defence, became the lead agency for managing both the offensive and defensive biological warfare programmes. The People's Health Commissariat (Ministry of Health) was ordered to obey all orders and requests from the military. It operated a biomedical research network of some thirty-five institutions working in epidemiology, genetics, immunology, microbiology and virology. This meant that the Soviet anti-plague programme was closely tied with the biological warfare programme. The people in charge of the anti-plague programme were the same as those tasked with creating offensive germ warfare weapons. The extensive and highly secretive effort far exceeded that of the Japanese.

In 1936, the Military Chemical Agency created the Vozrozh-deniye Island test site in the Aral Sea for open air testing of biological weapons. About a hundred people, led by Professor Ivan Velikanov, arrived on the island with special ships and two airplanes to conduct experiments on the spread of tularemia and other related microorganisms. In the autumn of 1937, the expedition was abandoned when Velikanov and other specialists were arrested under the purges. One former Soviet bioweapons scientist, Ken Alibek, formerly Kanatjan Alibekov, claimed in 1992 that tularemia was successfully deployed against the Germans besieging Stalingrad from August 1942 to February 1943.

By 1933, the Japanese had turned Korea into a colony, and this overseas empire was now extended to Manchuria, which was earmarked for settlement by Japanese civilians. Here the military, the Kwantung Army, set up an ambitious research and testing programme through the Epidemic Prevention and Water Purification Department. It established Unit 731 near Harbin, with facilities for biological weapons production, testing, deployment and storage.

Estimates of those killed by Unit 731 and its related programmes range up to half a million people. At Unit 731, now a museum, 300 researchers, including doctors and bacteriologists, worked in a very extensive complex of buildings. Plague-infected fleas were bred in the laboratories. To breed the fleas, the unit became home to millions of rats infected with the plague. After the camp was closed down, the rats escaped and started epidemics in the surrounding districts, which cost many lives.

The Japanese scientists tested biological weapons on prisoners, notably by trying to breed ever more virulent strains of bubonic plague. Bombs were each loaded with 30,000 fleas that had sucked blood from a dying prisoner. The fleas were packed in dust and sealed inside clay bomb casings, which were dropped by low-flying airplanes. This was to ensure that the fleas survived being dropped, and would be able to start an epidemic of bubonic plague. In one raid, the Chinese village of Quzhou was attacked, and witnesses saw a fine reddish dust settle on the town. An estimated 2,000 people died of plague following this attack. Another 1,000 or so died in nearby Yiwu, after the plague was carried there by sick railway workers. Other attacks, using anthrax, killed approximately 6,000 more people in the area.

When Japanese troops reach the Nationalist capital of Nanking, they spread typhoid and paratyphoid germs into the wells, marshes and houses of the city, as well as infusing them into snacks distributed to locals. Epidemics broke out shortly after, with the Japanese concluding that paratyphoid fever was the most effective weapon. There were further biological attacks with anthrax, typhoid, dysentery, cholera and other deadly pathogens. Infected food supplies and clothing were dropped by airplane into areas of China not occupied by Japanese forces. In addition, poisoned food and candies were given to unsuspecting victims.

During the final months of the Second World War, Japan planned to use plague as a biological weapon against San Diego, California. The plan was scheduled to launch on 22 September 1945, but Japan surrendered five weeks earlier. It was called Operation Cherry Blossoms at Night.

Following Japan's surrender, the Red Army took over Manchuria and seized the materials and scientists from Unit 731. Some of the scientists were put on trial. The Americans also interviewed some of the Japanese scientists and gave them criminal immunity in order to benefit from their research, but came away with little useful information. It's not possible to conclude that biological warfare influenced the course of the war or proved to be an effective weapon. When the Japanese Kwantung Army seized Nanjing in December 1937, they massacred the civilian inhabitants, killing hundreds of thousands with swords, bayonets, bombs and machine guns. The Japanese did not need the biological weapons to terrorise the Chinese population and indeed in one case, thousands of Japanese troops were infected and died of plague.

After the establishment of the People's Republic of China, the Communists did not play up the atrocity of the Rape of Nanjing until the late 1970s, and did not establish the museum at Unit 731 until 1985. Instead, the Chinese Communist Party developed a huge propaganda campaign during the Korean War (1950–53) that alleged that the United States was waging biological warfare. The US forces were accused of dropping bombs containing flies, beetles, spiders, crickets and other insects carrying various life-threatening pathogens, from the plague bacillus to cholera, anthrax, encephalitis and yellow fever. They were supposedly doing this not only in Korea but also in China. The Chinese presented evidence that convinced all kinds of prominent experts around the world, who loudly condemned the United States.

It is now generally accepted that this was entirely a disinformation campaign. Soviet archive documents released after 1990 revealed that Soviet, Chinese and North Korean officials knew that the Korean War germ warfare charges against the United States were false, as they were made in 1952. Among the archives are memos in which Soviet leaders promptly informed Chinese leaders that the accusations were made up and urged the Chinese to shut down a propaganda campaign based on false charges.

The international campaign relied on the testimony of top Chinese scientists as well as concerned groups of prominent Western scientists led by biochemist Dr Joseph Needham, the author of a multi-volume history of Chinese science and technology, at Cambridge University. They either deliberately fabricated evidence or allowed themselves to be misled or used. Too many experts abroad preferred to believe what Mao or Stalin said, rather than the American government.

During this period in the 1950s, China also launched into a series of mass mobilisation campaigns to eradicate 'the four pests'—rats, flies, mosquitoes and sparrows—which seemed closely modelled on the Soviet anti plague campaigns. China mobilised people to get rid of cockroaches, bed bugs and the water snails that cause schistosomiasis. These numerous 'patriotic public health campaigns' which everyone including school children had to participate in, together with biological warfare propaganda, naturally left a deep impression on the public consciousness. The Chinese government also began to campaign against pets, and it soon became rare to see even dogs or cats in Chinese cities.

All this propaganda certainly convinced everyone of the link between animals and disease, but it is difficult to evaluate how effective it really was in other respects. Foreign trained doctors and nurses, except those educated in the Soviet Union, lost all influence, and were soon persecuted and sent to labour in the countryside. Without qualified staff, the public health system in the 1960s and 1970s remained rudimentary. Propaganda took the place of proper epidemiological research. Statistics were propaganda. China continued to suffer from serious floods and famines in the 1950s, and in the Great Leap Forward, launched in 1958, around 40 million perished. Starving people are naturally extremely vulnerable to infectious diseases.

The Communist Party was able to build on work done after 1910 by Dr Wu and by various imperial as well as Republican era governments, but it mainly concentrated on copying the Soviet model in this and everything else. The Mao era left China with a particularly strong institutional machinery to run patriotic health campaigns and to enforce compulsory quarantining through its grass roots neighbourhood committee machinery. This could be turned on when needed, in a way that is available to few other large countries. Beijing can also easily switch on a well drilled and funded public information apparatus, and it has always been very hard for any dissenting voices to make themselves heard. All these things were visible from the start of the COVID-19 pandemic.

On the other hand, the propaganda campaign about America's supposed deployment of germ warfare during the Korean War has also left a legacy of distrust. This is one reason why Western intelligence agencies are likely to doubt or at least question official accounts about the origin of the virus and the role of the Wuhan Institute of Virology. While the Chinese and Soviet governments pushed a completely false story of its enemies waging war with bioweapons against civilians, they actively pursued their own germ warfare programmes in secrecy, and, indeed, in contravention of international law. It is worth looking at this in more detail, as it forms the context in which the suspicions about the real nature of the Wuhan Institute of Virology are aired. American intelligence continues to believe that China has a large and secretive biological warfare programme in breach of its international treaty obligations.

4

THE ASTONISHING SIZE OF THE
SOVIET BIOWARFARE PROGRAMME

After Japan's surrender, the Soviet Union tried to learn from the knowledge it gained from the Japanese Unit 731. In 1946, it used this expertise to set up a new biological warfare research centre in Sverdlovsk (now Yekaterinburg), called the Centre for Military-Technical Problems of Anti-Bacteriological Defense. This institute would later become notorious when, in April 1979, its staff accidentally released spores of anthrax, which killed at least 100 people. The outbreak was long blamed on the sale of tainted meat. The authorities did everything to cover it up, including removing all the medical records of the dead. The government was determined to prevent anyone from finding out that the USSR was breaking the Biological Weapons Convention just four years after it had signed it. The incident was only confirmed in 1992.

In 1947, a smallpox weapons factory was established at the Centre for Virology in Zagorsk (now Sergiyev Posa). It was part of a system of closed cities and military research complexes. Its work was to develop offensive weapons, with a focus on testing the most extremely dangerous viruses on animals. For this, it sent scientists to India in search of the most virulent strains of smallpox. It also designed vaccines that could be used to inoculate troops.

During the 1960s, the anti-plague system became the lead agency of a programme to defend against biological warfare, codenamed *Project 5*. This responsibility grew and, by the mid-1970s, came to include the undertaking of tasks for the offensive biological warfare programme, codenamed *Ferment*. It was administered by an organisation called *Biopreparat*, which concentrated on offensive research and development. The Soviet Union did not limit itself to developing biological weapons to sicken and kill human beings. The USSR Ministry of Agriculture was also responsible for a programme codenamed *Ekology*, which aimed to develop biological weapons against animals and plants. All the different programmes were highly secretive, and people working in one part of them knew nothing of what was happening elsewhere.

In the early 1970s, the Russians abandoned the bogus theories of the Soviet scientist Trofim Lysenko and embraced modern genetics. Initially, they concentrated on the 'classic' microbiological techniques of mutation, selection and propagation to weaponize anthrax, the plague, tularemia, rickets, typhoid, Ebola etc. This involved exposing a microbe to X-rays, UV light and chemicals to create mutations that would, say, make it more infectious or deadly to human beings.

The discovery of recombinant DNA technology in the West stimulated the Soviet government to redouble its efforts in the new field of biotechnology, especially when it came to devising military applications. So in 1972, the Soviets started a very large and costly effort to expand their bioweapons programme. A lot of it was the stuff of science fiction fantasy and implausible spy novels.

This violated both the spirit and the letter of the 1972 Biological and Toxin Weapons Convention (BWC), which

Moscow had ratified in 1975. When the Soviet representative to a UN disarmament conference announced that his country had ratified the BWC, he declared that the USSR had never possessed an offensive biological weapons programme and therefore had no stockpiles of weapons to destroy. However, the Treaty allows some ambiguity, because governments are permitted to perform research, development, testing and production of anything that can be justified as being for defensive purposes.

Moscow established the 15th Main Directorate of the Ministry of Health, which was designated as Post Office Box A-1968 to help keep it secret, to take charge of all biological defence and offense work. Some of this research under the Biopreparat programme was carried out by the ministries of agriculture, health and others. Since most of it was obviously for offensive purposes, and hence illegal, the Soviets went to great lengths to establish a civilian cover, or in spy jargon a 'legend', which, if necessary, could 'explain' how this or that research really had a legitimate peaceful or defensive purpose.

Soviet scientists spent years investigating ways to make pathogens work better as weapons. One way of doing this is to figure out how to create a laboratory 'chimera', which is a new virus or a bacterium made out of genetic material taken from two or more organisms. Others worked to eliminate the epitopes—the regions of proteins that can trigger a cellular immune response—on the surface of existing bioweapon agents, so they cannot be recognised by regular diagnostic techniques. In other words, they wanted to make microbes that the enemy would be unable to either identify or prepare for, or at least not until it was too late. They used the newly discovered molecular biology techniques to manipulate genes to breach the barriers separating species.

If, somehow, this work into creating a deadly new virus should ever be discovered and come to the notice of the outside world, then the Soviet government would have a ready cover story to hand, a 'legend': they would explain that the laboratory was really working on creating a peaceful vaccine.

One of the most vicious projects, codenamed *Hunter* (Okhotnik), focused on an even more devilish design: to build hybrid bacteria and viruses that would respond when the enemy used an antibiotic to kill an infection by releasing a deadly virus.

The arms reduction treaties which Western governments and the Soviet bloc negotiated in the heyday of the 1970s détente and peaceful co-existence policies went hand in hand with a global Cold War propaganda battle. In many Western countries everything about it became politicised, with left and right-wing parties making competing claims, and of course, scientists became drawn into it. Some believed the Soviet propaganda that it was genuinely attempting disarmament, and that it was the warmongering Western military industrial complex that was undermining these initiatives. Unilateral disarmament movements sprang up which were able to bring out huge numbers of supporters, and even more took part in protests against the installation of medium-range missiles in Europe in the 1980s.

Later, Soviet propaganda organs launched a very successful disinformation campaign, which alleged that the United States had created HIV/AIDS as part of a biological weapons research project at the US army bioweapons research centre at Fort Derrick in Maryland. The disinformation campaign was called *Operation Infektion* or *Operation Denver*. Moscow used allies and friendly 'agents of influence' across the world to plant the story that in America, genetic engineers had synthesised two retroviruses to create the deadly virus. In other words, the KGB accused the Americans of doing what they themselves were doing. In fact, the British offensive biological warfare programme closed in the late 1950s, and the American programme centred at Fort Derrick ceased operating in 1969. The Soviet programme was around ten times larger than the American one ever was.

THE SOVIET BIOWARFARE PROGRAMME

Against this background, many were hesitant to believe the sketchy evidence for a huge chemical and biological warfare programme by the Soviet Union. This changed when, in 1989, a senior Soviet biological weapons engineer, Vladimir Pasechnik, knocked on the door of the British embassy in Paris. When he was debriefed, Western intelligence was astonished to learn that the Soviet biological weapons programme was ten times larger than anyone had ever imagined.

Pasechnik explained that it was a vast programme extending over fifty-two clandestine sites that employed over 50,000 people. Annualized production capacity for weaponized smallpox, for example, was 90 to 100 tons. He said the aim of the enhanced programme, started after 1972, was to create an artificial virus, and that its being new meant that the enemy would have had no defences against it. He revealed that the Soviet Union had developed a genetically engineered strain of plague that was resistant to antibiotics and non-virulent in its stored form, but which could easily be converted into a deadly antibiotic-resistant form when needed for weaponization.

The Biopreparat programme created weaponized strains of the deadliest viruses known to man such as anthrax, Ebola, Marburg virus, the plague, Q fever, Junin virus, glanders, tularemia and brucellosis. The scientists even looked at ways of weaponizing the AIDS virus, HIV.

In the 1980s and 90s, many of these agents were genetically altered to resist heat, cold and antibiotics. In the 90s, Boris Yeltsin admitted to an offensive bio-weapons programme as well as to the true nature of the Sverdlovsk 1979 anthrax outbreak. Later, other Russian scientists turned up in the West who revealed that even after Yeltsin's admissions, Russia continued to hide its biological weapons programme.

The threat of bioweapons (and chemical weapons) did not end with the Cold War. In some respects it became even greater.

Saddam Hussein used chemical weapons against the Kurds and in the 1980s pursued an extensive biological weapons programme. It employed just 300 scientists, engineers and technicians, mostly at the Biological Research Centre for Military Defense at Salman Pak. There, they conducted applied research with the bacterium that causes anthrax, *Clostridium botulinum* (the bacterium used to produce botulinum toxin), and *Clostridium perfringens* (the bacterium that causes gangrene). At the Al Hakam Single-Cell Protein Plant, the biological weapons were developed and produced on a large scale. After extensive production of B. anthracis, botulinum toxin and other biological weapons agents, they were stored in refrigerated tanks, after which they could be loaded into munitions. The actual filling of bombs, missiles and other munitions with pathogens or toxins took place at the Muthanna State Establishment, Iraq's major chemical warfare production and testing facility. United Nations inspectors reported that Iraq may have produced up to 10 billion doses of anthrax, botulinum toxin and aflatoxin, a staggeringly large amount. Iraq did use both smallpox and anthrax during its war with Iran.

What this means is that even a relatively modest bioweapons programme can be terrifyingly dangerous. Since then, new technology means that small bioreactors can easily produce enough to kill many millions, and that the release of a biological weapon can go undetected for hours, days, or even weeks. It also means that it is within the even more limited ability of a modest terrorist group, such as Japan's Aum Shinrikyo cult, to acquire cultures of the bacteria that cause plague and anthrax. The cult even attempted to acquire Ebola virus from Zaire. Inevitably there are fears that an individual, a terrorist, could also start an epidemic. Militant Islamic groups are believed to have plotted to use such weapons.

So far this hasn't happened, but this is not true for chemical weapons such as the nerve agent sarin. The Aum Shinrikyo cult used sarin in a subway attack in Tokyo in 1995. During the Syrian civil war, the Syrian government stockpiled several hundred tonnes of sarin and many tons of VX, another nerve poison invented in the Soviet Union, according to French intelligence. Cuba was responsible for deploying VX against Angolan insurgents during the Angolan Civil War. The Syrian government also weaponized chlorine as well as blister agents such as sulphur mustard against civilians. North Korea assassinated Kim Jong Nam, a member of the ruling family, while he was travelling through Malaysia in February 2017 using the VX Nerve agent. Another deadly poison, Novichok, only came to light after its existence was revealed by the chemist Dr Vil Mirzayanov in the 1990s, via the Russian media. He later defected to the US, where he published the chemical formula in his book, *State Secrets*. Russia has used Novichok (banned under the Chemical Weapons Convention) to kill its enemies living abroad, such as in the well-publicised attack against the Skripal family in Salisbury.

5

DOES CHINA HAVE A
BIOWARFARE PROGRAMME?

Inevitably, some believe that China also has a bioweapons pro-gramme and that the Wuhan Institute of Virology is part of it. It could be that Chinese scientists have, like the Russians, been experimenting with creating chimeric viruses and, again like the Russians, gone to great lengths to establish a civilian cover story for this work. A part of this 'legend' could be the story of the zoonotic transmission of SARS and COVID-19 through wet markets, with the virus carried by bats, civet cats and pangolins. The Wuhan Institute of Virology could be a dual use facility that carries out both civilian and military research, and its staff could therefore be under military discipline. This was the conclusion reached by the US State Department in a fact sheet issued on 15 January 2021: 'Despite the WIV presenting itself as a civilian institution, the United States has determined that the WIV has collaborated on publications and secret projects with China's military. The WIV has engaged in classified research, including laboratory animal experiments, on behalf of the Chinese military since at least 2017.'[1]

This may be a case of a wild conspiracy theory. The fact sheet was issued in the last days of the Trump administration. There may, however, also be a certain reluctance in the overseas scientific community to recognise what exactly China has been up to, especially given the many ties with Chinese students, researchers, universities and companies that have been built up over recent years.

Many Western scientists in the 1950s were taken in by Chinese evidence that the Americans had been spreading the plague during the Korean War, or later refused to believe that the Soviet Union ran such a large biological and chemical weapons programme. As we know, even those who suspected the worst underestimated the extent of the Soviet programme by a factor of ten. The CIA and others also underestimated the sheer size and scope of the Soviet nuclear weapons programme.

The intelligence resources of the United States are far greater than those of its allies, such as Britain or France, so almost all publicly available information usually comes out of Washington in the form of annual reports and testimonies before Congressional panels. After China signed the BWC in 1984, the US government produced annual assessments of its compliance.

In the 1995 report, *Adherence to and Compliance with Arms Control Agreements*, the US Arms Control and Disarmament Agency said: 'China maintained an offensive biological weapons program throughout the 1980s. The program included the development, production, stockpiling or other acquisition or maintenance of biological warfare agents.'

In 1993, US intelligence officials stated that it was highly probable that China had an active and expanding offensive bioweapons programme, and claimed that two civilian-run biological research centres were actually controlled by the Chinese military. These research centres were known to have engaged previously in the production and storage of bioweapons.

DOES CHINA HAVE A BIOWARFARE PROGRAMME?

The *Washington Post* reported in February 1993 of the concerns of American intelligence when they noted that in 1991 one of the possible biowarfare centres was enlarged. Next, Beijing made, according to a US official, a 'patently false' declaration to the United Nations that it had never made any germ weapons or conducted any work to bolster defences against a biological attack.[2]

On 9 May 2002, the US government imposed sanctions on eight Chinese companies for engaging in transfers of sensitive equipment under multilateral export control lists to the Middle East. The sales occurred between September 2000 and October 2001 and violated the Iran-Iraq Arms Non-Proliferation Act of 1992.

The Act bars US companies from conducting business with the sanctioned entities or issuing export licenses to them for two years. Two of the sanctioned companies, Jiangsu Yongli Chemicals and Technology Import and Export Corp., and CMEC Machinery and Electric Equipment Import and Export Co. Ltd., denied the US allegations. China may have helped other countries with their biological warfare, such as Iraq, Syria, Egypt, Libya and North Korea. It is accused of actively helping Pakistan and North Korea develop nuclear weapons and the missiles to deliver them.

At a hearing on China's proliferation practices in 2003, the US–China Economic and Security Review Commission was informed as follows:

> The US believes that despite being a member of the Biological Weapons Convention, China maintains a bioweapons program in violation of its BWC obligations. The United States believes that China's consistent claims that it has never researched, produced or possessed BW are simply not true, and that China still retains its bioweapons program.

In 2005, the US Department of Defence again reported that it had specific and credible information that China was continuing to develop its biological weapons, despite its UN statements. The Pentagon also published a similar paper, entitled *Proliferation:*

Threat and Response, which claimed that China's BWP includes manufacturing of infectious microorganisms and toxins.

Even though China has submitted its voluntary annual BWC confidence building measure (CBM) data declarations every year, the US Department of State assessed in 2005 that the information given therein continued to be 'inaccurate and misleading'. Further, 'BWC CBMs since 1991 have called on the States Parties to declare, among other things, their past offensive activities, which China has not done. On the contrary, China insists it never had such a program at all'.[3]

The report said:

– The United States reaffirms its judgment that China maintains some elements of an offensive BW capability in violation of its BWC obligations. Despite China's BWC CBM declarations to the contrary, indications suggest that China maintained an offensive BW program prior to acceding to the Convention in 1984.

– China's current research activities and dual-use capabilities raise the possibility that sophisticated BW work could be underway. For example, because of the possible offensive applications of aerosolization techniques, the United States' concerns are underscored by publications indicating military involvement in such research.

– Although China has submitted its voluntary annual BWC CBM data declarations every year and did so again in 2002 and 2003 we assess that the information submitted therein continues to be inaccurate and misleading. BWC CBMs since 1991 have called on the States Parties to declare, among other things, their past offensive activities, which China has not done. On the contrary, China insists it never had such a program at all.

– In its October 17, 2002, announcement on the promulgation of "Regulations on Export Control of Dual-use Biological Agents and related Equipment and Technologies," for instance, China stated that it "has always fulfilled earnestly its obligations under the Convention" and "has never developed, produced or stockpiled any biological weapons, and never assisted any country to acquire or develop these weapons." These claims, we believe, are inaccurate.

– China has a number of civilian and military facilities that could be associated with an offensive BW program. For example:

- The Chinese Ministry of Defense's Academy of Military Medical Sciences (AMMS) Institute of Microbiology and Epidemiology (IME) in Beijing is acknowledged as a biodefense research facility.
- The Lanzhou Institute of Biological Products (LIBP) has been identified as a vaccine producer. We believe that LIBP has several BL-3 laboratories and dual use capabilities.

In 2007, the Defense Intelligence Agency (DIA) testimony for the US Senate, the Select Committee on Intelligence, entitled *Current and Projected National Security Threats* (in both open and closed sessions), said that the DIA believes that China 'continues to maintain some elements of an offensive biological weapons program'.

The Chinese Foreign Ministry has repeatedly described all this as groundless, and has denied that China has or ever had a germ weapons programme. The United States continues to state that China has an active bioweapons programme with an existing arsenal.

It is possible that China missed an opportunity to come clean about its biological warfare programme after 1979, when it demobilised a large part of its military and cancelled most of the weapons procurement programmes. If it had acknowledged its existence, then it would have had to demonstrate the elimination of its programme just as the United States had to do. This was difficult, because it would have had to explain the reasons for the programme to its own citizens. For half a century, they had been told all about the inhumanity of Japanese biological warfare crimes and the war crimes of the Americans during the Korean War.

China may have chosen to maintain the lie that the programme never existed, or it may have calculated that the BWC was so full of holes that coming clean would be unnecessary. Most pathogens can be used both for civilian and military purposes, and a great deal of work can be permitted by arms controls treaties for defensive reasons, or to maintain public health. Further, the Treaty is a gentleman's agreement, as it has no mechanism to enforce any inspections or penalties, making it quite different from the arms limitation treaties for chemical or nuclear weapons. Under this treaty, if the United States was worried about China (as it is), it was meant to resolve the concerns through mutual consultation. If that failed, then Article Six of the Convention would allow the United States to report China to the United Nations Security Council. The Security Council could then choose to investigate the allegations, but since China is a permanent member of the Security Council, it has a veto, which it would use to block that. In order to get around that, the United States would have to appeal to the court of public opinion by presenting undeniable physical evidence. But with laboratories and microorganisms this is very, very difficult. A satellite photograph of a laboratory is no sort of convincing evidence, unlike a photograph of a missile or a nuclear reprocessing plant.

After the Soviet Union dissolved, the evidence about its bioweapons programme became available through the documents in its archives and the testimony of those who worked in its laboratories. As the Communist Party is still in power in China, the archives are closed and there are no scientists who have come out in the open to explain the details of the research programme.

We do know that in the early 1950s the China's People's Liberation Army (PLA) sent delegations and students to the USSR for training in microbiology and infectious diseases. They returned to set up identical research institutions and possibly a copycat biological warfare programme. We also know that China in the 1950s was extremely concerned about protecting its troops and civilian population from biological warfare.

Scientific cooperation between the USSR and the PRC ceased in the early 1960s with the Sino-Soviet split, and China became cut off from scientific developments in the rest of the world. Not much is known about China's bioweapons programme, but China's military expenditure ballooned as it prepared to withstand a nuclear attack by the Soviet Union and a possible American invasion while it bankrolled the Vietnam War. It is believed that the bioweapons programme continued, both for defensive and offensive purposes. It may even have been greatly expanded, since germ warfare is often described as a 'poor man's nuclear weapon'.

A total militarisation of Chinese society and its industry took place in the 1960s and 1970s. China moved its scientific laboratories and factories out of the main urban centres into the interior, which became known as the Third Line. Many of these were housed in remote valleys or built inside limestone caves, of which China has many. It was thought they would be safe from a coastal invasion or from forces crossing the Soviet-China border in the north-east. They were also protected from bombers, including those carrying nuclear devices, as well as from aerial surveillance. The Chinese military invested heavily in developing space and missile industries, and even tried building nuclear powered submarines. It developed a capacity to build large amounts of Soviet designed artillery, tanks and aeroplanes, which in numbers at least matched that of the Soviet Union.

At the centre of the known scientific military endeavour was China's successful effort to build a nuclear bomb, the rockets to launch weapons with missiles, and long range bombers. The key research and production facilities were in Xinjiang, Yunnan, Gansu, Shaanxi—all in areas far from China's industrial centres.

The scientists and workers lived in towns much like the Soviet closed cities, which were only known by their highly secret code names. They weren't marked on maps, and the residents had no contact with the outside world.

A 2015 article in the *Journal of Defense Studies* by Danny Shoham listed thirty-two facilities in China connected to bio-weapons programmes and concluded that:

> China is capable of developing, producing and weaponizing, on the whole, some 40 anti-human pathogens and toxins either intact or genetically upgraded, if not largely engineered. In actuality, it is highly plausible that, at present, China possesses a lessened inventory of employable weaponized biological weapons agents. Presumably, it comprises a first generation of biological weapons agents (for example, plague and brucellosis germs) in an operational state; a second generation of biological weapons agents (for example, Hantan and Japanese Encephalitis viruses) in an operational state; plus a third generation of biological weapons agents (for example, SARS, Ebola and Influenza viruses) still under development, in part or entirely.

Among the facilities affiliated with the defence establishment that the author lists are:

– The State Research Centre for Viro-Biotechnology Engineering;
– The Biological Engineering Design Institute;
– The China National Biotech Corporation;
– The Lanzhou Institute of Biological Products;
– The Changchun Institute of Biological Products;
– The Wuhan Institute of Biological Products; and
– The Chengdu Institute of Biological Products.

According to the Department of Defense 2013 annual report on military and security developments involving the People's Republic of China, China has prioritized the development of ground and air attack cruise missiles, and so it is not far fetched to suspect that China is able to arm a stealth missile with a bio-warhead that would be very hard to destroy after it was launched.[4]

China has a number of biological research institutes that have been identified as factories producing bioweapons, such as the Yan'an Bacteriological Factory, which reportedly makes aerosol bombs as well as paper canister-type containers. There are others in Kunming, Changchun, Chongqing and Wuhan, which generally go under the name of 'biological products' institute or factory as in 'Changchun Biological Products Factory' or the 'Wuhan Biological Products Factory'.

Kanatjan Alibekov, former director of one of the Soviet germ-warfare programmes, wrote in his book *Biohazard* that he read in Soviet intelligence reports that China had suffered a serious accident at one of its biological weapons plants in the late 1980s. Soviet reconnaissance satellites identified a biological weapons laboratory and plant near a site for testing nuclear warheads. This must refer to the Lop Nur test site in Xinjiang. The Soviets also suspected that two separate epidemics of haemorrhagic fever that swept the region in the late 1980s were caused by accidents in a lab where Chinese scientists were weaponizing viral diseases, which might have been Marburg fever or Ebola.

Such reports, and the claims of various American intelligence agencies, have little impact in the absence of witnesses, Chinese documents, defectors, and photographs or video materials. A number of organisations such as the 'Wuhan Institute of Biological Products Factory' are named, but what might once have been a purely military-run enterprise could now refer to a commercial enterprise. The Wuhan Biological Products Factory, for instance, is indeed a large-scale commercial enterprise that belongs to the Sinopharma group of companies. This does not exclude the possibility that it, or a company like it, could produce biological weapons if requested to do so, even though the means to deliver them in a battlefield would have to be manufactured somewhere else. The equipment—vats, incubators, freezers, and so on—would probably look much the same, and the staff would have a similar training or background. Further, it is reasonable to assume that, if the PLA had created a new virus for offensive purposes, it would require a plant like the Wuhan Biological Products Factory to produce vaccines for its own troops. Certainly, the Wuhan Biological Products Factory has been at the forefront of developing a vaccine for COVID-19.

Once China stopped being a militarized economy in which microbiologists worked in closed secret cities, held military ranks and wore uniforms, it all becomes rather murky. If you add in the strict control over information in China, an outside investigator would find it very difficult, without the help of a whistleblower, to discover very much about a covert military bioweapons programme.

Dany Shoham notes in his 2015 article: 'The PLA has been able to mask a potent, self-sustained biotechnological system for the research, development and production of biological weapons within civilian entities. The PLA continues to operate programmes researching medical microbiology, veterinary microbiology, aerobiology, epidemiology, genetic engineering, biotechnology, and toxicology.'

We see a similar problem with investigating China's nuclear weapons programme. For decades, China has maintained that it has fewer than 300 nuclear warheads, a far smaller number than the thousands that Russia and the United States possess. Yet many suspect it is not being open. In 2011, a three-year study by Georgetown University raised the possibility that China has 3,000 nuclear weapons, which are hidden in a sophisticated network of tunnels. The study was based on state media footage showing tunnel entrances, and estimated a 3,000-mile network. China could have built thousands of nuclear weapons that it has not acknowledged, simply by preparing all the parts but stopping short of assembling them into a completed weapon. Technically, until it does so, these are not nuclear weapons. China would not need to declare them under arms limitation treaties.

China could easily have continued operating bioweapons laboratories and factories hidden underground after the 1980s, when it began to downsize the military. During the Mao era, China built hundreds if not thousands of huge underground bomb-proof shelters to house, feed and clothe its civilian population, especially the urban population, in case of a nuclear war. It also moved enterprises making tanks, artillery, ammunitions, planes, rockets and other military related enterprises inside mountains to protect them against attack. Vast caverns were excavated to house the entire nuclear cycle. Other underground facilities accommodated aircraft, navy vessels, submarines, tanks and rockets.

One of the largest of these is in a suburb of Chongqing, which opened as a tourist attraction calling itself the 'world's largest man-made cave' in 2010. The 816 nuclear plant was originally designed to manufacture plutonium in the 1960s, part of a military mega-project which occupied 60,000 soldiers for seventeen years. They built a million square feet underground structure spread over twelve levels with 20 miles of roads. All this was to stop Soviet intelligence from tracking down the facility. To keep it secret, China erased the town of Bailang from every map for nearly two decades until the project was called off in 1984.

Another vast underground project, 456 metres below ground, was constructed about 50 miles from Wuhan with the code name 131. A system of tunnels with meeting rooms, command and control centres were built underneath one of the hills. Villas for Mao Zedong and his Number Two, Lin Biao, were erected above the entrances.

Many of these projects were abandoned after the 1980s, but others are still in use and continue to be identified by satellite imagery, like those used in the Georgetown study. Compared to a tank factory, a few pharmaceutical laboratories would require a relatively modest amount of space and would be hard to identify. All of this is simply to say that there is a lot we still may not know about China's bioweapons programme.

It would also be very difficult, even for a UN investigation team, such as the one that investigated Iraq's nuclear, chemical and biological weapons programmes under Saddam Hussein (UNSCOM), to operate in China unless it fully cooperated. It was hard enough for UNSCOM to work in Iraq, even when Saddam Hussein faced the huge military might of the United States and its allies. Even there, the United States was still not able to verify that all the weapons of mass destruction had been found, so it launched an invasion of Iraq during the second Gulf War. With China, any similar investigation on the model of UNSCOM would be impossible without its full consent and cooperation. This leaves the United States and other countries in a strange situation, in which China knows that its claims that it does not and never has had a biological weapons programme are not believed. Its major economic partners, such as the United States and Japan, consider it to be in contravention of the BCW Treaty. It thus creates an awkward climate of mistrust, in which suspicions about the origins of COVID-19 can flourish. The lack of transparency and the mistrust will have consequences that will be discussed in later chapters.

American intelligence reports can be very wrong. Before Saddam's invasion of Kuwait in 1990, the United States had underestimated how close Iraq was to testing a nuclear bomb, but before the 2003 invasion of Iraq, its intelligence overestimated its readiness and capacity to restart the nuclear weapons programme. In a similar way, it had underestimated the danger posed by Saddam Hussein's secret biological weapons programme prior to 1990, and then before the 2003 invasion, it overestimated (or exaggerated) the likelihood that Iraq was about to resume production of deadly pathogens.

With this in mind, it is reasonable to assume that China would have started the 1950s with the goal of matching the bioweapons development programme of the Soviet Union and the capacity that it believed the United States possessed before 1969, when America shut its programme. It is also plausible to assume that during the early 1970s, when the Soviet Union abandoned Lysenkoism and expanded its research into genetic manipulation and the quest to create new deadly viral 'chimeras', China would not have been able to keep up. Besides, it had virtually no contact with the Soviet Union, as the two neighbours were on the brink of war. Beijing was probably unaware of the huge ambition of Moscow's *Biopreparat* programme, and even if it did know, it seems very unlikely that China could have mounted a matching programme.

China was cut off from scientific developments in the West, more isolated even than the Soviet Union, and its qualified scientists were labouring in the countryside. We can see from the sort of tanks and aeroplanes China was building in the 1970s that it was still working with the technology it had acquired from the Soviet Union in the 1950s.

In the 1980s, China's leaders certainly had the wish to acquire the technology and know-how of its neighbours and rivals, but everyone knew that this was going to take some time. China first had to open the country and send a new generation abroad to study in the West before it could start catching up. The generation of scientists who had studied abroad before 1959 were now on the verge of retirement, and there was no one ready to take their place.

The whole of the military industrial complex had to be reorganised. The Soviet Union probably dedicated a third of its GDP to its military industrial complex, but China devoted an even greater share, as it was actively fighting proxy wars across South East Asia, and preparing to fight off both the United States and the Soviet Union. China's military and its associated factories and enterprises employed something like 30 million people at the peak. After Mao's death, Deng Xiaoping began to slowly demo-bilise millions of troops and to shift the military factories towards producing goods for the consumer economy. The next chapter looks more closely at how this was done.

6

THE COMMERCIALISATION OF CHINA'S MILITARY ENTERPRISES

The vast investment in the Soviet Union's biological warfare programme, which stretched over decades and at its height employed some 70,000 people, came at the expense of its civilian pharmaceutical industry. The Soviet Union never managed to produce enough drugs, not even enough basic medicines such as penicillin. Routine procedures like root canal were carried out without anaesthetics.

Its citizens suffered perennial shortages of basics such as aspirin, children's cough medicine and simple antibiotics. Soviet pharmaceutical companies churned out billions of units of questionable drugs that were only partially effective at normal dosages, weakening bacteria but not killing them outright—thus creating an environment that was perfect for spurring antibiotic resistance. In 1956, Soviet health officials declared that penicillin no longer worked against venereal diseases. Even long after the dissolution of the Soviet Union, Russia still does not have a significant pharmaceutical industry. It relies on imports of foreign medicines.

China was in a very similar situation in 1979 when Deng Xiaoping came to power and promised to reform China with the 'four modernisations' and the Open Door Policies. The schools and universities had been closed for nearly twenty years. The best hospitals and pharmaceutical laboratories had been commandeered by the military. The provision of basic medicines and vaccinations to the population had continued, but few modern drugs or treatments were available to anyone but the elite.

In the 1980s, almost all consumer goods were still rationed, and priority was given to the residents of the big cities. Slowly a private sector was allowed to grow, but industries like pharmaceuticals and medical equipment remained under tight state control. Those who worked directly for the government as administrators or in state-owned factories generally enjoyed a privileged access to medical treatment. The prices of their medicines and treatments were set by the state and did not reflect either demand or the cost of production.

Deng set about cancelling most of the overambitious military procurement programmes and began the process of transferring the enterprises from their caves and tunnels in the remote interior, as well as putting them in new enterprise zones in the coastal belt outside the cities. Over the years, many factories that had been deliberately built in the centre of major cities, including steel plants, electronics factories, chemical plants and some pharmaceutical plants, were also moved into these new industrial zones. This switch enriched certain cities and provinces, often those in the south at the expense of those in the north-west or north-east. It involved a huge transfer of wealth and of population too. Those involved in light industry, making anything from shoes, buttons, clothes, bicycles, furniture, kitchenware, and all kinds of household goods began to prosper, while those in heavy industry, such as steel, began to suffer increasing losses.

In the early 1990s, the state admitted that these giant state-owned enterprises were going bankrupt along with the state banks. The government could no longer afford to subsidise many of these failing factories and institutes or pay the pension of the vast body of retirees. The state enterprise sector, which employed nearly 200 million people, was bankrupt. Tens of millions were effectively laid off, or their pensions cancelled and replaced by a tiny survival allowance. The state hospitals, which served the needs of these workers and pensioners, were in trouble too, as were their suppliers in the pharmaceutical and medical instruments sector.

The military-industrial sector faced especially difficult challenges. Its factories were over-manned and had rudimentary transport links to the main markets. Some were kept going by selling weapons during the Iran-Iraq War, but others tried to switch to producing goods for the consumer market. One tank factory in Shaanxi that I visited tried, without much success, to produce golf carts. The whole state sector was ordered to 'jump into the sea of commerce'. Everyone went into business. The navy started large-scale smuggling of coal, cars, cigarettes and TV sets. The Foreign Ministry went into catering and business consultancy. The Great Hall of the People touted itself as a conference and marketing venue. The secret Xichang satellite-launching centre in a remote area of Sichuan started inviting visitors and winning contracts to launch commercial satellites for the American company Loral. Even the military units in charge of China's nuclear weapons, the Second Artillery Corps, went into business. It was a way of offloading surplus personnel—all of them were burdened with far too many retirees, generals, managers and support staff—who could now be pushed sideways into these new businesses.

The whole process was accompanied by a dual pricing policy. This meant that there existed simultaneously a market price and a price fixed by the state for all goods and services. Lots of Chinese could therefore do well by arbitrating from one to the other. So, you could obtain coal at a low fixed state price and then sell it in the market at a hefty mark-up. In an economy where everything was in a short supply, these 'briefcase companies' could make a lot of money quickly. Besides, there were also huge differences between prices within the country and those outside. And all these state organisations owned lots of assets, such as land, housing, office space, vehicles, machinery which they could lease, or they could trade in permits and licenses by working as business consultants or fixers.

While all this was going on, the People's Liberation Army's General Logistics Department also took the plunge into 'the sea of commerce', and in 1992 backed the Sanjiu (Three Nines) Pharmaceuticals Group, which was set up in the Shenzhen Special Economic Zone. It had been founded a few years earlier by Zhao Xinxian, who had previously run the pharmacy department in a PLA hospital. Together with five colleagues, he made a success of marketing a medicine called *Sanjiu weitai* based on a traditional Chinese medicine treatment for gastric disorders. He promoted it everywhere and claimed to be the first Chinese company to put up a billboard in Times Square. It became a runaway success, allowing Zhao to take over or set up 100 companies with the ambition of creating a pharmaceutical giant. The General Logistics Department made Zhao's company take over businesses in hotels, property development, food and beverages, construction and printing that it had started. Unfortunately, some of these went sour and the group eventually collapsed, with Zhao ending up being arrested for economic crimes. But among the ventures that Zhao set up, several were in biotechnology.

However, at the peak of the military business craze in the late 1990s, just before the Asian financial crash, the PLA ran 400 pharmaceutical companies. Under Maoist policies of self-sufficiency and autarchy, every province had to be able to make its own medicines, so it could survive in case of a war. Together, these companies had a 10 per cent share of the domestic market and were especially good at trading in traditional Chinese medicines. The Second Artillery Group (which operated the nuclear rockets) had the Shanhaidan group, which was a runner up competitor to Sanjiu. Eventually, all these military-linked pharmaceutical companies began to be outplayed by new challengers who teamed with Western companies, and the Communist Party began to order the military to divest itself of its businesses. By this time, some of these former military factories had acquired foreign partners and were busy trying to find export markets.

The Chinese medicine industry was a particularly profitable niche, if only because it required none of the research and trials that make the development of new Western medicines so vastly time consuming and costly. The minimum cost of bringing a new Western drug to market is around $600 million, but in most cases it is closer to a billion. Soon lots of enterprises, mostly operated by local governments, found it easier to jump into the business of producing Chinese medicines or generic drugs. Until 1993, any Chinese company could copy a drug, as there was no law of patent protection.

The Chinese (and Asian) economic crisis began to abate, and after 2000, a new boom started, spurred by a new wave of reforms. As the state lifted price controls, thousands of new enterprises sprang up in the pharmaceutical sector, often quite small, producing drugs and other basic medical instruments and supplies. Many drugs and products could easily be copied because the original patents had expired. Such generic drugs are cheap to produce and very profitable, with margins averaging 18 per cent. Consequently, the shortages of basic over-the-counter drugs and prescription drugs turned into a surplus.

Most of these new enterprises, which sprang up almost overnight, were quite small. They produced common medicines such as vitamin C, aspirin, paracetamol, ibuprofen, basic vaccines and common antibiotics like capreomycin, streptomycin and sulfadiazine. China produced generic drugs at a very competitive price, even if sometimes the quality was not the best or the companies breached patents or stole IPR. In the United States, around 90 per cent of all prescriptions are generic drugs, but many of these are actually made in India, not China.

India was the first country to start making drugs whose patents had expired, initially for its domestic market. It started in 1970, when its then leader, Indira Gandhi, passed laws preventing medical products from being patented in the country. This spurred the creation of a new industry of local manufacturers, who found ways to produce patented drugs, but at a much lower cost. Soon India started making inroads into overseas markets, and by 2019 it was exporting drugs worth $20 billion a year. To stay competitive, these companies started sourcing materials from China.

India imports almost 70 per cent of its bulk drugs and intermediates—the chemicals that make a finished drug work. In particular, it buys all its paracetamol, metformin (a diabetes treatment), antibiotics such as amoxicillin, ampicillin and ciprofloxacin and ibuprofen from China. India has lower labour costs, but it's far less efficient, as electricity is more expensive and erratic, the transport system is poor and full of choke points, and its time consuming constrictive bureaucracy makes it a more difficult place to do business.

In China, the erosion of the state's monopoly over the distribution and pricing of every kind of medical supplies was a critical factor in encouraging real competition. There was a sudden scramble to create reliable brand names and to set up commercial marketing and distribution systems. By 2007, China had up to 7,000 producers and 14,000 distributors. The state-owned pharmaceutical enterprises struggled to compete with their nimbler private sector competitors.

On the other hand, Chinese companies developed a reputation for poor quality controls, and indeed for deliberately falsifying data. The American Food and Drug Administration (FDA), which carries out inspections at home and abroad, reports that inspections of drug plants in the United States uncovered violations of the FDA's data integrity rules about 15 per cent of the time. These rules stipulate that all manufacturing data must be preserved—unaltered—and made available to regulators. In India, about 25 per cent of the plants inspected committed some sort of data violation, while in China, that figure hovers just above 32 per cent. In the United States, about 28 per cent of plants cited for data integrity problems exhibited truly deceptive behaviour. In India, that number rose to 55 per cent, and in China, to 65 per cent. At the manufacturing plants themselves, data integrity violations can mean profound deceit: tearing up records of failing drug tests and smuggling them from the plant; or inventing data to indicate that a plant is sterile, without actually doing the required microbial testing of the surfaces, air, and water. It is worth recalling that such fraudulent activities take place in a system where FDA inspectors have to give advance warning of their visits.

Many Chinese companies have been caught out making and selling faulty vaccines, often with deadly consequences. In 2018, China launched a crackdown and singled out the country's second-biggest maker of rabies vaccines for harsh punishment. Inspectors from the State Drug Administration made a snap visit to Changchun Changsheng Bio-technology based in Changchun, in the northern province of Jilin, which supplies a quarter of the market. They found that the factory was forging manufacturing data to hide that it was using out of date vaccine fluid and blending it into new vaccine shots. So the State Drug Administration withdrew its manufacturing licence, the Good Manufacturing Practice (GMP) for medical products certificate. In its defence, the company said that the batch discovered by the inspectors had not been put on the market. The company recalled all the rabies vaccines it had delivered to disease control centres and hospitals and said that 'no adverse effects related to the quality of the vaccine have been found from years of adverse effects monitoring'.[1]

In another scandal, the Wuhan Institute of Biological Products (the company named as a bioweapons factory) was caught selling a substandard DPT vaccine. It sold 190,500 of these vaccines to the Chongqing Centre for Disease Control and Prevention and 210,000 to the Hebei Provincial Centre for Disease Control and Prevention.

In 2017, the WHO analysed drug samples and found that 10.5 per cent of pharmaceutical drugs in low and middle-income countries are fake or substandard. China is regarded as the largest production centre for counterfeit medicines. In 2001, the state media said that Chinese authorities had closed 1,300 factories after investigating 480,000 cases of counterfeit drugs worth $57 million. The State Food and Drug Administration (SFDA) of China announced that in 2005 it had banned 114,00 unlicensed drug manufactures and destroyed 461 illegal pharmaceutical factories. It is estimated that in China between 200,000 and 300,000 people die each year as a result of counterfeit or substandard medicine. And these are reported cases: the true number of cases is likely to be far higher.[2]

In 2008, China saw another scandal involving the adulteration of milk and infant formula with melamine, a chemical that was added to diluted milk so that it would seem to have a high protein content and could pass quality control tests. Some babies died from damage to their kidneys, and 54,000 others were hospitalized.

During that same year, the Chinese government decided that there were far too many pharmaceutical companies competing with each other, and they should be consolidated into a handful of big companies, national champions, which would be easier to control and manage. This is an industrial central planning strategy that China has applied to many industries—supermarkets, cars, TV manufacturers, coal mines—in fact those producing just about every consumer product.

Price liberalisation would unleash an investment craze in some sectors marked by shortages and therefore high margins. This sucked in a lot of capital and competitors, many with poor qualifications, which eventually led to an over-investment boom. This in turn led to rapidly falling prices, cut-throat competition and cutting of corners, low margins and finally a crash in which investors and banks lost their shirts. The state would step in and then favour a handful of companies with cheap credit, who could buy up their competitors—that is those that were still standing.

China is one of the last countries run by five-year plans in the style of Stalin, and these are the work of China's central planning board, currently called the National Development and Reform Commission. In this instance, the decisions are handled by the state-owned Assets Supervision and Administration Commission of the State Council (SASAC). It ordered the pharmaceutical industry to merge into a handful of big national players. By 2020, China had more than a dozen pharmaceutical companies with revenues of over a billion USD.

One of these is the CR Pharmaceutical Group Limited, which belongs to a giant state-owned conglomerate, the China Resources Group with over 400,000 employees. CR Pharma took over our old friend, the Sanjiu (Three Nines) Group plus others, such as the Double-Crane Pharmaceutical, which in the Mao-era was the military's Beijing Pharmaceuticals Factory, and a dozen other companies with similar pedigrees. The conglomerate has its own national network of pharmacies to distribute its many brands of traditional Chinese medicines.

The biggest fish is the state-owned China National Pharmaceutical Group—the Sinopharm Group—formed out of a compulsory merger of many companies including the Wuhan Institute of Biological Products (the company identified earlier as a bioweapons factory). The group has 150,000 employees and 1,500 subsidiaries. Among the largest of those are the China National Medicines Corporation Ltd., the China National Accord Medicines Corporation Ltd., the Beijing Tiantan Biological Products Co. Ltd., the Shanghai Shyndec Pharmaceutical Co. Ltd., and the China Traditional Chinese Medicine Holdings Co. Ltd. The group does everything from operating a nationwide chain of pharmacies to running advanced research laboratories and patenting new treatments.

Vaccine development is done through two institutes of a Sinopharm subsidiary, the China National Biotec Group. These are the Beijing Biological Institute and the Wuhan Institute of Biological Products. Later, the Wuhan Institute of Biological Products became the first institute worldwide to enter clinical trials for a COVID-19 vaccine in April 2020.

For Sinopharma and other giants, profits come from generic drugs, traditional Chinese medicines and active pharmaceutical ingredients. Traditional Chinese medicine takes around 40 per cent of the drug market in China, despite the fact that the absence of reliable clinical studies to prove that any of it works, or tough manufacturing standards and testing. Margins are high, and this reflects an abiding popular belief in the ideas behind Chinese medicine—and the consumption of many animals or animal related products. This is blamed for the outbreak of both SARS and COVID-19.

A closely related industry that expanded very fast is the manufacturing of all kinds of medical devices and equipment. China's medical equipment market is worth around $67 billion a year, and its exports tripled in the twenty years up to 2018 to total $25 billion a year. As with other industries, there are a lot of small players crowded at the lower end of the market. Not surprisingly,

Chinese manufacturers dominated the global supply of masks and other supplies needed to deal with the COVID-19 pandemic, and China was later accused of using its strong position to divert supplies to its domestic needs. This led to calls to localize production of essential supplies in America. An outbreak of fighting in the Himalayas between Chinese and Indian troops meant there were calls in India to stop relying on Chinese imports, and instead to boost the Indian generic drug industry.

At the same time that China has been busily building up a dominant place in the lower end of the pharmaceutical industry, foreign pharmaceutical companies entered the Chinese market, first to supply new drugs, then to manufacture, test and finally to carry out research and development. Gradually, tens of thousands of Chinese who studied abroad began to return, which created a pool of expertise that foreign pharma giants could employ. Next, China began to nurture ever-larger ambitions for its industry. It aspired to dominating the higher end of the pharma industry, until now the reserve of Western pharma giants in America, Switzerland, Germany, Britain and Japan. It wanted to leap frog into a commanding position in the biotechnology industry—and that is where the trouble started.

7

MADE IN CHINA PLAN

Plans, plans, plans. China out-produces the rest of the world in many things, including plans. It is still run by a Communist Party that never lost its love for central planning. There are five-year plans, ten-year plans, fifteen-year plans, thirty-year plans, national plans, regional plans, provincial plans, city plans, sector plans, industry plans, export plans, not to mention all kinds of targets and quotas—and secret plans which the Party keeps to itself.

All this is backed by an equally deep devotion to gathering and announcing statistics at every level. The quality of the statistics is so poor that even China's top leaders despair of ever seeing reliable economic statistics. Inevitably, everyone is under the compunction to twist the statistics, so as to make sure they exactly meet the targets set out in the plan. GDP statistics always matched those in the plan or exceeded them. They were never subsequently revised. It gives the impression of an all-knowing, all-powerful state.

To try and understand what was really going on in the economy, Chinese leaders started looking at shadow statistics, which they thought would be harder to falsify, such as electricity consumption or freight train movements. Others went abroad to study other countries' trade statistics in order to deduce what was happening inside China, because they might cast a more reliable picture of, say, energy consumption or manufacturing. Still others pored over night-time satellite photographs, comparing them day by day or month by month, to try to measure the amount of economic activity.

Despite the fetish with statistics, they don't necessarily provide a simple answer to a basic question: how much of China's growth and prosperity should be credited to the private sector, and how much to that owned by the state? How much to private entrepreneurial initiative and how much to top-down big state intervention?

It is hard, if not impossible, to provide a simple answer to this question, but, depending on one's standpoint, China's plans to dominate biotechnology are either a folly or a dire threat to Western interests.

One of the plans which has caused the greatest stir in recent years is the one called 'Made in China 2025', which was released in 2015. It aims to increase the domestic market share of Chinese suppliers for 'basic core components and important basic material' to 40 per cent by 2020 and 70 per cent by 2025. The plan focuses on cars, biotechnology, aviation, space, semiconductors, IT and robotics. This is because the CCP considers these the sectors where China must challenge the strength of foreign companies.

This is one piece of a complex architecture of plans and policies aimed at generating 'innovation-driven development'. There are ten priority sectors, which include new generation information technology; advanced numerical control machine tools and robotics; aerospace technology, aircraft engines and airborne equipment; and biopharmaceuticals and high-performance medical equipment.

Semi-official documents related to the strategy set very concrete benchmarks for certain segments: 40 per cent of mobile phone chips on the Chinese market are supposed to be produced in China by 2025, as well as 70 per cent of industrial robots and 80 per cent of renewable energy equipment.

Washington takes all this very seriously. In 2018, the Council on Foreign Relations stated that China is a 'real existential threat to U.S. technological leadership'.

China is already the dominant manufacturer in many sectors including textiles, garment making, shoes, phones, computers, electrical appliances, light industrial goods, rare earths, building materials, generic drugs, steel, coal, motor vehicles, ship building—at least when it comes to volume. China produces two thirds of the world's chemical fibres, 38 per cent of the world's textiles, a third of the world's apparel exports, two thirds of the world's shoes, more than half the world's steel and coal, a quarter of the world's mobile phones, and so on.

Until now, the global division of labour allowed the United States, Germany, Japan and other developed countries to dominate the top end, capital and knowledge intensive products—China may make mobile phones, but the most valuable parts are the chips, which are designed and made by Western companies. But China has set itself the ambition of ending the West's dominance over every part of the market.

China's National Integrated Circuit Strategy calls for at least $160 billion in subsidies to create a completely closed-loop semiconductor industry in China, including explicit plans to halve Chinese imports of US-manufactured semiconductors by 2025, and eliminate them entirely by 2035. The Made in China 2025 Strategy is supported by some 800 state-guided funds to the tune of more than $350 billion, including for projects in advanced-battery manufacturing, wide-body aircraft and robotics.

In the past, China's ambitions might have raised a polite smile, but this is no longer the case. American hi-tech companies and leaders such as former President Clinton had scoffed at the idea that China could cut itself off from the world wide web, which was dominated by American companies. In 2000, Clinton declared that trying to control the internet in China would be like trying to 'nail Jell-o [jelly] to the wall', in a speech on the China Trade Bill that paved the way for the US to normalize trade relations with China, and for the latter to join the World Trade Organisation in 2001. He sarcastically wished the Chinese 'good luck' for trying to crack down on the internet. 'In the new [21st] century, liberty will spread by cell phone and cable modem', he said.

Yet the Chinese government went on to build the so-called Great Firewall of China—a very large and sophisticated system that completely walls out Google, Facebook, YouTube etc., to the extent that it became nearly impossible for Chinese people to visit foreign media sites. In their place China created its own social media giants like Tencent QQ, Baidu, Wechat, Alibaba, Zhihu, Sinaweibo, Qunaer, Zoom, Ant, Didi Chuxing, TikTok and more. These were set up by Chinese entrepreneurs, but they also exist because the government created the digital Great Wall, and they can only flourish under tight Party supervision.

The Chinese government also confounded sceptics by dominating the market for solar panels after it had defined it as a 'strategic industry'. More than 60 per cent of solar panels are made in China, even though American companies invented the technology and hold most of the patents. China bought solar companies and invited others to move there, where they found cheap, skilled labour. Instead of paying taxes, they received tax credits. The central government subsidised the industry with $47 billion to help build the economies of scale to bring down prices quickly. The growth was helped by large-scale imports by Spain, Italy and Germany, who wanted to subsidize a quick expansion of solar power capacity.[1]

The result was a glut of solar panels on the world market. Prices crashed and many European and American companies, who often had better technology, went bankrupt and left the industry. China had effectively captured a new industry in the same way that it had earlier captured older industries such as textiles, shoes, garment and apparel making by providing its manufacturers with export credits, a cheap currency, cheap land, non-unionised labour and so on.

It is a policy mix pioneered by Japan after 1945—entrepreneurs backed by guidance from a central planning board, which in Japan was MITI—the Ministry of International Trade and Industry. Japan was almost always under one party, the Liberal Democratic Party, and it worked closely with banks, as well as the private sector, to protect the home market with non-tariff barriers. This created a launch pad to capture a series of industries—textiles, steel, ship-building, consumer electronics, integrated circuits, motorbikes, cars, machine building—which it still dominates fifty years later. The Japanese acquired Western technology by hook or by crook, and were then willing to suffer losses to undercut their competitors with 'predatory' pricing. If this succeeded, and they weakened their rivals, the Japanese could then raise their prices and start making profits.

The big Japanese conglomerates were also able and efficient manufacturers who earned a reputation for precision and reliability at a time, especially during the 1970s, when British and American competitors were crippled by waves of strikes and underinvestment. Later, some Japanese companies, such as Sony, became famous for innovative products like the Sony Walkman.

The Japanese and the small tiger economies of Taiwan, South Korea, Hong Kong and Singapore were also helped by the Cold War. America was fighting a series of wars in South East Asia, which meant it was willing to bolster the economy of these countries to defeat the Communist threat, even at the expense of some of its own industries. South Korean conglomerates such as Hyundai and Samsung then proved adept at following in the footsteps of the Japanese.

The American global strategy must be recognized as a success overall. Although it was defeated in Vietnam, East Asia remained staunchly anti-communist, and finally the Soviet Union collapsed. China was forced to demilitarize and switch to establishing a consumer-led economy. Washington then believed that, if it offered the same sort of economic and political aid to China, it would reap similar benefits. The creation of a thriving middle class with a strong private sector would inevitably bring about a political liberalisation in China, even under the continuing rule of the Chinese Communist Party.

In the event, the student-led uprising of 1989 failed. The pro-democracy protests were crushed by the PLA in the Tiananmen massacre. Those in the CCP leadership who wanted liberalisation lost power. Deng Xiaoping and his allies resolved to tighten political control, which meant more than strict censorship and a ban on any kind of organisation outside direct Party control. From now on every company, irrespective of its ownership, had to be kept under the control of its Party secretary. This is different from Stalin's model and more akin to Benito Mussolini's national corporatism—the merger of state and corporate power. The Italian dictator once said: 'Everything in the State, nothing outside the State, nothing against the State'.

A succession of Chinese leaders argued that without their political monopoly, the country would break apart or descend into chaos. Western governments, in the burst of optimism that followed victory in the Cold War, gambled that the Party would sooner or later have to succumb to the domestic demand for change and more freedom. Besides, as China opened up, it offered Western companies the huge and unique opportunity of conquering potentially the world's largest single market.

Chinese leaders saw things differently. They were not interested in Western political slogans or models, they wanted access to Western technology and know-how. Huge numbers went abroad to study in Western universities. In 1978, it started with the departure of 3,000 students and by 2018, there were over 600,000 studying abroad. Many chose to stay on in their host country to gain work experience or to take foreign citizenship.

Western companies, initially lured to set up shop in special economic zones, were compelled to take on Chinese partners and to share their technology and know-how. Even if they did, they often found that, after their partners had copied everything, they set up a rival company and let the joint venture fail. Those joint ventures that succeeded created job opportunities for the returning students.

China also argued that because of its size and history it was exceptional. It would therefore do things its own way, and it was free to ignore the advice and example of other countries. The Party followed political slogans such as 'socialism with Chinese characteristics' or the 'socialist market economy', or 'reform and opening up'—which it could interpret any way it wished.

In practical terms, China's sheer size and the human resources that it could mobilise did indeed make it unique. Take infrastructure: China really can build infrastructure at a speed that no other country could. It can commandeer a workforce to work three shifts round the clock seven days a week. It could select a technology and then throw a huge weight behind it on an unequalled scale. Such as trains, for example.

China barely built a single new (passenger) train line during the 1960s and 70s. It was still relying on old steam engines in the 1980s and had the slowest passenger train service in the world. Then, once it decided to build a new railway system, it managed to build the world's largest high-speed rail network in the world in just fifteen years. First it established a government 'Action

Plan for the Independent Innovation of Chinese High-Speed Trains'. Then it created a powerful national champion, the Chinese Railway Construction Corporation (CRCC), which as a result became the largest rail producer in the world. It managed to build its high-speed network at an average cost of $17m–$21m per km—about two thirds of the cost found in other countries. The CRCC built up a debt of a staggering $4.7 trillion, leading many to suspect that China has built a series of white elephants. Only one in six of its high-speed train lines can cover its operating costs. Yet China is now in a position to export its trains and know-how around the world. The China Export-Import Bank now offers $30 billion to finance the exports of the CRCC.

Japan was the first country to build high-speed trains with the Shinkansen Bullet Train in the 1960s, but China now has two thirds of the world's high-speed trains. In early 2004, when China wanted to introduce high-speed trains to the whole country, it was not able to do the design and manufacture on its own. So the Chinese railway ministry organized an international bid.

Many international bidders such as Kawasaki (Japan), Siemens (Germany), Bombardier (Canada) and Alstom (France) participated in the bid. Instead of choosing a single bidder, the Chinese railway ministry asked each company to design and produce their own type of high-speed trains. The conditions were that they would have to be manufactured in China, and to accept the signal standard from China.

In other words, the Chinese pressured foreign producers into giving Chinese state-owned enterprise competitors key technology and IP in what it called 'exchanging market for technology'. After two years, Kawasaki decided to quit and keep its own technology. It later claimed that China had stolen its technology.

The Chinese wanted Kawasaki to build a train that could run at 350kmph, like the new Shinkansen E2, but the Japanese only offered the older technology that allowed trains to run at

250kmph. It hadn't yet completed a new line for the Shinkansen E2 in Japan.

In response, China's railway ministry and Ministry of Science and Technology set up 'Project 226' bringing together dozens of universities and research laboratories, hundreds of researchers and thousands of engineers as well as its chief manufacturers Qingdao Sifang and CR Tangshan. They designed their own vehicle integration, aerodynamics topology, load-bearing system, dynamic transmission and braking system, train control operating system, traction power supply, key materials and components. The result was the CRH380A that appeared in 2010—a train that looked exactly like the Shinkansen E2.

Yoshiyuki Kasai, honorary chairman of the Central Japan Railway Company, then admitted that the transfer technology scheme had been a blunder. 'The Shinkansen is the jewel of Japan. The technology transfer to China was a huge mistake', he said.

The Chinese were then determined to show that their new train could travel faster than anyone's, at 360kmph. In 2011, two high-speed trains collided near Wenzhou in Zhejiang province, killing at least forty people. One of the trains involved was the 380A. The accident was blamed on signalling and a lightning strike.

Two other companies involved in partnering with the Chinese, France's Alstom and Germany's Siemens, have also come to regret their involvement in the Chinese market. The Chinese tried to reduce their dependence on supplies from these companies and then mounted an attack on their overseas markets. China went on to patent a remarkably similar high-speed-rail technology in the US and other countries, meaning that Japanese and European train makers now find themselves frozen out of international markets, including their European markets. Faced with being undercut by their erstwhile Chinese partners, Alstom and Siemens have been considering a merger.

Countries such as the United States and the UK have struggled to build high-speed train lines, and when they do try, progress is measured in decades. Overcoming the regulatory burden can consume a quarter of the cost, compared to around three per cent in China.

Under President Trump, Washington hit back with tariffs that often targeted goods made under the Made in China 2025 plan—especially IT and robotics-related products. Some Americans fear that China might move faster in adopting new breakthroughs in the fast-evolving field of intelligent manufacturing, and become more competitive. The Chinese government is throwing money at various projects such as electrical vehicles, lithium batteries and advanced manufacturing. There is, for instance, an Advanced Manufacturing Fund, worth 20 billion RMB ($2.8 billion). Or the National Integrated Circuit Fund, worth 139 billion RMB ($20 billion). These national level funds are complemented by a plethora of provincial level financing vehicles.

This compares well with the €200 million of federal funding that the German government has provided for research on Industry 4.0 technologies so far. While Chinese high-tech companies enjoy massive state backing, foreign companies in China face many non-tariff barriers to doing business in China—they are excluded from local subsidy schemes and also struggle to maintain any commercial secrecy. Some fear that, as China's own smart manufacturing capabilities mature, it will discriminate against foreign competitors even more. Many countries could find their technological lead quickly hollowed out.

In the struggle between China and America over who controls the future of 5G and integrated circuits (chips), Huawei became a key battleground. After it was founded by a former PLA officer, Ren Zhengfei, who had jumped into the sea of commerce, it grew from nothing to generating annual revenues of $100 billion. Ren had started out working in the PLA's Information Technology Research Bureau, but was demobilised in 1983 and went to Shenzhen to set up his own company selling and servicing server switches. Sometime in the 1990s, his company was selected out of thousands of start-ups to receive the backing of the state as the mobile phone industry began to take off in China, leapfrogging the whole stage of fixed line telephone connections. The *Wall Street Journal* estimated that the state gave it as much as $75 billion in subsidies. A *Bloomberg Business Week* story reports that Huawei partly owes its rise to technology from Canada's Nortel.[2] At its height, the Canadian telecom equipment manufacturer employed 90,000 people and 'dominated the market for fibre-optic data transmission systems; it had invented a touchscreen wireless device almost a decade before the iPhone and controlled thousands of fibre-optic and wireless patents'. Then Chinese hackers stole all its technology, downloading everything. The data leak was traced back to a district in Shanghai near a Chinese military unit tasked with spying on computer networks in the US and Canada.

Around the same time, Huawei turned from being a manufacturer of cheap imitation mobile phones to becoming a giant in making the routers and switches that direct data, servers that store it, components for the fibre-optic cables that transmit it, radio antennas that send it to wireless devices, and the software to manage it all. Soon Nortel fell victim to predatory pricing, and it went bankrupt in 2011. It even lost its own domestic market to Huawei. The Chinese company became the world leader. It is poised to own much of the world's critical telecom infrastructure and to set the international industry standards. Eventually Ren's daughter, Meng Wanzhou, would be arrested in Canada, from where the United States wanted to extradite her to face criminal charges relating to breaching the embargo against Iran.

The United States government has set out to prevent Huawei's further growth, and is demanding that its allies cease awarding contracts to the company. It argues that Huawei poses a huge long-term security risk, because the Chinese government can force it to spy on its customers or even sabotage critical infrastructure.

Huawei commands the latest technology, which it can offer at the lowest prices. The company generated revenue of more than $105 billion in 2018, an almost 20 per cent increase over the previous year. Huawei does business in more than 170 countries and regions; approximately half its income comes from outside of China. It controls 29 per cent of the market, while its nearest rival, Nokia, has a 16 per cent market share. Huawei's market share would have been even higher but for the fact that the US, Australia, New Zealand and Japan banned Huawei's 5G infrastructure. It has few rivals capable of building a 5G network: ZTE in China, Ericsson in Sweden and Nokia in Finland.

China has also been quicker and more determined to invest in upgrading its mobile phone network. Since 2015, China outspent the US by $24 billion in wireless communications infrastructure. Its three network operators have built 350,000 new cell phone tower sites, while the US built fewer than 30,000. China intends to keep spending on building a 5G mobile network that is quicker and better than that of any other country.

The mixture of low cunning and vaulting ambition, hubris and nemesis, is evident in this and many other industries. China is willing to gamble big on new technologies. Its size alone can help it to dominate any industry it wants to and then take control of its future. But it is China's ambition for the pharmaceutical industry, and especially for the new world of biotechnology, which may be deeply connected to the emergence of COVID-19.

8

WUHAN AND THE PHARMA INDUSTRY

Europe was the unquestioned centre for pharmaceutical research and development for centuries. The only challenge came from Japan in the 1960s and 70s. In the 1970s, the big European companies came up with 149 new drugs, compared to sixty-six created by Americans. Very few new active substances were first approved in the United States. Until 1990, the Europeans simply invested far more than the Americans.

American pharmaceutical companies are now the most dynamic and innovative. The United States stepped up spending until it accounted for 57 per cent of global research expenditures. European and Japanese firms began shifting some of their research work to the United States. Eleven of the top twenty-five global pharmaceutical companies now have their headquarters in the United States. The US remains the predominant powerhouse of drug discovery and production, ranking first in nearly all measures of innovation. In the 2000s, more new chemical entities were developed and approved by regulatory authorities in the United States than in the next five nations—Switzerland, Japan, the United Kingdom, Germany and France—

combined. Over the twenty years to 2016, US-headquartered enterprises were responsible for 42 per cent of new chemical and biological entities introduced and approved around the world, far outpacing contributions from European Union member countries, Japan, China and other nations. More than 350 new medicines have been approved by the (American) Food and Drug Administration (FDA).

How have the Americans done this? Mostly by making their regulations, laws and tax environment more attractive to the industry than anywhere else. For instance, in 1981 Washington encouraged private sector R&D spending with a special tax credit. This was followed up in 1986 with an orphan drug tax credit to encourage drug companies to develop drugs for rare diseases, those affecting 200,000 or fewer (American) patients. Then in 1992, the Prescription Drug User Fee Act allowed the Food and Drug Administration to collect fees from drug manufacturers to fund the new drug approval process. This cut the length of time it takes the FDA to approve a new drug from an average of thirty months to just ten. Next, American intellectual property laws give better protection for companies that develop 'biopharmaceutical' products—twelve years compared to five for chemical drugs—as well as protection for companies making generic drugs—those for which patent protection has expired. The American drug pricing system allows companies to earn enough from one generation of biomedical innovation to invest in the next one. In other words, limited government price controls made it more attractive to invest in this industry compared to other countries. Additionally, in the late 1990s and early 2000s, the National Institutes of Health (NIH) doubled research funding grants.

There has also been a shift away from chemical to organic compounds. The industry started with Germany's Bayer synthesizing the molecules to make aspirin in 1897, a drug which previously had been made from willow bark. After that, the industry concentrated on finding and making new chemicals.

The biotechnology industry—biotech—started in Silicon Valley with the development of human insulin by Genentech in 1976. Genentech was a company founded by a venture capitalist—Robert Swanson together with biochemist Herbert Boyer—to commercialize the new technology of recombinant DNA. This led to the creation of synthetic human insulin. The biochemists found a way of using recombinant DNA to change the DNA of living cells, altering their internal biochemical pathways so that they produce certain useful molecules. Biotech drugs are usually various kinds of proteins that are made by growing large batches of cells in a nutritive medium (a kind of yeast) and then filtering out the desired molecule. A biotech plant therefore looks more like a hi-tech brewery than a chemical plant.

This kind of drug is also known as a biologic medical product, or 'biologic', which means that they are extracted or semi-synthesized from biological sources. They include vaccines, blood, blood components, allergenics, somatic cells, gene therapies, tissues, recombinant therapeutic protein, and living cells used in cell therapy. Biologics can be composed of sugars, proteins, nucleic acids or complex combinations of these substances, or may be living cells or tissues. They are isolated from natural sources—human, animal, or microorganism.

All the big pharmaceutical giants now cover both sides of the industry, and the biopharma industry is particularly strong in the United States. But the biopharma know-how is shared with the 'biotechnology industry', which involves making products from microorganisms using different scientific processes like fermentation, gene cloning, genetically modified plants and animals to produce certain proteins or enzymes. The United States is the biggest adopter of biocrops. Americans more readily buy modified potato varieties that don't bruise and resist blight, or sugarcane that has been altered so it is more insect resistant and drought tolerant.

The US has strong competitors in Switzerland, Germany and the UK, but it is China that poses a threat. As part of its ambitions to capture new technologies and to be pre-eminent in all industries, Beijing earmarked the pharmaceutical industry for accelerated growth. President Xi Jinping described his country's reliance on foreign drug imports as a critical issue. China is already the second largest pharmaceutical market behind the United States and has a large ageing population, so he has intended this as a platform to build a powerful industry with globally competitive firms. China set out to make the biotechnology sector worth more than 4 per cent of the country's gross domestic product by 2020.

Under the China 2025 plan, China has crafted a mix of policies that it hopes will work just as well with biotechnology as it has with high-speed trains, solar panels, lithium batteries, or 5G IT. Wuhan was chosen to become a national centre of the new biotech industry, and its research laboratories and factories came under pressure to make rapid progress. Chinese biotech companies were given leeway to carry out risky experiments if it could help them steal a march on their overseas rivals.

The Chinese government set out to replicate some of the favourable policies that helped nurture the US industry. The regulations governing new drug approval were changed to make it quicker and cheaper to get approval. The Chinese Food and Drug Administration was replaced by a new body, the National Medical Products Administration, which aimed to streamline and improve the Chinese pharmaceutical industry.

Between 2001 and 2016, China approved 100 new drugs, while in the same period, Western countries approved over 300. It cut the approval times by half to just two or three years. One way of doing this was by allowing data from trials conducted overseas instead of forcing foreign companies to start again with fresh tests inside China. It strengthened the safety and testing requirements, making them more expensive but more trustworthy. China joined the International Council for Harmonization (ICH) in mid-2017 to demonstrate that its standards now met global benchmarks. All this spurred industry consolidation and forced companies to spend more on R&D. At the time, China dramatically expanded the share of its citizens eligible for health insurance.

The international pharmaceutical giants had already been investing in research centres and manufacturing facilities in China, but while they welcomed these changes, they became convinced that China was undermining their patent protection rights in order to force them to share know-how with Chinese competitors. For example, independent of patent protection, the United States and European Union both provide a period of marketing exclusivity (known as 'regulatory data protection') for a drug, as well as patent term extension to compensate for the loss of a patent term during the approval process. China does not do this, and this means that the lifespan of a patent can be shorter by 40 per cent. China also provides only a six-year data exclusivity period for drugs that contain new chemical entities, compared with twelve years (for biologic drugs) in the United States. However, China generally does not live up to even this commitment, which helps Chinese companies become competitors earlier.

China also uses procedures to invalidate patents based on heightened 'enablement' and non-obviousness requirements. This means that the applicant must show that an invention is new, inventive (non-obvious), and enabled to be considered patentable subject matter. This is particularly tricky in biotech, because it uses microorganisms that occur naturally. China made it more difficult than patent offices in other major countries to file supplementary data with the patent application (post-filing data supplementation), which invalidated more patents.

China also set about persuading the students who had gone abroad to study to return home and work in the domestic life sciences industry by offering all kinds of financial incentives under the Thousand Talents Plan. It increased the number of university places available to study relevant subjects. Chinese universities now produce around 150,000 life sciences graduates annually, compared with America's 137,000. And it channels ever-larger amounts of research funds into medical science. By 2016, Chinese biopharma R&D spending had shot up to $7.2 billion, from just $163 million in 2000. Soon, Chinese researchers were producing as many research papers as Americans. Slowly but surely, China began registering its own patents, especially in fields such as anti-cancer drugs and cell therapy. More and more start-ups appeared, sometimes set up by returning Chinese students or professors. The state is also providing incentives for expatriates in the industry to return to China to conduct research.

Through its Thousand Talents Plan, between 2012 and 2018 an estimated 250,000 Chinese life scientists returned. Many of China's biotech start-ups have founders who were educated abroad. Nearly all the top twenty pharmaceutical companies in the world set up manufacturing facilities and R&D centres in China. AstraZeneca, for example, had 18,000 employees in China in 2019 and recorded 21 per cent of its 2019 sales there.

To conquer the pharmaceutical industry, China created more and more biological science research parks. The Ministry of Science and Technology (MOST) spent around $1.45 billion by 2020 to support twenty biomedicine science parks. Local governments chipped in a similar amount. Other local governments are also targeting the industry, offering cheap land, infrastructure, tax incentives, free office space and direct subsidies. Innovent, a successful biotech based in Suzhou's BioBay, for example, was given the financing by the local government to build a $120 million biologics manufacturing facility. The company agreed a ten-year $1 billion deal with Eli Lilly to co-develop and commercialise oncology medicines and treatments for diabetes.

These biotech parks come in addition to the over 100 national-level life science parks and more than 400 provincial-level parks. Shanghai, for example, has its 'Pharma Valley', which is a 10km^2 industrial zone that houses more than 500 biotech companies. The city also has another five 'parks'; in different corners of the city, each is devoted to another sub-industry—biomedical innovation, precision diagnosis, high-end medical equipment, and pharmaceutical logistics. About 25 million people work in various kinds of hi-tech zones across China.

The inspiration behind these parks is the Silicon valley effect of innovation clustering for creative entrepreneurs, with the aim of fostering a supportive culture that will produce high risk but high reward start-ups. While elsewhere in the world these communities formed spontaneously, in China they are top-down projects in a country known for a high degree of social control and a lack of political freedoms.

Wuhan in Hubei province also committed to building a portfolio of science and manufacturing parks. These are in the Wuhan East Lake High-tech Development Zone, also known as Optics Valley of China. It is the self-proclaimed birthplace of China's incubator business, the first 'hundred billion yuan-output level' industrial park. Its website claims that it covers an enormous 518km^2 development zone that is home to forty-two universities, fifty-six national and provincial research institutions, sixty-five academicians and more than 300,000 professionals. The park consists of twenty-two sub-parks devoted to high-tech industries such as optical communications, lasers, integrated circuits, the mobile internet, software innovation and financial services and is about 'constantly improving the innovation industry chain and creating an innovation industry cluster'. It also includes a port with its own free trade area and bonded warehouses and other logistics facilities.

Inside this complex is the Wuhan National Bio-industry Base, also known as the Biolake, which claims to be China's second largest state-level biotech industrial base. Biolake's seven industrial parks have formed an industrial cluster devoted to biomedicines, bio medical engineering, bio agriculture, precision medicine, smart medicines and bio services. Some of these companies are just making products used in the generic pharmaceutical industry, often for export to India.

Wuhan had previously been noted as a centre for the car industry, which was drawn by its large steel plants. The Dong Feng Motor Corporation, one of the big four Chinese car manufacturers, is based there. It has strong ties with France, as Dong Feng has partnerships with Peugot-Citroen and Renault.

The whole East Lake project is an impressive sight marked by landmark modern architecture, including one striking building that looks like a gigantic five leaf clover. Another building, shaped like a giant silvery lotus bud, houses an Agricultural Science and Technology Museum. A lot of it looks like it is modelled from Disney World's EPCOT—a 1960s vision of the Experimental Prototype Community of Tomorrow with its silent gliding monorails, concrete plazas, lakes, high density housing, and silvery geometric public buildings.

Many of the production facilities are on a huge scale, clean, gleaming, new and equipped with the latest manufacturing equipment. It is a testament to China's energy and its commitment to switch to a knowledge-based economy. It all demonstrates its ability to marshal huge resources to quickly throw up new housing blocks, roads and metro lines to build its Progress City of Tomorrow.

The Biolake project started with only a dozen or so small companies; within seven years it had attracted nearly a thousand. The industry took off very quickly, not just in Wuhan but across China. The city government claims that by 2020, the Biolake plants had developed thirty Class I new drugs—meaning they had never been marketed in China or overseas—and were entering the stage of clinical trials. Additionally, there were more than 500 Class I and II medical devices, fifty-nine new veterinary drugs and sixty-nine state-approved new varieties of crops.

A stalwart of the project is, of course, the Wuhan Institute of Biological Products, which sprawls over 36 hectares. It is the national engineering technology research centre for vaccines, with over a thousand employees.

Some of the pharma products made in Wuhan and neighbouring cities are involved in small molecule API manufacture. There are in all about forty-two pharma contract manufacturing facilities in the province. Innovative pharmaceutical products whose APIs are manufactured in Hubei include the French company Ipsen SA's Onivyde (irinotecan hydrochloride), a semisynthetic derivative of an alkaloid originally extracted from a Chinese tree, which is manufactured at a Hubei Haosun Pharmaceutical Co Ltd facility, as well as Abbott Labs' clarithromycin, a semi-synthetic macrolide antibiotic that uses APIs manufactured at an HEC Pharm facility in Yidu, Hubei. Hybio Pharmaceutical Co Ltd (Guangdong, China), JHL Biotech Inc (Zhubei, Taipei, Taiwan), and Wuhan Biocause Pharmaceutical Development Co Ltd each have biologic API facilities in the province.

These investments are part of a wave of money flooding into the sector. Something like $45 billion was invested in biotech companies in China, making them the second largest investment field, behind only information technology. A third of it was coming from Chinese venture capital and other private firms. Further investment came through cross border deals, mostly in biologics. A few companies have been able to raise quite substantial amounts by listing on America's stock markets. Chinese biotech company BeiGene raised $756 million with an IPO on Nasdaq in January 2016, and Chi-Med raised $650 million in the same year. Both offered plenty of oncology treatments that were going through clinical trials.

Between 2016 and the end of 2018, Chinese biopharma companies raised $2.3 billion through IPOs. The Hong Kong Stock Exchange had prohibited companies without revenue from listing, which applied to biotech companies, as they are still developing their products. But after it lifted that restriction in 2018, the Chinese company BeiGene raised approximately $900 million, and Innovent raised $400 million.

A particular focus of Western companies going into the China market with local partners, and Chinese companies tapping overseas funding to develop new drugs, is the great potential market in China for cancer, immunology, neurology and diabetes treatments.

WuXi AppTec, which was founded in Shanghai in 2001 and set up a plant in Biolake, has a joint venture with Juno, a leading American company with various kinds of cancer treatments, as well as others with Medimmune, the biologics arm of AstraZeneca, and Eli Lilly. Heading in the opposite direction, in 2015 the Jiangsu Hengrui Medicine Co. has licensed a preclinical immunotherapy drug, PD-1 antibody, to an American company, Incyte Corp., for $795 million. Jiangsu Hengrui is also one of the first Chinese biotechs to have started clinical trials in America.

China also wants to become the best location for drug companies to carry out clinical trials by speeding up approvals for trials and new technologies. A key area is CAR-T trials which refers to chimeric antigen receptor T-cell therapy. This focuses on developing a treatment specifically tailored for an individual patient by reprogramming a patient's own immune system cells so they target their own cancer. This is a very complex and potentially risky treatment, but in some trials it has cured some patients, even those with advanced cancers. It is used when everything else has failed. China approved 300 CAR-T clinical trials by 2019, far more than in the United States.

Another new and risky procedure is cell therapy. This is where human cells, in particular stem cells, are transplanted to replace or repair damaged tissue or cells. In China, there is no need to get a regulator's approval to start a trial.

China also quickly became a hotbed for gene therapy, in which a faulty gene is replaced or a new gene added in an attempt to cure a disease. It may also treat a wide range of conditions like cancer, cystic fibrosis, heart disease, diabetes, haemophilia and AIDS. Over 1,000 clinical trials were under way in China in 2019 and at the time of writing the country produces more patents and academic papers on this than almost anyone else.

China also helps its companies in other ways. Americans believe the Chinese government has funnelled government funds into what it claims are 'private' entities in order to bypass World Trade Organisation rules on government subsidies. The United States Trade Representative's office sent seventy questions to the WTO about Chinese subsidies, including those in biotechnology. Some of these investments were allegedly offered with very easy terms, much easier than you would find in a normal commercial deal.

This meant that all at once, Chinese venture capital firms were racing to buy up American biotech firms. The Chinese internet giants Alibaba and Tencent also jumped into early-stage US technology projects. In the first three months of 2018, Chinese-based venture-capital funds pumped $1.4 billion into US biotechnology companies. From just $0.2 billion in 2015 total investment shot up to $2.6 billion in just the first nine months of 2018, with stakes in 300 life sciences and biotech firms. These included California's GRAIL Inc, an early-stage cancer detection company, which in May raised $300 million in a Series C round (meaning third stage) led by the Chinese healthcare fund Ally Bridge Group. The immuno-oncology company TCR2 Therapeutics of Cambridge, Massachusetts, received $125 million in March in a Series B round co-led by 6 Dimensions Capital, which is a large Chinese health care fund partly capitalised by a provincial government. It has also invested in the Maryland biotech Vielo Bio, which was spun out of AstraZeneca's biologics R&D arm. The idea seemed to be to grab new and possibly key technologies and then speed up development with the backing of a government willing to take big risks in order to capture a new technology.

In fact in 2018, Chinese venture capitalists splurged more money on American start-ups than they did on Chinese ones. Inside China, the funding for biotech ventures, both private and government, also shot up from $0.5 billion in 2015 to $2.5 billion in 2018. Much of it was done through IPOs. These firms have also been taking large stakes in American biotech firms. Further, China is investing in American universities, often with the backing of local state governments, such as that of Maryland. It granted $600,000 to the Maryland International Incubator specifically to attract high-tech companies from China and elsewhere to collaborate with University of Maryland researchers. Of the eighteen companies in the incubator, nine are from China, mostly biotech enterprises. There have also been numerous reports of Chinese biomedical researchers working at American universities, often on American government grants, taking the IP their labs develop to China.[1]

At the same time, foreign biopharmaceutical companies in China have found it difficult to protect their intellectual property from predatory Chinese rivals, including those in the generic pharmaceutical sector. Foreign companies only win one in five cases brought against Chinese generic companies, and even when they do win, the losers only face small penalties. According to a 2019 report by Information Technology and Innovation Foundation, an independent think tank in Washington:

> Invalidating foreign patents appears to be a key way for China to enable its generics industry to gain market share [...] This high rate of invalidation has generated the creation of a "reverse patent troll" industry in China wherein individuals threaten to challenge a patent unless they are paid in cash or given a free license (which they usually sell to a Chinese generics company). As one private practice lawyer in China stated, "It's a protection racket".

The report points out that Chinese law requires products actually to be sold in China before a patent holder can bring an infringement action. Thus, even if a Chinese company produces an infringing product and gains regulatory approval, a foreign drug company can be limited in bringing action if the company has not yet sold the drug in China.

The report's authors believe that China's core strategy is to promote Chinese generics companies, and that the weak intellectual property protection system has been deliberately designed to facilitate that strategy. New rules on data exclusivity favour companies that first launch in China, which are not going to be foreign companies in the general run of things. At the same time, the system does encourage foreign companies to seek approval for their products in China first, ideally by developing drugs in China or at least doing clinical trials there.

The report says that Chinese regulations help Chinese biotechs in other ways. American regulations drawn up under the Health Insurance Portability and Accountability Act make it very difficult to collect and use patient data for research but, in contrast, China has made the generation and sharing of medical data a top priority. The reason is that, if you have a lot of data like this, you can get a computer to mine it for useful information.

This is not as easy as it sounds. A new field of artificial intelligence is being developed that enables computers to learn on the job and create better and better biopharma algorithms. For example, after Chinese researchers got hold of 600,000 patient records from a paediatric hospital, they used them to 'train' an AI algorithm to diagnose children's diseases. Ultimately, AI will be used to discover and develop entirely new drugs.

China has also set out to create a DNA repository of over 70 million individuals, mostly men, which allows the state to construct the genetic links to China's entire male population of roughly 700 million. It will form another tool in the state's growing ability to mesh its surveillance powers, such as its facial recognition systems and its network of advanced security cameras. Nothing on this scale is happening in any other country. The Chinese government can also use access to this massive database to attract foreign genetic research companies to China, in addition to tracking down criminals, or indeed anyone else.

Chinese law makes it extremely difficult for genomics data or genomics material to leave the country (e.g., by being published in scientific journals) to the extent of prosecuting a number of companies for doing so. Moreover, foreign companies that want to use genetic data from Chinese persons are now obliged to enter into cooperative agreements with Chinese organizations.

Yet there is also a growing fear that China is trying to steal bio-data from American pharmaceutical and health-care companies, especially DNA data gathered from patients. The Chinese government could be working with DNA sequencing firms to secretly amass enormous amounts of data sets of American DNA and health information. Chinese firms have set themselves up as DNA sequencing factories, conducting testing for individuals and back office analysis for major American health-care firms and academic institutions. Chinese hackers could also be at work. In 2014, Community Health Systems, which runs 206 hospitals across the country, reported that hackers stole data on 4.5 million patients. In 2015, Premera Blue Cross said hackers may have accessed data of 11 million people, including clinical information and specific insurance claims.

'For years, we have witnessed China's voracious appetite for the personal data of Americans, including the theft of personnel records from the US Office of Personnel Management, the intrusion into Marriott hotels, and Anthem health insurance company, and now the wholesale theft of credit and other information from Equifax', the former US Attorney General William Barr said at a press conference in February 2020, announcing charges against four Chinese military officers. 'The scale of the theft was staggering.'

The Pentagon has asked military personnel to stop using at-home DNA kits for health and ancestry purposes, fearful about where that unchangeable, unalterable genetic data may end up now or later.

China is accused of stealing know-how, often through universities and the university research grant system. Chinese hackers have penetrated the systems at US biopharma companies, including Abbott Laboratories and Wyeth (now part of Pfizer). They have targeted biopharma firms to steal their know-how through cybertheft or with the help of rogue employees.

Chinese scientists working at biopharma companies in the United States have taken the IP back to China. In 2002, a Chinese national was charged with stealing biological materials from Cornell University. In 2013, two Chinese nationals working at Eli Lilly were charged with theft and with providing trade secrets to a Chinese pharmaceutical firm.

In 2018, Yu Xue, a leading biochemist working at a GlaxoSmithKline research facility in Philadelphia, admitted to stealing company secrets and funnelling them to Renopharma, a Chinese biotech firm partly funded by the Chinese government.

In 2019, MD Anderson and Emory University both dismissed Chinese-born scientists for theft of IP.

A 2019 report to the US China Economic and Security Review Commission notes: 'Ventria Bioscience, GlaxoSmithKline, Dow AgroSciences LLC, Cargill Inc, Roche Diagnostics, and Amgen have all experienced theft of trade secrets or biological materials perpetrated by a current or former employees [sic] with the intent to sell it [sic] to a Chinese competitor. In the academic sector, researchers have stolen information or samples from their employers at Cornell University, Harvard University, and UC Davis.'[2]

In another case, a former Genentech employee was charged with trade-secret theft and passing on critical information to a Chinese competitor. A former Chinese employee of a leading medical device firm was convicted of stealing IP and then travelling to China to obtain financing from the Chinese government to open a rival company using the stolen IP—even though the government knew the technology was stolen.

A US Department of Justice release in early January 2020 detailed the capture of three Harvard University researchers who had been developing biological weapons for China. One of them, Zaosong Zheng, a Harvard-affiliated cancer researcher, was caught leaving the country with twenty-one vials of cells stolen from a laboratory at Beth Israel Deaconess Hospital in Boston. Another person accused of pirating IP was Yanqing Ye, who, prosecutors said, hid the fact that she was a lieutenant in the People's Liberation Army, and continued to carry out assignments for Chinese military officers while at Boston University. Ms Yanqing was charged with visa fraud, making false statements, acting as an agent of a foreign government and conspiracy.

According to the FBI, the Wuhan University of Technology paid Harvard Professor Charles M. Lieber, chair of the Department of Chemistry and Chemical Biology, $50,000 per month and a lump sum of $1.5 million under the Thousand Talents Plan.

Lieber is alleged to have concealed this from both Harvard and the US government. He is known for finding ways to make new nano materials and for developing applications in medicine and biology. US prosecutors further allege that Professor Lieber agreed to open a lab in Wuhan with a grant of $1.5 million.

That China plans to create a handful of pharmaceutical giants, to switch from making generic copycat drugs to becoming a drug innovator, is not particularly shocking or surprising. It wants to use the sheer weight of its market and its human resources to power this change, as it did in other sectors. Nor are the accusations and evidence of state-directed industrial espionage something entirely unexpected. What is unusual, and sometimes frightening, is to consider the extent to which China has fused together the activities of civilian and military entities, party and state organisations, all to serve its ambitions. It is equally worrying to see the goodwill of Western countries being exploited.

In General H. R. MacMasters' recent book *Battlegrounds: The Fight to Defend the Free World* (2020), he endorses the view that 'Chinese cybertheft is responsible for the "greatest transfer of wealth in history".'

He reports that the Chinese Ministry of State Security used a hacking squad known as APT10 to target US companies in the finance, telecommunications, consumer-electronics and medical industries as well as NASA and Department of Defense research laboratories, extracting intellectual property and sensitive data. For example, the hackers obtained personal information, including Social Security numbers, for more than 100,000 US naval personnel.

'China's military has used stolen technologies to pursue advanced military capabilities of many kinds and drive U.S. defense companies out of the market. The Chinese drone manufacturer Da-Jiang Innovations (DJI) controlled more than 70 percent of the global market in 2017, thanks to its unmatched low prices. Its unmanned systems even became the most frequently flown commercial drones by the U.S. Army until they were banned for security reasons', he wrote.

Even so, discovering new drugs, getting them past the trial stage and then persuading doctors around the world to use the drug before its patent protection expires, is an enormously costly and high-risk enterprise. In the world of medicine and pharmaceuticals, a great deal of information and knowledge is in any case freely exchanged and openly available. Medicine has historically always been an 'open-source' profession. A lot of medical research is publicly funded and openly evaluated. Swiss doctors don't (generally) keep their medical techniques secret from their French colleagues in the hopes of attracting more patients. Knowledge that can save lives is always shared. The world of defence is the exact opposite. Knowledge that can destroy lives is not shared. In the military world top-secret weapons, or the mere threat of possessing some secret weapons or technology, are the most desirable ones. In the Soviet Union's bioweapons programme, not even the scientists working in these closed science cities were allowed to know what other microbiologists in the same project were researching. This is ultimately why the enormous research effort proved of little practical value.

When it comes to creating a new and successful cure in medicine, there is only so much any company can gain from industrial espionage. After all, the majority of drugs fail. Only five in 5,000 drugs that enter preclinical testing progress to human testing. Only one of these five drugs gets approved. The chance for a new drug to actually make it to market is thus only one in 5,000.

The odds of success, however, began to change, dramatically and unexpectedly, just as China was launching its 2025 plan. All of a sudden it became possible to reduce the risk, the time and the cost of developing new cures. The hunt for pharmaceutical compounds was overtaken by an overwhelming excitement about the potential of biotechnology. China scrambled to join what became a scientific land rush. To stake its claims first, Chinese companies exploited China's lax laws to take great risks. This may well be connected to the Wuhan virus, as the next chapter explains.

9

ILLUMINA AND CRISPR

If you've ever pondered whether it is government plans, or individuals with a clever new idea and a dash of private enterprise, that change history, consider two inventions that have transformed biotechnology. One is the invention of a cheap and easy way of gene sequencing. Another is a clever way of cutting and pasting genes, called CRISPR. It is these discoveries that started a scientific and commercial boom—one that could change our lives just as the internet and mobile telephony have done.

Every microbiology lab, including those at the Wuhan Institute of Virology, now has a machine about the size of a kitchen fridge or an office photocopier. It is there to sequence a genome, that is, identify the genes—the DNA and RNA—that make up any organism. This machine is now made by a listed American company called Illumina, but it started out with some blue sky thinking by some academics in Cambridge (England) having a drink in the pub in the summer of 1997.

A few years earlier, in June 2000, the Human Genome Project was launched by President Clinton with great fanfare. It set out to sequence all the base pairs of a human being. The fifteen-year project was a big-government, big-science project, which would cost $3 billion. It didn't actually read a real genome of an individual, but sequenced a composite genome—and the sequence was riddled with hundreds of gaps. It was a historic milestone but was mostly symbolic. Yet it spurred scientists to think of a better and faster way to read genes.

The Cambridge scientists Shankar Balasubramanian and David Klenerman were using fluorescently labelled nucleotides, the building blocks of DNA, and watching how an enzyme acts on a molecular level when it synthesizes DNA molecules. They hit on a new idea of breaking up the DNA into small fragments, and copying and amplifying these fragments on small pieces of glass trays so that each fragment could be read. Finally, the fragmented sequences could be assembled into a cohesive whole.

DNA is composed of four chemical building blocks, or 'bases', abbreviated as G, A, T, and C, with the biological information encoded within DNA determined by the order of those bases. The genome of E. Coli, a bacterium that lives in the gut, consists of about 5 million bases (also called megabases), while that of a fruit fly has about 123 million bases and that of a human has nearer 3,000 million bases.

The next year, Balasubramanian and Klenerman approached a venture capital firm and set up a company called Solexa. A few years later, it acquired the technology from another company to help amplify single DNA molecules into clusters. In 2005, Solexa acquired Lynx Therapeutics in a reverse merger and got listed on NASDAQ. The new company brought the know-how to build and sell instruments, and in the following year the first commercial product, the Genome Analyzer, was delivered. It gave its owners the ability to sequence one gigabase (Gb) of data in a single run. In 2006, Solexa was acquired by Illumina, a company which currently dominates the field. By 2014, the machines could sequence 1.8 terabases (Tb) of data in a single sequencing run. That year the company brought out a new model—HiSeq X Ten—which enabled users to sequence over forty-five human genomes in a single day at a cost of approximately $1,000 each. The price has since dropped to hundreds of dollars, and almost every year the machines have become smaller and cheaper.

Illumina's machines are not the only method of carrying out these tasks. A rival system has been developed by Oxford Nanopore Technologies. It was founded in 2005 by Dr Gordon Sanghera, Dr Spike Willcocks and Professor Hagan Bayley as Oxford Nanolabs with some seed capital from a venture capital group, IP Group PLC. They set out to read the DNA molecules by passing them through tiny pores as an electric current is passed. The tiny differences in the readings of the current reveal the identity of a molecule. These are interpreted by a special chip, which can then give a quick reading.

The origin of the idea came from an American professor, David Deamer, who first hit on it in 1989. The initial patents were filed in America after research done at Harvard and the University of California. Deamer thought of using a doughnut-shaped protein whose hole is just a billionth of a meter wide—a nanopore—embedded in cell membranes. By perforating it, it is possible to detect the molecules that pass through its inside channel. When the pore is open, ions can flow freely through it, creating a tiny but measurable current. But if something blocks the pore—for example a strand of DNA—that current collapses. The four bases of DNA—A, C, G, and T—each change the current through the pore in unique ways. So, as a DNA strand threads its way through the pore, the rising and falling current reveals its sequence.

The work of all this multinational, multi-disciplinary research resulted in the creation, in 2012, of the first hand-held MinION device. It became commercially available three years later. A series of new products have since been launched on the market, making it cheaper and easier to use. The technology has become steadily more accurate and reliable. It means that by 2020 anyone could go into the field, even the International Space Station, taking a small device, that can plug into a phone or laptop, and get an instant readout from a sample of any kind of DNA, such as from saliva, or from an animal, plant or microbe, or just a swipe of trace DNA left on a surface. A starter kit can be bought for just hundreds of dollars. It is already good enough for food quality control, or to identify any viruses that are damaging crops. Researchers in rural Africa use it to test cassava for damaging viruses on the spot and in real time.

The small portable device meant that the transmission of the Ebola virus could be traced across West Africa during the 2013 outbreak, without the need to send samples back to the lab for analysis. It is easy to sample milk or other foods, or to look for dangerous viruses or bacteria while out in the field.

These new gene sequencing technologies have opened the door to personalised medicine. It is feasible to investigate your personal genome to find, say, rare hereditary diseases such as sickle cell or cystic fibrosis, or to screen for the first signs of cancer, to anticipate future problems like rheumatoid arthritis, or to identify sepsis or TB in hours rather than days. Early treatment is vital to curing such diseases. By simply sequencing a sample of blood, these devices can avoid the need to undertake an expensive, time consuming and painful biopsy. They can be used to replace the extraction of amniotic fluids during pregnancy. The foetal DNA that circulates in a pregnant woman's blood can be used to screen for foetal disorders resulting from, for example, an extra chromosome, as with Down syndrome. It can be used to detect conditions resulting from an extra sex chromosome, a missing part of a chromosome, and even for conditions resulting from a single gene mutation.

The more people agree to carry out individual gene sequencing and the more this information is shared and processed, the more useful it becomes. The better it is analysed, the more reliable the conclusions that can be drawn from it. Suddenly, people realised that possessing a vast data bank of DNA is such a powerful tool that it becomes a strategic asset, much like an oil field.

With so much biodata piling up, people began to look at how best to extract useful information from it. This gave birth to the new field of bioinformatics. This is all about programming computers so that they 'learn' how to get better and better at analysing patterns in a flow of data. This could be algorithms that learn how to study data that could be uploaded into the cloud from all over the world. This data might be blood test samples, or it might be biomedical imagery such as lung scans. Eventually, the computer becomes able to interpret this data faster and more accurately than a human expert, so it can forecast if or when someone will fall ill. The more times it does this, the better it becomes at the task, so having a vast data bank is very important.

It allows researchers to trace the evolution of many organisms by measuring changes in their DNA. In 2016, a team of British and Brazilian researchers went to Northeast Brazil to study an outbreak of the Zika virus, which is carried by mosquitoes. They took the MinION device with them. They were then able to conclude that the first case of Zika virus infection in Brazil probably took place a year before the disease was first recognized.

Josh Quick at the Institute of Microbiology and Infection at the University of Birmingham used this method to date the COVID-19 outbreak in Wuhan. 'Gene sequencing can reconstruct the processes that drove its global spread and determine when it first arose within a population', he said in an article published in STAT, an online bio-pharma magazine.[1]

Using the mutation rate, the most recent common ancestor of all COVID-19 cases is dated back to mid-November 2019. The date can be worked out because the virus has a predictable rate of evolution, accumulating on average two mutations per month. 'Sequencing also makes it possible to read these mutations to identify different sub-lineages of the virus as it evolves, branching like a tree [...] An analysis by the COVID-19 Genomics UK Consortium was also able to identify 1,350 separate introductions of the virus into the UK in March 2020', he wrote. Quick also points out that no close relative to the COVID-19 virus has been isolated anywhere in the world that allows us to identify an animal host.

The next invention has changed the future of biochemistry, and may also hold the answer as to where the COVID-19 virus came from. Around 2012, scientists discovered a cheap and simple way of gene editing. In 2020, two of the leading pioneers in this field, the American Jennifer Doudna, and France's Emmanuelle Charpentier, were both recognised with the Nobel Prize in Chemistry. Scientists can now use a technology called CRISPR to insert, edit or delete the associated gene in virtually any living plant's or animal's genome. This process is far simpler and more effective than any other gene-manipulation technology to date. It can now be done in a lab by an undergraduate student for hundreds of dollars, or indeed in your own garage using kits bought online.

For thousands of years, people only had one tool—selected breeding—when they wanted to change an animal such as a pigeon, or a goldfish, or many of the fruits and vegetables we eat. More recently, scientists tried another method of starting high frequency random mutations. China would justify its costly space programme by claiming that it could improve crops by sending seeds into space, where they would be exposed to radiation, which would lead to beneficial mutations.

From the 1970s onwards, new techniques of genetic engineering were developed, mostly in America, but it took years, as well as a great deal of expertise and money, to make them work. The CRISPR technique sweeps all that away. It is a quick way of finding a specific bit of DNA inside a cell. Next, this can be altered in almost a scissors and paste operation. It can be used to turn genes on or off without altering their sequence.

It started with the search for a way of using the natural defences of bacteria to fight off invading viruses. In 1993, Francisco Mojica, a microbiologist at the University of Alicante in Spain, noticed peculiar repetitive DNA sequences in the genome of a primitive single cell microbe called *Haloferax*. He then discovered that similar sequences can be found in all kinds of microbes. Later he suggested that these sequences were part of a microbial immune system. He called these sequences 'clustered regularly interspaced short palindromic repeats'—shortened to CRISPR.

For billions of years cells and viruses have been engaged in an endless battle, constantly evolving new methods of attack and defence. Scientists are still arguing whether viruses or cells came first in evolution. A virus is essentially a string of DNA or RNA wrapped in a protein coating. It replicates by inserting its genome into a fully-fledged cell, which proceeds to treat this new and foreign set of raw genes as if it were its own original genetic material. The viruses must invade the cells if they are to reproduce. One way they do this is through rapid random mutation of their unstable RNA, until they by chance discover a combination that allows them to unlock the defences of a particular microbe. Strictly speaking, it is the enzymes' sloppy copying of the RNA that leads to mutations.

The research breakthrough of the Nobel Prize winners was to understand how to use the different 'Cas' proteins found in bacteria that are used to destroy viral DNA. 'Cas' is short for CRISPR-associated genes. The Cas9 protein is the one most widely used by scientists and is found in the Streptococcus bacteria—a species which is used to make Swiss cheese.

In 2007, scientists at Danisco, a Danish food manufacturer later acquired by DuPont, infected a milk-fermenting Streptococcus with two virus strains. Many of these bacteria were killed by the viruses, but some survived and replicated, which meant that their descendants were all resistant to the viruses. As researchers discovered, the survivors had inserted DNA fragments from the viruses into their 'spacer' sequences, which enabled them to defeat the invaders.

In the laboratory, the Cas9 protein can be instructed to find almost any sequence that you want to target, simply by introducing a stretch of 'guide' RNA to help it seek out and bind to the same sequence. When the Cas9 protein is attached to the guide RNA, it marches along the strands of DNA. When it finds the same twenty-DNA-letter long sequence as the guide RNA sequence, it binds to it. It is quite a feat, since our cells have DNA with 6 billion letters and, unwound, it would stretch out over two metres. Next, it uses an enzyme to chop up that bit of DNA, knocking out a gene. When the cut is repaired, you end up with a new and genetically modified cell. And one that can defeat a virus.

An organism's entire DNA content, including all its genes, has thus become almost as editable as a simple piece of text, according to Jennifer Doudna. She called the process 'an incredible molecular machine that could slice apart viral DNA with exquisite precision'. 'Practically overnight, we have found ourselves on the cusp of a new age in genetic engineering and biological mastery—a revolutionary era', she wrote in her book *A Crack in Creation* (2017).

For the first time, Doudna and Charpentier were able to show that they could use different RNAs to programme Cas9 to cut and edit different DNAs. Customised Cas proteins are now available online that do not cut DNA or alter it in any way, but that can turn genes on and off. Others, called base editors, can change one letter of the DNA code to another. The technology allows scientists to actually 'paste' a new piece of DNA at the cut site. It also allows researchers to alter several genes in a single experiment.

This makes it possible to manipulate many different genes in a cell line, plant or animal very quickly. It means the process can take weeks instead of years. And it can be applied to any species.

In 2008, Danisco started using its discovery to protect the bacteria used in fermentation of cheese and yoghurt against viruses. Many other food manufacturers now do the same—it saves them time and money and results in a better quality.

Next, scientists started trying to modify plants to help protect themselves against insects, viruses and herbicides, and to be tolerant of heat, cold or drought.

Soon other scientists became more daring and moved on from bacteria and plants to modifying DNA in human cells grown in petri dishes. Others started using the techniques to add a foreign gene into various creatures like mice, rats, zebra fish, pigs and monkeys. Before long, scientists began experimenting with human embryos, and not just in the lab.

The quick and easy DNA sequencing of a cellular genome allows storage of the genetic instructions of life as a digital file. You could read it and quickly identify minute errors. Now there was an equally quick and easy way of fixing them. And you could start taking desirable genes from somewhere else and try to add them. Anything became possible. Like producing human organs from transgenic pigs. Or engineering mosquitoes to stop them transmitting malaria or the Zika virus. Or bio-engineering microbes to eat plastic or produce biofuels or exotic materials.

Even more sophisticated forms of bio-engineering sprang up, such as synthetic biology which enables scientists to synthesize *ex vivo*, without cutting and pasting, the exact biopolymer constructs, such as proteins or nucleic acids, they are interested in.

The arrival of these two new technologies at the same time started a gold rush in biotechnology. Billions of dollars were quickly raised both in China and America, indeed everywhere, as governments and companies scrambled to stake their claim.

Patent lawsuits multiplied. Law-makers and regulators struggled to catch up. And many of the leading scientists like Doudna became seriously alarmed that a dangerous genie had been unleashed from the laboratory test tube.

10

CHINA'S BIOTECHNOLOGY RACE

China immediately started directing resources into exploiting this new opportunity, and it encouraged, or at least did not stop, its scientists taking steps that more cautious countries shied away from. The 2016 five-year plan highlighted gene editing, and Chinese scientists responded to the call to arms. Dozens, if not hundreds, of Chinese institutions both in research hubs like Beijing or Wuhan and further afield enthusiastically deployed CRISPR.

China's researchers quickly racked up a long list of CRISPR firsts in dogs, mice, rats, pigs and rabbits. So far, many of the animals are simply proofs of concept, but it was possible to do this research because animal researchers in China face less public scrutiny than their counterparts in the United States and Europe.

The regulatory regime was so loose that scientists elsewhere became quite alarmed. A storm over bio-ethics became so heated that China was eventually forced to rein in some of its scientists.

In 2015, the Beijing Genome Institute (BGI), the world's largest gene-sequencing organisation, used CRISPR to bio-engineer a new breed of miniature pig, the size of a small dog, to sell as pets. BGI is funded in part by local government incentives and in 2010 received a $1.5 billion line of credit from the China Development Bank.

The Shaanxi Provincial Engineering and Technology Research Centre used CRISPR simultaneously to disrupt four genes of the Shaanbei Cashmere goat to create a new kind of goat with bigger muscles and longer hair. In early-stage goat embryos, scientists successfully deleted genes that suppressed both hair and muscle growth.

The same year at the Guangzhou Institutes of Biomedicine and Health, CRISPR was used on a pair of beagles to create two super-muscular dogs. Another experiment deleted the gene inhibiting muscle growth in sheep. Over forty different genetic modifications have been made to pigs, some to increase their fat, others to make them resistant to viruses such as classic swine fever.

The Shanghai Institute of Biological Sciences used CRISPR to genetically engineer silkworms, allowing them to fight off a deadly virus—the Bombyx mori nucleopolyhedrovirus (BmNPV)—responsible for more than 80 per cent of unnatural deaths of domestic silkworms. Scientists injected the system into worm eggs and produced a new transgenic species capable of generating Cas9 in its cells. The new genes are passed on from one generation to another. In another project, Chinese scientists modified silkworms to make them produce a thread as strong as spider web thread.

The China Agricultural University introduced human genes into 300 cows to produce 'human' milk, which is known to contain high quantities of key nutrients that can help boost the immune system of babies.

China now has at least four groups of CRISPR researchers doing gene editing with large colonies of monkeys—far more than anywhere else in the world. At the Yunnan Key Laboratory of Primate Biomedical Research, they have been creating monkey embryos with a gene mutated so that, when the animals are born five months later, they will age unusually fast. Researchers have been using CRISPR to create a range of monkey models to study human diseases such as autism, cancer, Alzheimer's disease and muscular dystrophy. The Institute of Neuroscience in Shanghai used gene editing to disable a gene in macaque monkeys crucial to their sleep-wake cycle. Its scientists then cloned one of those monkeys to produce five primates with almost identical genes.

This was the first time researchers cloned a gene-edited monkey on the way to create populations of genetically identical primates that might revolutionize biomedical research. Another group at the Institute disabled a gene in monkeys that is linked to autistic behaviour in people. Others knocked out the gene for the immune cell protein CCR5, a mutation that makes humans resistant to infection by the most commonly transmitted variant of HIV. This kind of research into non-human primates is tightly regulated in Europe and America, and the costs are much higher.

China was also first off the block when, in 2015, a team at the Hangzhou Cancer Hospital started treating cancer patients with blood modified using CRISPR. The team took blood from oesophageal-cancer patients, and shipped it to a lab that deleted the gene that interferes with the immune system's ability to fight the cancer. The cells were then infused back into the patients in the hope that the cancer would be defeated. At least eighty-six patients had their genes edited. A few survived, but most died. This is just one of at least nine trials on human patients.

In 2015, the Sun Yat-Sen University in Guangzhou used CRISPR on eighty-six human embryos to precisely target the gene responsible for producing beta globin in order to show that a blood disorder disease called beta thalassaemia could be stopped. Also included was a piece of synthetic DNA with which to repair the broken gene, as well as a jellyfish gene encoding green fluorescent protein. This last ingredient allowed the researchers to analyse the embryos that continued to grow and divide after the gene editing was done; all they had to do was look for glow-in-the-dark cells. The experiments didn't work, but they led Doudna to call for a moratorium on further experiments in germline gene editing. The research was legal within China, which bans experiments on human embryos more than fourteen days old, and was supported in part by government grants.

In November 2018, the Chinese researcher He Jiankui at the Southern University of Technology and Science in Shenzhen shocked the world by announcing that twin girls had been born from embryos that he and his colleagues had edited. He became the first to modify two human embryos. The embryos were edited for their CCR 5 gene in the hope of providing genetic resistance to HIV. The gene is also linked to enhanced memory function. Later, he was charged and found guilty of forging documents and unethical conduct. He was sentenced to three years in prison with a fine of 3 million yuan.

This led to bans on similar experiments and a spate of reports that He's work was government funded and possibly connected to the military. It is not clear whether He Jiankui received approval or even funding from the government, but he edited embryos that became the world's first genetically modified humans. The news provoked serious concerns and backlash around the world and in China, where new legislation has been introduced to increase oversight over such research.

A lot of the research using CRISPR gene editing techniques takes place at PLA medical institutions, such as the 301 General Hospital in Beijing. It is organised by the PLA's Academy of Military Medical Sciences (AMMS), which is controlled by the Academy of Military Science. The Chinese military not only trains doctors, but also tries to bring in medical science and new technologies such as gene editing to create projects that can serve the military. The PLA has been thinking hard about how these technologies can strengthen China's military power.

For example, an AMMS doctoral researcher published a dissertation in 2016—'Research on the Evaluation of Human Performance Enhancement Technology', which claimed that CRISPR-Cas might be deployed to enhance the combat effectiveness of troops. This could be done, for example, by using the drug modafinil, which can counter tiredness and make troops smarter and more alert. The article claims that there is 'great potential' of CRISPR-Cas as a 'military deterrence technology', in which China should 'grasp the initiative' in development.[1]

China has certainly launched far more clinical trials using CRISPR, mainly for cancer, than any country. From 2011 to 2015, China ranked second in the world behind the United States in international biomedical publications. It quadrupled its global share of biomedical articles between 2006 (2.4 percent) and 2015 (10.8 per cent). In 2016, it was responsible for almost as many biotechnology and applied microbiology publications as the United States.

The biggest impact of CRISPR gene editing and similar methods is not on humans or animals but on plants. The new treatments being trialed on humans would only target a relatively small pool of patients with rare hereditary diseases. China's biggest push is in agriculture. China's public funding of agricultural research approached $10 billion—double that of the United States—and it supports over 1,000 agricultural research institutes. Many are trying to adapt vegetables, fruits, wheat, corn, rice and other staples to make them more commercially productive. China was, for instance, able to develop mildew-resistant wheat with 'targeted mutations' using CRISPR-Cas9 without inserting new genes. The Huazhong Agricultural University alone registered twenty-four CRISPR patents to knock out genes with the purpose of increasing crop yields.

The benefits could be huge. The European Courts consider such crops to be genetically modified organisms that need strict regulation, but the US Department of Agriculture has exempted them from regulations that cover GMO—as long as they were produced not by transferring DNA from other species, but by inducing mutations that could have occurred naturally or through conventional breeding. Consequently China has 60.5 per cent of the patents for CRISPR-Cas changed plants (2012–18), followed by the USA with 26 per cent, while patents of European origin represent only 8 per cent—Germany had six and the Netherlands five patents. Japan and Korea had just five patents between them.

The scope of China's ambitions was made obvious when, in 2017, the giant state-owned company ChemChina bought Switzerland-based Syngenta—one of the world's four largest agribusinesses, which has a large R&D team working with CRISPR—for a staggering $43 billion. It was the biggest ever purchase of a foreign company by China. It will enable China to quickly transfer research into the market, and it creates a rival to giants such as Monsanto.

ChemChina also added Israel-based Makhteshim Agan (renamed to ADAMA Agricultural Solutions), the largest manufacturer of generic pesticides, a $2.4 billion acquisition of a 60 per cent stake in the company; the Adissero Group, a leader in animal feeds, especially biological enzymes; Strider, a Brazilian agtech company; and Floranova, a British flower and vegetable seeds breeder. In September 2019, the company acquired all the assets of the Cropio Group, an agri-technology company.

The Chinese mega corporation could now take a leading role in the global market for crop seeds, including hybrid seeds and genetically engineered seeds, such as corn seeds resistant to insect pests and biofuels. In August 2020, the US Department of Defense listed ChemChina as one of the 'Communist Chinese military companies' operating directly or indirectly in the United States.

China also set up one of the world's largest gene-sequencing organisations, a challenger to Illumina. The Beijing Genome Institute (BGI) is based in Shenzhen, and was originally set up so that China could take part in the Human Genome Project. It was funded in part by local government incentives and endowed, in 2010, with a $1.5 billion line of credit from the China Development Bank.

Early on it bought over a hundred Illumina Hi Seq machines. It claims a number of firsts. It was the first Chinese institution to sequence the SARS virus. It sequenced the first giant panda genome, equal in size to the human genome, in less than eight months. By 2010, it had sequenced the genomes of rice, cucumber, soybean and sorghum. It went on to sequence the genomes of other creatures including the silkworm, honey-bee, water flea and lizard. By 2014, it had sequenced over 1,000 bacteria, part of a project to sequence 10,000 microbes. The BGI also started cloning hundreds of pigs a year to test out new medicines. Another of its projects, run by an eighteen-year-old when it started, is the Cognitive Genomics Team, an international team that investigates the relationship between DNA and IQ. It is about identifying the genes in super-gifted child prodigies. The team collects blood samples for their DNA from gifted children, such as those who take part in the mathematics Olympics. The team wants to investigate a total of 2,000 DNA samples in the search for the intelligence gene.

In 2012, BGI acquired Complete Genomics, an American start-up and rival to Illumina, for $118 million. Three years later, BGI launched BGISEQ-500, a larger desktop sequencing system, which a year after that received an approved registration as a medical device by the Chinese authorities. The following year, it claimed to have received over 500 orders. In November 2016, BGI launched a miniature version of its desktop sequencer, called BGISEQ-50. In 2017, BGI launched a simpler machine that could sequence a whole genome in twenty-four hours and generate six terabytes of sequencing data.

BGI owns the China National Genebank, which contains 11 million human, plant and animal DNA samples. It was opened by BGI and the Chinese government in September 2016, and quickly bought 150 sequencers from BGI. Beijing Genomics Institute has grown into one of the world's largest genomics companies. It is now challenging Illumina by offering personal genome sequencing for lower prices, just a few hundred dollars. At stake in this rivalry is a global market for population sequencing for genetic disorders and personalized medicine that is growing fast—even before the COVID-19 pandemic pushed the demand for coronavirus testing kits—and could be worth $64 billion by 2030.

Australia says that its purchase of 10 million coronavirus test kits from BGI will not risk patient privacy, as researchers hope for greater price competition in a biotech market dominated by a US rival.

11

BIOETHICS AND GAIN OF FUNCTION DEBATE

Not long after CRISPR started being used around the world, a group of scientists got together to issue warnings that this was dangerous and untested technology. They were less concerned about what they called 'loss of function'—that is, when a certain gene is knocked out—as they were about 'gain of function'—when a gene or more is added.

Soon, evidence began to emerge that their caution was justified. Scientists at Nanjing Agricultural University used CRISPR to edit the MSTN gene out of rabbits to make them meatier, resulting in fourteen of the thirty-four genetically engineered offspring being born, inexplicably, with enlarged tongues, dislocated teeth and a strange pelvic tilt.

Since 2012, Chinese scientists had been reverse-engineering cells from adult Chinese pigs to their embryonic stage, a common process when cloning animals, and then knocking out the MSTN gene. The edited cells were then infused into eggs, chemically fertilized in a lab and implanted into the womb of a surrogate. Their meat indeed was leaner, but one in five offspring who inherited the edited genes grew a piece of spine known as thoracic vertebrae. It turned out that the MSTN gene also controlled some part of skeletal formation. The pigs were not dangerous to eat, at least according to lab tests, but after cooking their meat was a little paler than normal.

Chinese scientists at another research facility deleted the MSTN genes from sheep and produced bigger, meatier lambs, but unfortunately, they could not be delivered naturally, only by caesarean section. Researchers in the Xinjiang region also used CRISPR to alter the ASIP gene in Merino sheep in the hope of creating breeds with black, grey or brown coats, to avoid the trouble of dying the wool. It didn't quite work as planned. The sheep turned out with odd colours. One had white hair, two were mostly black, and the other three had spotted fleeces like a panda. But it transpired that the genes also had something to do with reproduction, because only a quarter of the modified ewes gave birth.

What happens though when you genetically alter a virus or a bacterium? Would these mutant strains also have unexpected characteristics, like these rabbits pigs and sheep? And could they cause a pandemic?

In 2014, the Harvard epidemiologist Marc Lipsitch and seventeen other scientists formed the Cambridge Working Group to oppose gain-of-function research. They issued a statement pointing out that lab accidents involving smallpox, anthrax and bird flu in the US 'have been accelerating and have been occurring on average over twice a week'.

'Laboratory creation of highly transmissible, novel strains of dangerous viruses [...] poses substantially increased risks', the statement said. 'An accidental infection in such a setting could trigger outbreaks that would be difficult or impossible to control. Historically, new strains of influenza, once they establish transmission in the human population, have infected a quarter or more of the world's population within two years.'

Among the founders of the group are the virologist Michael Osterholm of the University of Minnesota, the Nobel Prize winner Richard Roberts of New England Biolabs, the former Harvard School of Public Health Dean Barry Bloom, and the activist Edward Hammond of the Third World Network. More than 200 scientists eventually endorsed the position.

The group urged that experiments that produce potential pandemic strains 'should be curtailed until there has been a quantitative, objective and credible assessment' of the risks, potential benefits, and alternatives. They call for a process akin to Asilomar, a 1975 summit that came up with guidelines for recombinant DNA technology.

Concerns about 'gain-of-function' experiments with influenza erupted in 2011 after two teams genetically tweaked the H5N1 avian flu virus. This strain of flu is found in birds in China and South East Asia, both on farms and in the wild. On 29 September 2005, David Nabarro, the newly appointed Senior United Nations System Coordinator for Avian and Human Influenza, declared that an outbreak of avian flu could kill anywhere between 5 million and 150 million people. The virus is very dangerous for such birds and spreads quickly, killing tens of millions of them. To curb its spread, farmers have culled over 100 million birds.

The virus does not spread between humans, but some farmers who regularly handle these birds have become infected and have died from it. If it mutates and becomes transmissible, some fear that it could be as lethal as the Spanish flu, called H1N1. The virus which caused the 1957 Asian Flu is H2N2 and the 1967 Hong Kong flu epidemic was caused by the H3N2 virus. So it is very closely related. As the virus was upgraded to highest risk, something that could potentially cause a global disaster, pharmaceutical companies spent billions of dollars researching H5N1 and preparing for a potential pandemic. One way of forestalling a potential outbreak was to gain an understanding of the process that might lead it to adapt and to allow it to jump species.

Ron Fouchier, a scientist at Erasmus University in Holland, set out to find out what it would take for the bird flu virus to mutate into one that would spread between human populations. What exactly made it transmissible?

The first step was to breed a version of the avian flu with mutations that enabled it to jump to humans. Then he used a technique called 'animal passage': instead of using cell cultures, the virus was passed between animals—*in vivo*. This way, he would be able to observe how the bird flu virus would make use of a chance to mutate. The animal he chose was a ferret: whatever can jump between ferrets could just as easily jump between humans.

He infected one ferret with the bird-flu virus and when it fell sick, he then removed a sample of the virus with a swab. As the virus multiplies in the body, its RNA mutates slightly, so the virus that was found in the ferret might be a bit different from the one that went into it. Flu viruses are basically eight pieces of RNA wrapped up in a ball.

Fouchier then thought he would take the virus from the first ferret and infect a second. Next, he took the mutated virus from the second ferret and infected a third, and so on. After passing the virus through ten ferrets, Fouchier noticed something important. A ferret in an adjacent cage fell ill, even though the two hadn't come into direct contact with one another, because the virus had passed through the air. It showed that the virus was now transmissible in ferrets—and, by implication, in humans. Fouchier had transformed a non-transmissible virus into one that was contagious enough to start a pandemic. By analysing the virus's genes in each generation, he could figure out the exact five mutations that led to H5N1 bird flu becoming airborne between ferrets.

When Fouchier published the results of his animal-passage experiment in *Science* in 2011, it alarmed everyone. Could a dangerous pathogen accidentally leak from Fouchier's lab, or someone else's?

These labs are given a safety rating depending on how elaborate their system of protections and inspections are. The more dangerous a pathogen, the higher the safety measures required. Fouchier had done his work in bio-safety level-2 labs (BSL-2), instead of BSL-4, which are intended to contain the most dangerous viruses, such as Ebola. BSL-4 labs have elaborate safeguards, such as their own air circulation systems, airlocks and so forth.

Everyone in the world of virology also knew that even in the most closely inspected laboratory facilities in the world accidents have been known to happen. In 2014, there were several breaches of protocol at US government laboratories—dozens of workers at the Centers for Disease Control and Prevention (CDC) might have been exposed to anthrax—vials of smallpox virus had been left lying around in an NIH storeroom—and the CDC had unwittingly sent out samples of ordinary influenza virus contaminated with H5N1.

The (American) National Institutes of Health (NIH) issued a moratorium on future research, but the debate raged in academic journals and at conferences. The scientists split into two factions, pro- and anti gain-of-function (GoF) experiments.

'We need GOF experiments', wrote Ron Fouchier in *Nature*, 'to demonstrate causal relationships between genes or mutations and particular biological traits of pathogens. GOF approaches are absolutely essential in infectious disease research.'

Scientists said they needed more GoF mutation research to better understand SARS and MERS, the coronavirus cousins of COVID-19. The highest priority, the top justification, was that GoF would help us understand how to avoid the next influenza pandemic. Fouchier claimed that we need to understand the kinds of flu viruses that could cause it. GoF mutation research can help by showing what kind of mutations might allow a virus to jump across species or to evolve into more virulent strains. It could therefore help us prepare and save lives.

Its critics complained, however, that so far no one has shown any evidence that gain-of-function experiments, especially with regard to dangerous viruses, have been of any use, certainly not given that they carry the risk of unleashing a pandemic. It was like looking for a gas leak with a lighted match, as one scientist quipped.

Animal-passage experiments with pathogens had started back with Louis Pasteur and his research into the rabies virus and a vaccine. Scientists went on to study the HIV virus in baboons and the SARS virus using mice, and in all these kinds of experiments more virulent types of virus emerged. In more than thirty BSL-4 labs around the world, scientists used them to enhance the transmissibility of respiratory tract pathogens. A top security lab is essentially an airtight cement bunker, negatively pressurized so that air only flows into the lab in case of any breach, which pushes the airborne viruses back in. All air flowing in and out of the lab passes through multiple filters. Researchers wear special protective equipment, including respirators. Anyone coming or going into the lab must go through an intricate performance of stripping and putting on various articles of clothing and passing through showers and decontamination.

Then another development added to the already existing concerns about these experiments. Scientists in some labs started creating synthetic viruses. It started in 2002 when scientists synthesized the genome of the poliovirus, which was more or less extinct, using a process called the *de novo* synthesis of a viral genome. Viral genomes, especially those of RNA viruses, are relatively short, often less than 10,000 bases long. This makes it relatively easy to assemble a whole genome with pieces of RNA or DNA (with the currently available technology) instead of the much more complicated animal genomes. The poliovirus genome has 7,500 bases, while a human being has three billion.

So researchers all over the world felt inspired to try out the new technology and make their own synthetic viruses. They even dared recreate the smallpox virus, perhaps the worst plague in human history. As it had been eradicated, the world stopped smallpox vaccinations in 1978, meaning that the roughly five billion people worldwide under the age of forty have never been inoculated. If it escaped, the consequences could be horrendous. Others resurrected the extinct 1918 strain of influenza virus, as well as a synthetic SARS virus.

These designer viruses can now be made anywhere for relatively modest amounts of money. Canadian researchers even revived an extinct cousin of smallpox, called horsepox, just by ordering DNA online. There does exist an International Gene Synthesis Consortium that works with government agencies to screen orders and buyers, but in practice anyone can buy potentially hazardous DNA samples on the black market after a simple Google search.

The synthetic genes for *de novo* synthesis are assembled from short custom-made single-stranded DNA oligonucleotides, or 'oligos', which are strings of a few nucleotides. A nucleotide is the basic building block of nucleic acids. RNA and DNA are polymers made of long chains of nucleotides. All of this means that it could be done by a skilled laboratory technician or by undergraduate students working with viruses in a relatively simple laboratory. Building a virus from scratch became like assembling Lego blocks.

In 2015, US national intelligence director James Clapper for the first time listed bio-engineered pandemics as one of his agencies' biggest concerns in a report named 'Worldwide Threat Assessment'. This meant that genome editing joined nuclear bombs on the list of weapons of mass destruction.

So over a few years, it became ever cheaper and simpler for anyone to set up a biolab in their own garage by getting their hands on a sequencer, DNA samples and CRISPR-Cas cut and paste tools to make Frankenstein microbes.

When the poliovirus synthesis project started in 1999, commercial gene synthesis was unheard of. It was far too difficult and expensive. Yet by 2010, the price for buying enough oligos to assemble and synthesise a virus had fallen to mere hundreds of dollars. And existing viruses such as the common flu could easily be tweaked in a lab to evade immune responses and resist treatments. That means creating viruses with properties that do not exist in nature. Like the COVID-19 virus, perhaps? Certainly, the GoF suspension in America led researchers to transfer the research work to China and take advantage of the looser regulations.

In October 2014 American government agencies started to review this gain-of-function research to assess the risk of changing pathogens to alter their virulence and transmissibility. The fear was that a modified virus could either escape or be stolen from a laboratory, or simply be put to purposes that threatened public health and national security.

The US government imposed a temporary suspension of funding for new GoF projects that 'may be reasonably anticipated to confer attributes to influenza, MERS, or SARS viruses such that the virus would have enhanced pathogenicity and/or transmissibility in mammals via the respiratory route'. The government asked researchers already carrying out GoF projects to 'voluntarily' postpone their studies until the risks were evaluated.

At a two-day meeting of the US National Academy of Sciences, there was a fierce debate on the ban. Ralph Baric of the University of North Carolina spoke out against it. He and his team were already engaged in investigating the SARS virus, which had suddenly emerged in China in 2002, and MERS—the Middle East respiratory syndrome, a deadly disease caused by a virus that jumps from camels to people. Professor Baric led a team at the Department of Microbiology and Immunology that had long focused on the relatively unfashionable study of coronaviruses, which include SARS and MERS. Research on coronaviruses had only started in the early 1960s. Baric was considered the world's leading expert on coronaviruses and was very surprised by the suspension of his work, protesting that the funding ban was unnecessary. Unlike commercial start-ups or big pharma companies, work at his lab depended heavily on public funding.

The absence of vaccines and anti-viral drugs for these kinds of viruses meant that if they ever mutated into becoming highly contagious among humans, there would be no tools available to fight an outbreak. Baric's challenge was to find a new way to deal with the problem, because there are no small animals like ferrets suitable for carrying out the kind of 'animal-passage' studies, as Fourier had done with avian flu.

So since 2001, his team focused on creating a chimeric virus adapted to infecting mice, making them ill with both MERS and later SARS. Then he could carry out animal-passage type experiments on real animals instead of cell cultures.

The chimeric versions needed modified spike proteins, the part of the SARS coronavirus that acts as a key to unlock entry into human cells. Its official name is angiotensin converting enzyme 2, and it is an enzyme attached to the membranes of cells located in the lungs, arteries, heart, kidney and intestines. It is the coronavirus' entry point into a cell—where the virus can unlock the door, allowing it to get into the cell and then to multiply.

The ACE-2 key doesn't work on mice or other animals such as civets in quite the same way as it does on humans. The purpose of the modification was not to make any virus more easily transmissible—something that Baric said was difficult to do in any case. On the contrary, he pointed out that a coronavirus adapted to make a mouse sick was inevitably going to be less infectious for humans. So he carried out experiments with a safer version of the virus. His GoF research was thus different from Fourier's. Cell receptors for influenza viruses—such as Fourier's H5N1 avian flu—are much the same for different species, including humans, so they can mutate and jump from ferrets to humans, or from birds to humans, with relative ease. In contrast, the ACE2 receptor interface for coronaviruses varies a great deal more from one species to another, because they do not share an evolutionary history.

Baric's appeal was successful. His work was allowed to continue because it was judged not risky enough to be bound by the moratorium. Then, in 2015, Baric and his collaborators made a successful breakthrough. His paper caused a stir and reignited the controversy all over again. Baric and his team created a chimeric SARS-like virus, which expresses the spike (attachment protein) of a bat coronavirus in a mouse-adapted SARS-CoV backbone. In other words, his team had succeeded in creating a chimeric SARS virus that could enter the lungs of a mouse and make it very sick, but not kill it.

The article 'A SARS-like cluster of circulating bat coronaviruses shows potential for human emergence' appeared in *Nature Medicine* in December 2015. It explained how the team created a version of the virus that Chinese scientists from the Wuhan Institute of Virology had obtained from swabs taken from horseshoe bats living in caves in Yunnan province. The project set out to evaluate the risk of SARS coronaviruses spreading from the viruses circulating in the bats.

The scientists investigated a strain of virus called SHC014 and took a surface protein of SHC014 as well as the backbone of a SARS virus that had been adapted to grow in mice to create their hybrid. This proved that the surface protein of SHC014 has the necessary structure to bind to a key receptor in human airway cells and to infect them.

This was startling, since almost all coronaviruses isolated from bats had not been able to bind to the key human receptor. In

2013, researchers had already reported this ability, but in a different coronavirus strain isolated from the same bat population.

'The findings reinforce suspicions that bat coronaviruses capable of directly infecting humans (rather than first needing to evolve in an intermediate animal host) may be more common than previously thought', the authors of the article concluded.

The North Carolina University group also reported that their hybrid SARS-like virus could indeed bind to and replicate efficiently in human airway cells, at least *in vitro*. In fact, in human cells the chimeric virus replicated just as well as epidemic strains of SARS-CoV did.

A news article in *Nature* magazine reported other virologists questioning whether the information gleaned from the experiment was really so useful that it justified the risk of unleashing a dangerous virus. Simon Wain-Hobson of the Pasteur Institute in Paris said that since the researchers created a novel virus that 'grows remarkably well' in human cells it meant that 'if the virus escaped, nobody could predict the trajectory'.

Wain-Hobson also argued that the study was not very useful, since it revealed little about the risk that the wild SHC014 virus in bats poses to humans. Baric and his team had reconstructed the wild virus from its genome sequence and found that it grew poorly in human cell cultures and caused no significant disease in mice. So, it was clear from the experiments that a virus in wild bats like this one had to evolve quite a bit before posing any threat to humans. Every virus has evolved to target a particular species, so it is very rare for a virus to be able to jump to another species.

Wain-Hobson was supported by Richard Ebright, a molecular biologist and bio-defence expert at Rutgers University in Piscataway and another long-standing critic of GoF research: 'The only impact of this work is the creation, in a lab, of a new, non-natural risk'. Harvard epidemiologist Marc Lipsitch said the work brings 'a unique risk that a laboratory accident could spark a pandemic, killing millions'.

The work was carried out jointly with the Wuhan Institute of Virology, which, after 2014, continued to pursue its own research into bat viruses, collecting more samples, and studying the chimeric virus created in the North Carolina lab. The Chinese research was helped along with funding from several American funding organisations—something that became particularly significant since the work in Baric's lab was suspended while it was being reviewed. But why were Americans so interested in bat viruses?

12

THE VIRUS HUNTERS

Battling the influenza virus in all its forms is the top priority for governments, international organisations such as the WHO, and big pharmaceutical companies. Interest in bats and other wild animals came later. Enormous efforts around the world are made to collect and collate data on the annual winter flu virus. This date is given to big pharmaceutical companies in time for them to prepare the flu vaccines for the following winter. They take around six months to prepare and produce them. Sometimes the vaccines work, perhaps on as many as half of those who take the shot, sometimes they are effective on as few as 25 per cent. It all forms part of a vast multi-billion dollar industry.

Unlike with the coronaviruses, scientists have no doubt that the flu virus is easily transmissible between people, as well as between domestic animals such as pigs, ducks, geese and chickens. It has no trouble jumping from one to the other. These animals are natural reservoirs or hosts of the flu virus. It is why the influenza virus is constantly mutating. Different strains can meet in one host and create a hybrid that can spread quickly. The virus is very contagious and can spread through dung, through touch or through the air.

Scientists have been studying the various types of the flu virus since 1933, when it was first identified at a laboratory in North London. There is still an immense amount about it that has yet to be learned, but it is currently believed that it started out in South China or South East Asia, as that is where fowl such as chickens and ducks were first domesticated, perhaps some 10,000 years ago. In this part of the world, for thousands of years, millions of households have lived closely together with both domesticated fowl and with a pig or two. Every farmer had a yard where he kept his pigs, chickens and ducks. Many illnesses such as cowpox or horsepox or indeed MERS are transmitted through close contact with domesticated animals.

South East Asia is where humans first started growing rice. Rice was domesticated in the deltas of the Yangtze and the Pearl River perhaps 10,000 or 15,000 years ago. Around 5,000 years ago, its cultivation began to spread throughout South East Asia. To grow rice domestically, you need to create paddy fields, by damming and flooding fields. This is very labour intensive and supports very high population densities compared to nomadic herder cultures, which require large expanses of pastureland to breed goats, horses and cows.

These paddy fields are most easily created in river deltas where there is already a lot of water—lakes and marshes—which attract large populations of migratory birds eager to feed on the fish, snails, insects, worms and other creatures that thrive in these wetlands. Vast numbers of birds from Russia, Japan, the Korean Peninsula and North China head south to winter and then return north (or in some cases westwards) in the spring to breed. Rice farmers naturally noticed that some of these fowl, in particular ducks, are very helpful in eating the pests that attack their rice crops, as well as being good to eat. The domestication of mallard ducks probably started 3,000 years ago. The chicken was probably domesticated even earlier, but also in South East Asia. The birds defecate in the water, and so can easily spread an avian virus to humans and other farm animals. On most farms, the chickens, ducks and geese are co-farmed.

The result is that China is home to huge populations of both domesticated and wild birds that are in contact with each other. They are managed by rice farmers who also breed pigs. Pork was until recently the primary staple meat in China, where the animal was first domesticated probably 8,000 years ago. In fact, the relationship was so strong that the Chinese character for the word family or house is composed of a roof above a pig. In recent decades, China has begun factory farming huge numbers of chickens, which have become the nation's favourite food. The influenza virus lives in the wild ducks' guts, but it can cross over into the respiratory tracts of a pig, and from there it can mutate a little, so that it can then infect humans.

All this makes the reassortment of new virus strains as they mutate in a melting pot of ducks, chickens, pigs and people, and then cross over, relatively straightforward to imagine. It also means that domesticated animals can be vaccinated but still be re-infected through contact with wild birds with a reservoir of viruses. Only rarely does a virus emerge, as it did with the Spanish flu in 1918, that is so dangerous that it kills its hosts in large numbers.

It is, however, notoriously tricky to be sure where and how exactly any new flu virus emerges. An outbreak in 1889 seems to have originated with horses in Kazakhstan. The 1900 virus seems to have come from an inter-human mixing of two preceding strains. The 1918 Spanish flu pandemic seems to have arrived from pigs, perhaps in America but perhaps in China. The 1977 Asiatic H1N1 pandemic strain appeared in the Soviet Union and China, and some virologists now think that the reason for its sudden reappearance is that it escaped from a laboratory attempting to prepare an H1N1 vaccine from a frozen sample of the virus that first appeared in 1949–50. The virus spread rapidly, but it was mostly dangerous to those under twenty, as most adults had immunity. Certainly, some flu viruses do appear then disappear for decades before they unexpectedly re-emerge. Some experts suggest that the virus survives in frozen lakes, from where it is picked up by migrating fowl.

The human genome is made up to a large part of old viruses and defences against old viruses, a sort of attic full of discarded old items. Some say that 50 per cent of our genome consists of this historical legacy, others put the figure much lower. It means that it is possible to imagine that China and South East Asia can both be breeding grounds for new strains of the influenza virus, while at the same time, the local rice-growing population may have an inherited natural defence against the virus.

We know, for example, that some of us are more likely to suffer badly from flu because of a variation in our interferon response genes. About one in 400 Europeans has a non-functional version of a gene called IFITM3, and variations of this gene are even more common in Japanese and Chinese people. These interferon-stimulated genes trigger cells to stop invading viruses including the swine flu virus, orthomyxoviruses, flaviviruses, filoviruses and coronaviruses. So, anyone lacking it is more likely to need hospital treatment. It is one piece of research that suggests why various populations do not respond in the same way to different strains of the flu and other viruses.

For a long time, the big guns of the WHO and the pharmaceutical industry were trained on the flu front. Western governments developed plans on how to defeat an outbreak and spent billions on creating emergency stockpiles of medicines such as Tamiflu, vaccines and other equipment. Yet a new front also opened after the HIV-AIDS pandemic started in the early 1980s. It took a long time to understand the virus, which can disguise itself and hide in the body for a long time. It was equally difficult to understand where it came from, but it was eventually traced to monkeys and apes living in West Africa.

Acquired immunodeficiency syndrome (AIDS) in humans is caused by two lentiviruses—HIV-1 and HIV-2. They are the result of multiple cross-species transmissions of simian immunodeficiency viruses (SIVs), which naturally infect African primates. It doesn't do them a great deal of harm. Most of these transfers resulted in viruses that spread in humans to a rather limited extent. However, one transmission event, involving SIVcpz from chimpanzees in south-eastern Cameroon, gave rise to HIV-1 group M—the principal cause of the AIDS pandemic (HIV-2 is mostly limited to West Africa).

The SIVs crossed from monkeys to apes and from apes to humans, mostly by hunters killing or eating these monkeys. It was then transmitted from person to person through direct exposure to infected body fluids (blood, semen) through sexual contact, sharing unclean needles etc. These lentiviruses cause chronic persistent infections in various mammalian species, including bovines, horses, sheep, felines and primates, and they date back millions of years. The HIV virus is a peculiar kind of virus because it initially appears as a brief flu-like infection and then reappears after a long incubation period. The virus is not lethal itself, but turns the body's immuno-defences against itself. The body overreacts and shuts down its defence against all kinds of other diseases—hence the term acquired immune deficiency. There is no vaccine against the virus per se, but there are now anti-viral drugs, which control the body's overreaction to the invasion.

All these discoveries led scientists and administrators to start worrying about what other kinds of lethal viruses might be found in wild animals. HIV wasn't the only emergency that fostered these fears. There were, too, the outbreaks of the deadly Ebola virus, which also emerged out of the forests of West Africa. It first appeared in 1976 near the Ebola River in what is now the Democratic Republic of Congo, and in 2014, there was a severe outbreak. It is thought that fruit bats are the natural hosts of the virus, but humans get it from chimpanzees, gorillas, monkeys, forest antelopes or porcupines. People either found these animals ill or dead in the rainforest, or went out to hunt and kill them. The virus is passed via contact with the blood, secretions, organs or other bodily fluids of this 'bush meat'. When someone falls sick, it is passed on through close contact with a carer, or relatives gathering for a funeral.

These two viruses led a group of virus hunters to devote greater efforts to studying wild animals, mostly in Africa, to stop or contain outbreaks of known or unknown viruses before they suddenly emerged from their hosts living in tropical forests. The virus hunters estimated that there are 600,000 unknown viruses, possibly more, which have the ability to jump from animals to people. They put forward the 'spillover' theory. This holds that such viruses suddenly emerge when their hosts or their hosts' habitat is threatened by climate change, deforestation, mining, road building, increased migration and travel, or other human activities. Destruction of forests and other encroachments on wildlife habitats, especially the hunting of wild animals and the sale of live animals in wet markets, is believed to force humans and animals into uncomfortable proximity. This is bad for vulnerable and endangered species, as well as for humans who are at increasing risk of contracting novel zoonotic diseases.

The idea is that, like the infected plague fleas, the virus mutates and, when its host is threatened or is 'under stress', it responds by shedding a larger viral 'load', so it can jump species as it seeks out a new host. Viral 'shedding' is when a virus replicates and then sends its progeny out of the host cell, often through the skin or through the air, or in some other way.

The principle sponsor of these new virus hunters was the US Agency for International Development, which in 2009 launched a five-year Emerging Pandemic Threats programme (it was renewed in 2014). It started in response to the 2005 H5N1 bird flu panic and largely focused on South East Asia and Central Africa. The US Center for Disease Control and Prevention (CDC), and the Department of Defense (DoD) also put money in a pot, which fluctuated at around $500 million per year. Spending rose if there was a fresh crisis, such as the 2014 Ebola outbreak or the Zika virus crisis. The World Health Organisation also had a hefty budget of around $100 million a year, and many other governments and universities around the world chipped in.

The USAID Emerging Pandemic Threats programme created four projects with catchy names—PREDICT, RESPOND, IDENTIFY and PREVENT. RESPOND was about institution building in trouble spots—helping local universities, public health workers, veterinary doctors, nurses and doctors collaborate with each other. This was termed the One Health Approach.

The PREVENT project focused on changing the behaviour of those people most at risk from catching these dangerous new diseases, such as stopping the trade in wild animals and bushmeat.

IDENTIFY was about linking up with the WHO, the UN Food and Agriculture Organization (FAO), and the World Organisation for Animal Health to create a network of laboratories operating in hot spots to identify outbreaks or new threats. It was designed as a sort of early warning system.

The University of North Carolina, where Dr Ralph Baric led the team that created the chimeric SARS virus, was a major beneficiary of USAID grants. In 2014, the university won the second largest five-year grant in its history, $180 million, for measuring and evaluating public health programmes around the world. The award will be used to continue the research required to target US spending on global health threats such as malaria and HIV. The actual research on the SARS virus was mostly funded by the National Institute of Health, but also by the PREDICT programme.

The PREDICT programme was the most exciting of the four programmes, involving, as it did, hunting for new viruses in exotic locations around the world. It was often dramatized as a race against time to find disease X before it wiped out human civilisation. Here, it was taken as a given that three quarters or more of any new threats would come from zoonotic diseases—the transmission of diseases from animal hosts such as bats and rats to humans. The virus hunters set off on difficult and some-times dangerous Indiana Jones type adventures to collect samples from wild animals, livestock and humans living in the back of beyond. With the advent of portable handheld sequencing devices like the ones made by Oxford Nanopore, this became ever more practical. It was no longer necessary to send swabs off to a distant laboratory and wait weeks for the results. A lot of work could be done on the spot.

Finding new viruses is not as difficult as it might sound. Inconceivably large numbers of viruses inhabit the world. New strains appear constantly. A drop of seawater contains billions and billions of viruses. Even our skins and guts are host to such extraordinarily large numbers of viruses, viroids, phages and bacteria that the whole thing is given a name—the human microbiome—much of which is uncharted. Our body consists of 37.2 trillion cells, and ten times as many microbes. Nearly all of these are harmless, and in most cases they are benign, if not useful or indeed essential to our wellbeing.

Viruses and the like have been on earth for billions of years and come in an almost limitless variety. Some viruses even have viruses. Some are as big and complex as cells. It is possible that 99 per cent of viruses are still to be discovered. The trick is to find the viruses that are dangerous. These are extremely rare.

Influenza was only isolated in 1933, Zika in 1947, chikunganya (a virus spread by mosquito bites) in 1952, the Hanta virus (carried by rodents) in 1953, the Marburg virus (from African green monkeys) was identified in 1957, the Ebola virus in 1976, the Nipah virus in 1999, HIV in 1983, SARS in 2003, MERS in 2012 and so on.

Only a tiny number of newly discovered viruses have led to epidemics, and even fewer to pandemics. This is all the more remarkable since the world's population has increased from one billion to over seven billion, and international travel has become so common. One might expect far more pandemics like the Spanish flu. On the other hand, like any risk insurance policy, it is only sensible to do everything possible to avert another devastating pandemic such as the one from 1918. The longer historians researched its history, the more often has its mortality been revised upwards. It is now thought that the global death toll was 100 million.

With a $200 million budget over ten years, the virus hunters collected more than 140,000 biological samples from various animals, including 10,000 bats and over 2,000 other mammals. The result of all these efforts provoked a mixed reception. PREDICT discovered hundreds of new coronavirus species and hundreds of potential zoonoses, although it is not always easy to assess what kind of risk any one of these poses. The programme led to the discovery of just one real threat, the Bas-Congo virus, which caused a deadly haemorrhagic fever in two inhabitants of a remote village.

The researchers became particularly interested in studying the viruses that live in bats. The most dangerous of these, rabies, is well known, at least by scientists. It still kills over 50,000 people a year. Scientists started looking at bats during the 1950s, when the Rockefeller Foundation and several governmental agencies backed researchers trying to find viruses that caused encephalitis and tropical fevers. Field laboratories were funded in many tropical countries, and eventually several new viruses were isolated, including the Rift Valley fever virus and the Japanese encephalitis virus, which are hosted by bats.

In general, bats and people have been coexisting for a very long time, without having very much to do with one another. And bat viruses don't easily cross over to humans. Since the discovery of the connection between rabies and bats in southern Brazil in 1906, bats have been killed to prevent the disease spreading to livestock and from cattle to humans. Elsewhere bats are hunted for food. Around 167 species of bats are hunted, but it is mostly the larger, fruit-eating species that are regularly caught and consumed, as these are the only ones with enough meat on them to make it worthwhile. They are still regularly eaten in Malaysia, Indonesia, the Philippines, Thailand and Vietnam. More often, they are treated as a pest because they raid valuable orchards. Recently, the fruit bats in these regions have been listed as endangered, which shows that they are not very common.

Interest in bats picked up again in the 1990s with the discovery of the Hendra virus, which affected horses in Australia. It was responsible for the deaths of two humans and fifteen horses during two separate outbreaks, and was eventually traced back to fruit bats. These are of the genus *Pteropus*, or flying fox, so named after the fox-like shape of their faces. They can have a wingspan of up to four feet, fly up to 50 miles at night in large flocks, and prefer flowers and pollen to fruit.

Next came the deadly Nipah virus (named after a village in Malaysia), which, starting in 1998, swept through numerous piggeries in Malaysia and killed over a hundred people. It was later discovered that the host was the same fruit bats, the genus *Pteropus*. Both people and pigs, it turned out, can contract the virus, either from the saliva of the bats left on palm trees, or from partially eaten fruit or excreta that fall into the feeding pens at the piggeries. A million pigs were slaughtered in order to contain the outbreak.

The PREDICT programme was particularly keen on taking bat samples around the world, and it was the top priority of a major grant winner, an NGO called EcoHealth Alliance, based in New York. EcoHealth Alliance (originally called the Wildlife Preservation Trust International) had been set up in 1971 by Gerald Durrell (1925–75), the author and naturalist whose memoir of his childhood in Corfu, *My Family and Other Animals*, became a bestseller. In 1999, it became the Wildlife Trust, and then merged with the Consortium for Conservation Medicine. It was set up after the launch of the Emerging Pandemic Threats Program and cleverly managed to offer funding organisations a way to hit two of the most fashionable concerns with one shot—pandemics and environmentalism.

EcoHealth Alliance presents itself in this way:

> Building on over 40 years of groundbreaking science, EcoHealth Alliance is a global, nonprofit organization dedicated to protecting wildlife and safeguarding human health from the emergence of disease. The organization develops ways to combat the effects of damaged ecosystems on human and wildlife health. Using environmental and health data covering the past 60 years, EcoHealth Alliance scientists created the first-ever, global disease hotspots map that identified at-risk regions, to help predict and prevent the next pandemic crisis. That work is the foundation of EcoHealth Alliance's rigorous, science-based approach, focused at the intersection of the environment, health, and capacity building. Working in the U.S. and more than 20 countries worldwide, EcoHealth Alliance's strength is founded on innovations in research, training, global partnerships, and policy initiatives.

It is run by Peter Daszak, a British scientist, whose success in attracting $100 million in various kinds of US government grants earned him a salary of just over $400,000. Some grants came from the Pentagon, but nearly half derived from the USAID Emerging Pandemic Threats programme. Peter Daszak and others researched the Nipah virus in Malaysia and discovered two new viruses, Tioman virus and Pulau virus, in bat excreta. They also investigated outbreaks of the Nipah virus in Bangladesh.

Dr Daszak argued that these fruit bats and the viruses they host present a grave danger, because the deforestation in Malaysia, Indonesia and elsewhere is driving the bats into closer contact with humans as they establish colonies close to town and villages. In fact the outbreak around Nipah was probably caused by a decision to plant fruit trees, lots of mango trees, around the piggeries. It was these trees that attracted the bats. Nothing similar happened in other parts of the region. No new outbreaks have been reported in Malaysia since 1999.

In this part of Malaysia—peninsular Malaysia—these large flying foxes are avidly hunted. About 1,750 hunting licences were issued between 2002 and 2006, permitting around 22,000 to be caught each year. Some are killed to protect valuable orchards—a bounty equal to US $2 is paid per bat—although the fruit bats are also key pollinators of many important and commercial species such as durian trees.

For the largely Muslim populations of Malaysia and Indonesia, bats are not a permitted food (nor is pork), but the ethnic Chinese population consider bats an exotic delicacy. Generally, though, Chinese culture celebrates bats because the character for a bat, fu, is a homonym for another word meaning prosperity or 'good fortune'. Bats are therefore painted as a decorative motif on all kinds of things, such as household furniture.

Even though the outbreaks of the Hendra and Nipah viruses killed relatively small numbers of people, Daszak argued that some yet undiscovered virus in a creature like a bat could be the next HIV, and start a terrible pandemic. Daszak diligently promoted the idea that bats are a particularly significant host for viruses. The more that was known about them, and the sooner, the better.

There is no known treatment for Nipah, and it is deadly. It became the inspiration for the 2011 thriller *Contagion*, where the wife of a businessman, played by Matt Damon, returning from a trip to Hong Kong, brings back a virus which turns out to be a reassortment of genes from pig and bat viruses. Then the hunt is on for a vaccine before everyone dies. In the real world, research for a vaccine for Nipah and Ebola is carried out at the newly built BSL-4 laboratories at the National Bio and Agro-Defence Facility in Kansas.

Fear about a new pandemic brought EcoHealth Alliance a $1.6 million grant from the Pentagon for 'Serological Biosurveillance for Spillover of Henipaviruses and Filoviruses at Agricultural and Hunting Human Animal Interfaces in Peninsular Malaysia'. EcoHealth Alliance also won a $1.7 million grant (2002–05) for 'Anthropogenic Change & Emerging Zoonotic Paramyxoviruses'. In 2012–14, Daszak also won a $569,700 grant from the National Fish and Wildlife Service for 'Development of a Great Ape Health Unit in Sabah, Malaysia'.

When, in 2002, the new SARS virus appeared in China, seemingly out of nowhere, Dr Daszak and his colleagues were already becoming established as experts on researching bat virus threats in South East Asia. The SARS virus also presented a perfect match up of the mission of EcoHealth Alliance—it brought together all their concerns: unknown viruses lurking in bats, the hunting, trade and consumption of endangered animals, deforestation pushing animals into closer contact with humans, and the importance of cross border cooperation to create an early warning system.

China had until then been much less willing to allow foreign researchers to work on its territory than governments in Africa or South East Asia. Researchers are obliged to form a close partnership with a Chinese organisation if they are to gain access. The 2002 SARS virus epidemic opened the door and accelerated the building of the first BSL-4 lab in China. It was built with French support in Wuhan. Daszak used a $2.6 million grant (2008–12), to investigate the 'Risk of Viral Emergence From Bats', from the National Institute of Allergy and Infectious Diseases to gain the support of the Chinese authorities. This allowed the scientists at the Wuhan Institute of Virology, like Shi Zhengli—dubbed China's bat woman—who had worked with Dr Baric at the University of North Carolina, to go out and find bats that might be a possible source of the SARS virus and other viruses. This project was followed up with a $3.7 million PREDICT grant (2014–20) for 'Understanding the Risk of Bat Coronavirus Emergence'.

Ecohealth Alliance was therefore able to back Dr Baric's research on gain of function on SARS, since his department was the acknowledged leader in coronavirus research, as well as the collection of samples from bats in Yunnan. Daszak became the Project Leader of the bat coronavirus surveillance conducted with the Wuhan Institute of Virology. And when the gain-of-function research moved from North Carolina to Wuhan, he was also able to support the bat coronavirus gain-of-function research in Wuhan with a $3.7 million grant.

Later, Daszak also won a new $1.5 million grant from the US National Institute of Allergy and Infectious Diseases for 'Understanding Risk of Zoonotic Virus Emergence in Emerging Infectious Diseases Hotspots of Southeast Asia'. The grant is intended for a South East Asia Research Collaboration Hub that 'brings leaders in emerging disease research from the U.S., Thailand, Singapore and the three major Malaysian administrative regions together to build an early warning system to safeguard against pandemic disease threats. This team will identify novel viruses from Southeast Asian wildlife and characterize their capacity to infect and cause illness in people...'

A belief that Dr Daszak and his colleagues share is that disease outbreaks are predictable and therefore preventable. The problems of human and animal disease are intimately linked and exacerbated by ecological change. His team produced the first ever global emerging disease 'hotspots' map to determine where in the world viruses with pandemic potential are most likely to emerge, and developed a strategy to identify just how many of those viruses currently exist.

Daszak also has his critics in the scientific community. They argue that virus spillover from bats is extremely rare, and that the gain-of-function research being carried out on the bat viruses is extremely dangerous, especially given the risk of laboratory accidents—above all in China, where standards are low. The country already had a reputation for recklessly encouraging, or at least tolerating, all kinds of experiments that are not permitted elsewhere. And when the biotech investment craze started, Chinese researchers seemed to be taking even more daring risks with gain-of-function experiments on animals and even humans. Besides, as everyone was aware, gain of function know-how has a dual use. Creating an unknown chimeric virus of which the enemy has no knowledge, let alone a vaccine for it, is exactly what the Russians were up to in their vast and secretive bioweapons research.

In a commentary published by the *Lancet*, Colin Carlson, an expert in emerging infectious diseases at Georgetown University, argued that work funded by PREDICT helped virologists rapidly isolate and classify the COVID-19 virus when it came out.

We can more rapidly contextualise where, how, and why new human viruses originate in wildlife. [...] Nonetheless, disciplinary tensions around accountability and rhetoric suggest that academic research on emerging wildlife viruses could be better positioned for a broader overall impact.[1]

On the other side of the debate is Professor Richard Ebright of Rutgers University in New Jersey. He told *Newsweek Magazine* that: 'The PREDICT program has produced no results—absolutely no results—that are of use for preventing or combating outbreaks. There's no information from that project that will contribute in any way, shape or form to addressing the outbreak at hand. The research does not provide information that's useful for developing antiviral drugs. It does not provide information that's useful for developing vaccines.'[2]

Some believed that the top priority should be influenza. The odds of a new and deadly cross-over virus emerging from the interaction between the many hundreds of millions of pigs, ducks and chickens in southern China are very high, much higher than the transmission of a bat virus. These huge numbers of domesticated animals live in close proximity to a dense human population of some 500 million. Compared with that, the odds of a virus from a rare bat living in a distant cave or forest spilling over into humans are always going to be low. Yet Daszak was able to counter this by pointing out what had happened with SIV virus and the AIDS pandemic—30 million cases and untold misery—from a virus in rare chimpanzees. And there is the case of the SARS virus outbreak, but, as the next chapter reveals, the mystery of SARS has yet to be solved.

13

THE MYSTERIOUS SARS OUTBREAK 2002–03

In late 2002, a strange pneumonia-like illness appeared in Guangdong province. It seemingly came out of nowhere, and disappeared in the same inexplicable way. Much about it remains uncertain. Even though only a very small number of people were infected and fewer died from it, it was very dangerous. There were officially just 8,422 cases, but the fatality rate was eleven per cent. It was dubbed severe acute respiratory syndrome (SARS), and it was caused by a virus. The victims suffered from fever, headache and respiratory symptoms including coughing, breathing difficulties and pneumonia. Not a single case of the severe acute respiratory syndrome has been reported after late 2004. The epidemic strain of SARS that caused at least 774 deaths worldwide by June 2003 has not been seen outside of a laboratory since then.

It was identified as a type of coronavirus, and genetically similar viruses were found in masked palm civets (*Paguma larvata*) that were sold in wet markets in Guangdong.

Some believe that the first case appeared in Foshan, a large but fairly dull city in the Pearl River delta. It is home to thousands of factories and migrant worker dormitories. The area is largely devoted to making products for the building industry, ceramics and furniture, which are exported around the world. The city and its environs are home to over seven million people. It rains a lot, and during the rainy summer months it gets unbearably hot and humid. There's a brand new high-speed train station—it is an important railway junction—that connects it to Guangzhou, the provincial capital, and Hong Kong. The city even boasts its own metro system, and it is also connected to a network of fast motorways.

The illness appeared on 16 November 2002, and the outbreak peaked the following February. The first place to officially report this atypical pneumonia was a hospital in Heyuan, another city in the province. The patient was a thirty-five-year-old cook working in a restaurant that offered exotic animals, including snakes, on its menu. Yet the restaurant was in Shenzhen, another industrial city bordering Hong Kong, and he first went to a hospital there before seeking treatment at the Renmin (People's) hospital in Heyuan. He was then sent to the Guangzhou Military Hospital. The first super spreader was Zhou Zuofen, a fishmonger who checked into the Sun Yat-Sen Memorial Hospital in Guangzhou on 31 January, where he infected thirty nurses and doctors. Another early patient was a waitress at a restaurant in Guangzhou that served dishes of palm civets, and another was a customer. The restaurant had eight animal cages in four stacks at the restaurant entrance, close to the pavement. The diner was a forty-year-old physician who ate at a table in the restaurant on 31 December 2003, within a few yards of the cages. He first showed symptoms on 7 January 2004.

What seems to have happened is that there were clusters of infections among people working in markets or restaurants, or people handling animals, who fell sick. Not all of the civets were wild animals, with some coming from breeding farms. The infected people then reported to hospitals, where medical staff fell ill and quickly spread the infection. A few went across the border to Hong Kong and then fell ill. In February 2003, Liu Jianlun, who worked at the Sun Yat Sen Memorial Hospital in Guangdong and had treated SARS patients, arrived to attend a family wedding. He checked into room 911 on the ninth floor of the Metropole Hotel, an ugly square concrete building in central Kowloon. Despite feeling ill he met his relatives, but a few days later, feeling worse, he walked to nearby Kwong Wah Hospital and asked the staff to put him in isolation. He died in the intensive care unit on 4 March.

Next, twenty-three other guests staying at the Metropole developed SARS, including seven from the ninth floor. Liu's brother-in-law was hospitalized in Kwong Wah Hospital on 1 March and died on 19 March. Around 80 per cent of the Hong Kong cases were traced back to Liu.

A Chinese-American, Johnny Chen, a resident of Shanghai who had stayed in a room across the hall from Liu at the Metropole, flew to Hanoi. He checked into the French Hospital in Hanoi on 26 February, where he infected at least thirty-eight members of staff. Even though he was evacuated to Hong Kong, he died on 13 March.

Carlo Urbani, an infectious disease specialist working for the WHO, was one of those who examined Chen. He saw that other hospital staff were already falling ill and realized that he was dealing with a new and dangerous disease. On 11 March, Urbani travelled to Bangkok to attend a medical conference but fell ill during the flight. He told a friend waiting at Bangkok not to touch him, to call an ambulance and take him to a hospital. He was isolated in an intensive care unit and died on 29 March.

On 23 February, another guest at the Metropole, Kwan Sui-Chu, flew back to Toronto. She died at home on 5 March, after infecting her son Tse Chi Kwai, who subsequently spread the disease to Scarborough Grace Hospital, and died on 13 March.

For reasons that are still not clear, the Metropole Hotel infection chain seeded a great many cases around the world. It infected 195 in Hong Kong, 71 in Singapore, 58 in Vietnam, 29 in Canada, and one each in Canada and the USA. In another case, 321 residents of a single apartment block in Amoy Gardens in Kowloon developed SARS.

On 12 March, the WHO issued a global alert about a new infectious disease of unknown origin in both Vietnam and Hong Kong. Three days later, after cases in Singapore and Canada were identified, they issued a heightened global health alert about a mysterious pneumonia. It warned international travellers, healthcare professionals and health authorities. The US Centre for Disease Control also issued a travel advisory warning people not to go to these areas.

The American Centre for Disease Control held its first briefing on SARS and said that fourteen suspected SARS cases were being investigated in the US. On 1 April, Washington called back non-essential personnel from their consulate office in Hong Kong and Guangzhou and warned its citizens from traveling to the region. The WHO also advised travellers to avoid Hong Kong and Guangdong during a press briefing. By this time, both Hong Kong and Singapore had shut down schools and colleges and started large-scale quarantining of residents and some visitors.

The day after the announcements by the WHO and American officials, China began reporting the outbreak. China's southern Guangdong province reported 361 new infections and nine new deaths, increasing the total previously reported at the end of February. By this time, travellers had carried the virus to Beijing and Shanghai.

In early April, the Chinese government changed tack and then launched a full-scale campaign to bring the disease under control. Health minister Zhang Wenkang, and Beijing's mayor, Meng Xuenong, were replaced and in Beijing, Shanghai and

Guangdong province, and indeed most of the country, a complete lockdown and sanitation campaign went into full swing. The draconian measures worked, and by early July, the Beijing government declared victory. The WHO dropped its travel warnings. On 16 August, with the last two SARS patients discharged from the Beijing Ditan Hospital, China, for the time being, was free from SARS.

According to the official statistics, which have never been revised, the pandemic generated 8,500 cases, 916 patients died world-wide, and the mortality rate was nearly 11 per cent, although in some places it was closer to 20 per cent. It struck those over sixty-five much harder. For them, the death rate was 50 per cent, while young adults under twenty-five only had a seven per cent chance of dying.

The pandemic revealed several disturbing things. The Chinese government was not to be trusted, and it was very reluctant if not unwilling to cooperate with the WHO. Secondly it showed that many countries were not sufficiently prepared to deal with the challenge of a super-infectious disease. As medical staff didn't have enough protective clothing and isolation wards, and didn't carry out the right sanitary procedures with sufficient vigour, they accounted for a fifth of the cases in Hong Kong, and 40 per cent of those in Toronto. The security controls in the labs of institutes and universities that worked with SARS were exposed. Researchers in labs in both Taiwan and Singapore managed to infect themselves.

By the middle of March 2003, laboratories around the world set out to understand what exactly was the disease. At the time everyone was watching to see a new influenza virus emerge from Guangdong province that would kill chickens and ducks. The SARS virus led to similar symptoms in people, but was different. It took five days to incubate, and did not become contagious until after fever and dry coughing had occurred. It took about ten days for it to peak, and there were asymptomatic infections. Yet with the flu, someone can be infected and pass on the virus a day or two before the actual onset of symptoms. And many people in an influenza epidemic get the bug without showing any signs of being sick. It also spreads much faster than SARS. This makes SARS easier to control, as, once an infected person has been identified, they can be isolated and will stop infecting others. That seems to explain why SARS could be contained much more easily than a flu outbreak.

The next question is, where did the SARS virus come from? A lot of the work on this was done by scientists in Hong Kong, which has a strong research tradition dating back to the discovery of *Yersina pestis*. The Sri Lankan professor Malik Peiris led a team at the Hong Kong University Pasteur Research Centre, which had dealt with the 1997 Avian flu outbreak. In early 2003, his lab was the first to isolate the SARs virus and to develop a rapid diagnostic test.

Professor Peiris was part of a research team led by a university colleague, Guan Yi, who went to a wildlife market just across the border in Shenzhen and took samples from a variety of caged animals—six masked palm civets, a raccoon dog and a Chinese ferret badger. They found that four of the civets tested positive for SARS, but they were unable to say if these were the primary host or just another susceptible species. Although the civets were kept in the wet markets to be sold to customers who wanted to eat them at a restaurant, Peiris said that as long as their meat was properly cooked, no one would be infected in that way.

The civet is a solitary nocturnal small mammal about the size of a domestic cat. It has dark fur, apart from a band of white fur above its eyes, making it look a bit like a cartoon masked bandit. It eats fruits and the sap of the palm flower—hence its name masked palm civet. Palm sap is fermented to make a popular drink called toddy. It is quite common all over South East Asia.

Some Chinese believe that eating civets provides immunity to influenza. People in Indonesia like to drink coffee made from beans that have been eaten and expelled by the cat, because a fermentation process takes place in the gut of the civet that alters the flavour. Lots of civets are captured and kept in cages just to make this coffee. Therefore, there are dozens of farms in both China and Indonesia breeding civets.

After that, however, the trail for the origin of the coronavirus went cold. Possibly the civets might have picked it up from contact with the flying fruit bats, as they share a liking for palm trees and various fruits. Yet there is no research indicating that civets play a role in transmitting SARS or other diseases anywhere else in the region. Or the civets at the Shenzhen wet market might have picked up the virus from some other creatures kept in a neighbouring cage. The animals sold there included donkeys, calves, goats, sheep, piglets, American minks, raccoon dogs, farmed foxes, hog badgers, porcupines, nutria, guinea pigs, rabbits and birds. It is true that they are kept in small wire cages piled atop one another, which facilitates transmission, but they are never there for very long, since they are displayed to be quickly sold and eaten. And the numbers of these creatures that are traded is very insignificant compared to, say, the billions of chickens raised and sold in China and neighbouring countries.

The wet markets selling live animals are rather common all over Asia and China. They are called that to distinguish them from markets that specialise in dry goods like grains, spices, pulses, dried sea foods etc. The wet markets usually have rows of fishmongers who may keep sea food alive in tanks or buckets, and butchers with squawking caged fowl for those who want to be sure the meat or fish is really clean and healthy. They are best regarded as a holdover from the days before refrigerated meat and supermarkets became common. Added to this, the rise of incomes has boosted the demand for household pets, so there are now markets selling the usual tropical fish, dogs and cats, caged song birds, crickets and all kinds of exotic animals.

The wet markets are not noticeably unsanitary, but Westerners are often shocked by seeing all kinds of creatures such as snakes, rats or scorpions, that are no longer part of Western diets. Cantonese are famous even in China for their willingness to eat anything. In some regions in southern China, wild-animal dishes on a single restaurant menu can run in the dozens. One Shenzhen restaurant, for instance, served everything from deep-fried baby pigeons to soy-braised civet steamed with ginger.

The most pernicious part of the wildlife market in China is the demand for products made from rhinoceros horns, tiger bones, musk deer, black bear bile, seahorses etc, which are used to treat various ailments. Even though many scientific studies have found that these are worthless cures with no medical benefits, the trade in endangered animals is fuelled by a state-sponsored belief in traditional Chinese medicine.

It was never really feasible to close either China's wet markets—they are an important source of affordable food and a livelihood for many—or the restaurants; but in May 2003, the authorities launched 'Operation Green Sword' and banned all wildlife sales. They went after the civet farms and ordered a cull. The state media reported that the police had confiscated 30,335 wild animals in nearly 1,000 markets around the country. They searched almost 7,000 hotels and restaurants and went after trucks and vans used for trafficking wildlife. In Shanghai's Fengxian district, one million partridges, mallards and pheasants were slaughtered during the wildlife crackdown.

Thousands of farmers, animal dealers, stall keepers and restaurant workers lost their jobs, and some staged public protests. Others simply carried on as a black market sprang up. The protestors had the support of some officials, who encouraged farmers to switch from growing low value staple crops into more profitable businesses, such as breeding wild animals.

The Guangdong province people's congress hosted a rare televised discussion. This gave environmentalists a platform to call for a permanent ban on the wild animal trade. Businessmen and farmers protested that they would starve, and besides, a ban could never be enforced. The congress passed a weak regulation that didn't amount to a ban, but instead issued a recommendation for people to stop eating wild animals.

In fact, the businessmen were right. Soon wild game was again being openly sold, and vendors handed out bribes to ensure there were no more 'surprise' inspections. Later that year, the central government lifted the temporary ban on fifty-four species—including civets, which, it declared, could be bred in licensed farms, subject to sanitation checks. The Chinese authorities not only dropped the whole wild animal-trade ban, but began offering export tax incentives to the multibillion-dollar animal products industry. China's Ministry of Finance raised the value-added tax rebates on nearly 1,500 Chinese products, including a 9 per cent rebate on the export of animal products such as edible snakes and turtles, primate meat, beaver and civet musk, as well as rhino horns. Beijing even promoted the use of traditional Chinese medicine in treating coronavirus patients, with China's National Health Commission recommending a remedy containing bear bile, goat horn and other ingredients for critically ill patients.

Surprisingly, the resumption of the trade in wild animals (and farmed civets), assuming it ever stopped, didn't lead to any fresh outbreaks of SARS. The public ceased worrying about it after the government declared the crisis over. Yet the panic had caused the country and indeed the whole world a huge loss, which one consultancy calculated at $40 billion.

The crisis led the government to spend two billion RMB ($250 million) for SARS prevention and control. The fund was used to upgrade county-level hospitals, to finance the treatment of farmers and poor urban residents infected with SARS, and to purchase medical facilities in central and western China. Another seven billion RMB ($875 million) was spent by local governments on free treatment for SARS sufferers.

The government kicked more money into public health. Apart from the billions of dollars devoted to SARS prevention and control, it invested 6.8 billion RMB ($850 million) for the construction of a three-tiered network of disease control and prevention. A nationwide SARS training programme started up, and the government initiated an Internet-based disease reporting system to allow local hospitals to directly report suspected SARS cases to the Chinese Centre for Disease Control and the Ministry of Health.

As China boosted its disease reporting system, it encouraged its scientists to start looking at solving the mystery of where the disease came from, and what exactly it was. SARS belongs to a family of very common viruses that cause mild to moderate upper-respiratory tract illnesses. In other words, the common cold. There are hundreds of coronaviruses, most of which circulate among animals such as pigs, camels, bats and cats. Since about the 1960s, we also know that two in particular—CoV-OC43 and CoV-229E—are to blame for between 10 and 30 per cent of everyday colds. Well over 200 virus strains can cause the common cold, and rhinoviruses are the most common. The infections spike between early winter and early spring—but no one knows why—and infect all age groups. Curiously, we can get reinfected time and time again, and there is still no vaccine for the common cold.

With the help of new gene sequencing techniques, it has become possible to trace back the history of these two viruses. In 2005, Belgian researchers suggested that the ancestor of CoV-OC43 which had crossed over from cattle to humans was connected to contagious bovine pleuropneumonia. This had started off two decades earlier as an infection limited to cattle. Many countries set out to eradicate it by a mass culling of sick bovines, and they eventually succeeded in bringing it under control. It is still rampant in Africa. This disease is caused by bacteria, as is often the case with pneumonia, but it is facilitated by a viral infection called bovine coronavirus (BCoV). (Victims of the 1918 Spanish flu pandemic contracted the viral influenza, which weakened them, but they were mostly killed off by a bacterial pneumonia that followed hard on its heels.) It is now thought likely that people involved with the sick cows caught this bovine coronavirus, as it is strikingly similar to HCoV-OC43. It sheds light on the pandemic known as Asian flu or Russian flu which suddenly swept the world around 1890 and is usually blamed on the H2N2 influenza. Over a million died, including Prince Albert Victor, Queen Victoria's grandson. In the last 130 years it seems to have become less dangerous, as we have built up immunity to it.

A German research team has come up with a theory that the other coronavirus that causes the common cold—CoV-229E— also originates from a common domesticated animal, the camel. The researchers at the University Hospital of Bonn who were interested in the new MERS coronavirus took samples from a thousand camels and found pathogens very similar to CoV-229E. They discovered that these could enter human cells via the same receptor used by the common cold virus—HcoV-229E. Yet the human immune system defends itself against the camel viruses, just as it does against common cold viruses. Most people already have immunity against the camel virus for the same reason that they are largely immune to the HcoV-229E common cold virus.[1]

The task facing the researchers investigating the mystery of SARS was to find the missing link—a domesticated animal like a cow or a camel that was the origin for the virus and responsible for transmitting the infection. It apparently wasn't the civets that were to blame, but if it wasn't them, then what could it be? This is where Peter Daszak enters the picture with his fascination with unknown but dangerous viruses harboured by bats living in wild jungles. In 2004, he helped bring together a multinational team from Australia, America and China on a mission to find the bats responsible.

14

GOING BATS IN CHINA

The team was led by Jonathan H. Epstein, the executive director of the Consortium for Conservation Medicine, one of the two forerunners of EcoHealth Alliance. It included Peter Daszak, China's Shi Zhengli who would later become famous as China's 'bat lady', and the Australian Hume Field from the Queensland Centre for Emerging Infectious Diseases. He studied the Hendra virus and Lyssavirus, both of which are blamed on the fruit bats known as flying foxes.

The team mounted a series of expeditions around China, hoping to find bats that could be the natural wild life reservoir for the SARS virus. An article in *Scientific American* published in 2020, 'How China's "Bat Woman" hunted down viruses from SARS to the new Coronavirus', gave this account:

> To Shi, her first virus-discovery expedition felt like a vacation. On a breezy, sunny spring day in 2004, she joined an international team of researchers to collect samples from bat colonies in caves near Nanning, the capital of Guangxi province. Her inaugural cave was typical of the region: large, rich in limestone columns and—as a popular tourist destination—easily accessible. 'It was spellbinding',

Shi recalls. Milky-white stalactites hung from the ceiling like icicles, glistening with moisture.

There are certainly a lot of bat species in the Karst limestone mountains of southern China, but few mega-bats like the fruit eating flying foxes. What the team found were mostly tiny insect-eating micro-bats of the horseshoe bat species. These hunt their prey in the darkness by echolocation, emitting a sound through their noses, or rather furrowed nose leafs—a feature that has shaped their faces so they resemble bent horseshoes. Some species are solitary, others roost in large colonies, but they are all very tiny and very hard to spot. Their bodies are anything from an inch to five inches in length.

The expedition knew that these bats are abundant in southern Asia, but they still struggled to find any of them. They trekked for hours around the steep mountains, following tips from local villagers and squeezing through small narrow crevices, hoping to find bat roosts. In one week, the team explored over thirty caves but encountered only a dozen bats. If they did find a bat cave, they then stretched nets across the entrance, hoping to trap some at dusk when they flew out to hunt insects. If that worked, they then grabbed them to take samples of their blood or saliva, or they would try to and collect urine or bat excrement.

They also set out to Hubei Province (of which Wuhan is the capital) to search for bats. Yet when they got back, none of the samples turned up any trace of the coronaviruses. 'Eight months of hard work seemed to have gone down the drain', Shi told *Scientific American*. 'We thought maybe bats had nothing to do with SARS.'

The team was about to give up when researchers at Hong Kong University took fifty-nine anal samples and ran them through a different testing machine—polymerise chain reaction (PCR)—and found 40 per cent of them showing signs of a coronavirus similar to the one found in civets. PCR testing is a kind of molecular photocopying, in that it creates huge numbers of a small sample of DNA. It is used to detect the presence of an antigen, the name for a substance that causes the host's immune system to produce antibodies. This showed, for the very first time, that bat-SARS-CoV is closely related to the SARS-CoV that is found in humans and civets. It suggested a common ancestor for two viruses, but it was clear that there were also significant differences in key areas.[1]

Samples from three horseshoe bat species contained antibodies to the SARS virus. 'It was a turning point for the project', Shi said. In October, the team co-authored an important article in *Science* entitled 'Bats Are Natural Reservoirs of SARS-Like Coronaviruses':

> Here we report that species of bats are a natural host of coronaviruses closely related to those responsible for the SARS outbreak.

They found these coronaviruses in different bats of the Rhinolopus species in Hubei and Guangxi provinces, but the difference to the human SARS virus was not insignificant—it was a 94 per cent similarity. The genetic difference between *homo sapiens* and a gorilla is 1.6 per cent of the respective genomes. The paper proposed that in some wet markets, a fruit bat had passed on a related virus to a civet cat in some sort of spillover, which was a little confusing since the two species are so different. However, everyone now agreed that the home of this virus was in bats.

The hunt was now on to get more and better bat samples, so as to fully understand the coronaviruses in bats. Shi's team looked around many Chinese provinces but finally settled on one particular bat cave for their research. This one was called Shitou Cave, about 60km from the provincial capital of Kunming to the south of the lake of that name in an area inhabited by the Yi minority, also known as the Lolo. They spent the following five years taking samples at different times of the year and identified hundreds of viruses, most of which turned out be harmless. Only a handful were similar to the SARS coronavirus. Photographs from the time show that the team took no protective measures to guard against infection, so they must have deemed the risk of getting infected quite low.

During this period, the team also investigated a derelict copper mine shaft in Mojiang county in Yunnan, which is not too far from the border with Burma. In June 2012, six miners fell ill and three later died from pneumonia after removing slag from the mine. 'The mine shaft stunk like hell', Shi said. This time the team decided to put on protective masks and clothing. 'Bat guano, covered in fungus, littered the cave.' It turned out that it was the fungus which had infected the mine workers, not any bat virus.

In the caves they identified six bat species: *Rhinolophus sinicus*, *Rhinolophus affinis*, *Hipposideros pomona*, *Miniopterus schreibersii*, *Miniopterus fuliginosus* and *Miniopterus fuscus*. Some of these bat species roost in big colonies pressed densely together, so large amounts of bat faeces pile up on the floor below. The team took lots of samples from this bat guano and identified many viral strains. One of these, a beta coronavirus, was particularly interesting. It was called RaTG13, and it bears a 96 per cent similarity to COVID-19. The RaTG13 genome, almost 30,000 bases long, is therefore the only bat virus that might be a direct ancestor of the COVID-19 virus. The only report of the existence of this particular virus was in a publication by Shi Zhengli and her collaborators in January 2020 and in *Nature* magazine. 'Discovery of a novel coronavirus associated with the recent pneumonia outbreak in humans and its potential bat origin' has nearly thirty authors. This new virus is important, as the authors confirm that it has the same cell entry receptor, ACE2 (Angiotensin converting enzyme II)—which is the key that allows the coronavirus to get into the human cell.[2]

However the timing of announcing the discovery of a new virus made seven years earlier aroused a great deal of suspicion. People naturally wondered why this was declared only after the Chinese government had recognised the pandemic in mid-January of 2020. There were questions, too, whether the purpose of the revelation was to support the theory that COVID-19 came from an animal rather than being made in a lab. After all, one would normally have expected scientists to rush to claim credit for such a discovery.

Meanwhile, work continued on taking samples from bats living in the Shitou cave, and on investigating the viruses found. This work had the funding and cooperation from Peter Daszak and EcoHealth Alliance. In 2010, Shi published a paper examining the sensitivity of different types of bat ACE2 to human SAR-CoV spike protein, using live virus and an HIV pseudo virus. A pseudo virus means an artificially created one, which, once it has entered a cell, can only replicate once. Wild viruses can replicate many times. They are not so virulent as the parent virus, which means that these particles will not cause an active infection. It also means they can be handled at a BSL-2 lab because they are not considered very dangerous.[3]

On 30 October 2013, *Nature* magazine published a paper called 'Isolation and characterisation of a bat SARS-like coronavirus that uses the ACE2 receptor'. The paper said that there is a bat SARS-CoV that uses the ACE2 receptor and which could therefore potentially infect humans. Furthermore, the building blocks for SARS-CoV were identified from eleven different SARS-CoV viral strains found in the horseshoe bats in Shitou cave. The paper stated:

> Our findings [...] provide the clearest evidence yet that SARS-CoV originated in bats. [...] However, the ability of SL-CoV-WIV1 to use human ACE2 [...] suggests that direct bat-to-human infection is a plausible scenario for some bat SL-CoVs.[4]

The trouble was that, if it was true that large numbers of bats really could pass on viruses directly to humans without the necessity of an intermediary host like a civet or a pangolin, or indeed a fruit bat, then there must be lots of people somewhere who had been infected by SARS bat viruses. After all, horseshoe bats have been around for tens of millions of years, they are very common around the world, and there are a lot of them.

In 2014, Shi received a $665,000 grant from the US National Institute of Health for a study entitled 'The ecology of Bat Coronaviruses and Risk of Future Coronavirus Emergence', as well as a $559,500 USAID grant for another study, 'Emerging Pandemic Threats', part of the PREDICT 2 China grants.

The next piece of evidence that came out of this research was a finding in 2015. In October that year, Shi's team collected blood samples from more than 200 residents of four villages in Jinning County, which borders the Dian Hu (Lake) next to Kunming, and who live about a mile from the Shitou cave. They discovered that six people carried antibodies against SARS-like coronaviruses from bats, although they had no symptoms, nor did they have any connection with bats, other than seeing them fly around.[5]

Others found this evidence quite unconvincing. The fact that a tiny handful of people developed antibodies does not prove that the bat viruses could infect people. 'Antibody production is not always evidence of a virus having got inside someone's cells, just inside their body', said the biotech entrepreneur Yuri Deigin in *GM Watch*, published on 17 June 2020. 'The presence of antibodies doesn't mean the virus could infect cells. You could have antibodies to a banana.' Deigin also noted that the antibody levels detected were 'pretty low'.

Peter Daszak, Shi Zhengli and others released another report in 2019 in which they took blood samples from 1,600 people living in three provinces between 2015 and 2017. The study targeted people whose work makes them very exposed to bats and other wildlife, including those who visit or work around bat caves, work in local live animal markets, raise animals, or are involved in wildlife trade (e.g. wild animal harvest, trade, transportation, and preparation). They found only six people who tested positive for bat coronavirus. 'This study provides serological evidence of bat coronavirus spillover in rural communities in Southern China. The low seroprevalence observed in this study suggests that bat coronavirus spillover is a rare event', the study concluded.[6]

To Daszak et al., all this was convincing evidence that bat virus spillover was a real risk and could happen any moment. To his critics, the same research proved the contrary: the fact that it was so rare meant it presented an almost negligible risk. Plus, there was no evidence that the new virus discovered in the bats living in the old copper mine (RaTG13) had infected local residents, even though it was supposedly adapted to entering human cells.

Yet on numerous occasions, Daszak argued that there might be millions of people in villages around South East Asia with a genuine risk of catching a deadly coronavirus from bats, and then spreading it around the world. 'We can safely estimate that between one and seven million people are infected with bat coronaviruses each year', he wrote in an op ed piece in the *Guardian* newspaper in June 2020: 'Ignore the conspiracy theories: scientists know COVID-19 wasn't created in a lab'.

The flaw in this theory that he and others had to overcome is that bat viruses are, primarily, bat viruses, tuned to infect the former rather than humans. Bats are very different creatures, with a peculiar metabolism. They frequently go into hibernation mode when their body temperatures drop, and when they fly around, their metabolism heats up beyond the temperature of human bodies. Additionally, unlike with domesticated animals such as chickens or pigs, we don't have much contact with bats. So how exactly could a bat virus evolve into one infectious to humans? This is where the research carried out by Ralph Baric's team described earlier in the book comes in. They set out to study the SARS virus in the lab in order to understand that evolution better. This led to a collaboration with Shi Zhengli, Peter Daszak and the others.

On 9 November 2015, Shi Zhengli, Ralph Baric and others jointly published the important paper in *Nature Medicine* mentioned earlier: 'A SARS-like cluster of circulating bat coronaviruses shows potential for human emergence'. It described their efforts (funded by EcoHealth Alliance) to create a chimeric virus from a Chinese horseshoe bat with the right entry proteins (ACE2) that could unlock the cell doors that would normally stop it from entering the human respiratory tract. Next, they tried to experiment with a live mouse to see if this man-made virus could enter the lungs of a mouse and infect it. And it did. They then concluded that this proved that the SARS virus from such a bat could infect humans, but also that it needed further adaption. In 2020, it also emerged that one of these infected mice bit the finger of one of the people handling them in the lab, although this person did not become infected.

The justification for the research was that in future an outbreak was possible and therefore further research was needed in order to develop a vaccine. The paper also hinted that the Wuhan Institute of Virology was doing similar research and creating man-made chimeric viruses and using HIV-based pseudoviruses. This is a common technology used when labs try to create vaccine candidates, and the technique makes them less dangerous. The discovery of some parts of the HIV virus in the COVID-19 virus would later heighten concerns that this was a lab-made virus, and thus connected to these experiments. It is time now to look more closely at what else was going on in the new lab in Wuhan, which opened in 2015.

15

THE STRANGE STORY OF FRANCE AND WUHAN'S BS4-LAB

In the wake of the SARS epidemic, the Wuhan Institute of Virology (WIV), a relatively obscure and modest institution attached to the University of Wuhan, was suddenly thrust into international and national prominence. Yet intelligence officials in countries such as France and America remained deeply suspicious of its real purpose, while others questioned its safety procedures.

After 2003, the WIV set up a whole new department devoted to studying emerging infectious disease, which was headed by Shi Zhengli. In addition to looking at bat viruses, the Chinese developed a new and strong interest in studying the world's most dangerous infectious diseases, including the deadly Ebola, Nipah, Marburg, Lassa fever virus, and Crimean-Congo haemorrhagic fever viruses. Very few of these diseases pose a threat to China.

In response to a very dangerous outbreak of Ebola in West Africa, China made an unprecedented effort to send hundreds of specialists to help stop it spreading. They set up hospitals and BSL–3 test labs, distributed medical supplies and carried out tests and medical treatments. Some of the Chinese specialists came from Wuhan.

As it developed its new role, the WIV was selected to run China's first level-4 biosafety lab, which the French offered to help build following the SARS outbreak. However, work on the project did not really get going until after 2014, and when it was finished, relations with France had deteriorated to the extent that all cooperation ceased. The WIV then developed strong ties with counterparts in America, Australia and Canada.

In July 2019, a big story broke in the Canadian press. Two Chinese-born scientists, Xiangguo Qiu and her husband Keding Cheng, the recipients of many Canadian grants, were escorted out of Canada's National Microbiology Laboratory. They were reported to have secretly smuggled samples of the Ebola and Henipah viruses back to China. Qiu made at least five trips to Wuhan over the academic year 2017–18 alone.

It is puzzling what the motive would be for smuggling the viruses to China. China already had samples of the Ebola virus after it sent scientists to West Africa. Canada owns the IPR rights to a number of patents for treating Ebola, and in fact Qiu had herself developed one such treatment. Information about treatments was either publicly available or could be acquired for modest amounts of money.

The Israeli expert on China's biological warfare programme, Danny Shoham, claims that the Wuhan Institute of Virology is a dual-purpose military/civilian institution, and has even suggested that SARS itself is the product of China's biowarfare programme. According to this line of thinking, China's new-found interest in exotic pathogens could therefore be attributed to an ambition to modify them using gain-of-function techniques, in order to make a deadly bioweapon, and that this work continued even as China took advantage of deepening cooperation with foreign countries.

The WIV started out in the 1930s as a small department at Wuhan University, one of China's oldest and most prestigious universities, which is graced with an attractive campus. It was founded by a handful of returning scientists, notably Professor Gao Shangyin (Harry Zanyin Gaw), who wanted to set up China's first microbiology research unit. Professor Gao had studied at Yale and returned home out of a sense of patriotism. He and others soon found themselves at the mercy of a series of historical events. After the anti-Japanese War broke out in 1937, the entire university relocated to temporary accommodation in a small town in Sichuan province. The staff returned to Wuhan after 1945, but then Professor Gao decided to move back to America to carry out more research at Princeton. Then, in another fit of patriotism, he returned to China, but his work had barely got started again when the Communists unexpectedly won the civil war. The new regime had little liking for intellectuals and was deeply suspicious of those with strong ties to America. Everything now had to be done according to the Soviet model, and soon there was wave after wave of political campaigns targeting anyone with a Western education.[1]

In 1956, the department was renamed the Wuhan Institute of Virology under the Chinese Academy of Sciences. Its research staff continued to focus on studying viruses that attack plants such as tobacco and insects such as silkworms—research that is important to local farmers and had the (ultimately successful) aim of developing biological insecticides. The institute built up one of the world's largest collections of insect viruses.

It is not clear if this work continued once the Cultural Revolution started, but people like Professor Gao would have been sent to learn from the peasants in the countryside. Of course, a few Western-trained scientists with a similar background continued to work on key military projects, like the one to build China's nuclear bomb. Professor Gao could conceivably have been employed in some such military research role, but it seems unlikely and there is no information to support that.

On the other hand, it is not impossible. We now know that the Soviet bioweapons programme, Biopreparat, used the purpose of tackling influenza preparedness as a cover story. For example, the Omutninsk Chemical Factory manufactured large amounts of influenza vaccine and crop production bacteria above ground, while plague and tularemia were researched in heavily guarded facilities that were hidden underground. The Omutninsk Chemical Factory had the capacity to mass produce viruses and bacteria, and it was able to produce 100 tons of each weapon annually.[2]

The Soviet military took great care to hide what it was doing from the outside world and to create a cover of plausible deniability. China could therefore conceivably be using an institution such as the WIV as a front for carrying out biological weapons research. Certainly, the head of the mission sent to West Africa was Chen Wei, a PLA Major General who heads the Institute of Bioengineering at the Academy of Military Medical Sciences. She is possibly the head of its biological warfare division.

Chen Wei is credited with developing a nasal spray against SARS. When the COVID-19 crisis started, she led a large military team to Wuhan to take charge. Three military transport planes with hundreds of doctors and nurses arrived, took over the WIV and set about developing a vaccine. To Chinese eyes, it is normal for the PLA to take a leading role whenever there is a major crisis such as a flood or an earthquake, but it would look different to Western intelligence agencies.

The WIV had come back to life again after 1978 following Chairman Mao's death, but its fortunes only really picked up in the wake of SARS. By this time, a new generation of researchers who had studied abroad began returning home. In 2005, the WIV was declared a state key laboratory and given more resources to expand.

It set up a whole new department devoted to studying emerging infectious diseases. The WIV also built up a biobank of pathogenic microbial species with1,500 viruses and 117,000 isolates. The bank includes human, zoonotic, animal, insect and plant viruses, phages, environmental microorganisms, virus-sensitive cell banks and virus genetic data banks. It became a WHO 'reference laboratory', linked to similar labs around the world: a key node in the global biosafety-lab network, as one official put it. It was also given the opportunity to move out of the university campus to new dedicated facilities in one of the industrial parks outside the city.

In the wake of the bird flu and SARS outbreaks, China began a determined effort to study how other countries monitored influenza, tested and reported swabs, developed vaccines and inoculated their citizens. It decided largely to copy the American approach with its Centre for Disease Control system. Thus, it set about building a bioinformatics deck to strengthen data analysis, publishing weekly online influenza surveillance reports in English and Chinese. The surveillance system collects between 200,000 and 400,000 specimens and tests more than 20,000 influenza viruses annually. It also obtained the help of other countries in training the 2,500 staff it needed, though it struggled as some staff complained of low salaries.

From the start, the ambitious programme was hindered by the lack of trained staff and by funding shortages, as well as the challenge of coordinating labs and hospitals that were funded by local and central governments. The network also had trouble ensuring that veterinarians, agricultural institutions and hospitals coordinated their actions when faced with avian and swine flus. In 2015 during an outbreak of H7N9 avian influenza, the Chinese CDC budget expanded to $157.5 million in a year, but, by 2019, it had fallen to just $40 million. China's CDC also had far smaller human resources than its American counterpart—just 2,120 full-time employees in 2016 compared to over 11,000 in America.

Funding became a problem for the Chinese CDC and its local bodies, because, after 2005, they could no longer charge anyone to give them a flu shot. Local CDC revenues took a big hit. It is striking, too, that less than 2 per cent of the population has a flu shot in China compared to 45 per cent in America.[3]

Despite the underfunded human resources, China announced a big building programme. It set out its intention to build a network of bio-security labs. By 2025, it wanted to have between five and seven biosafety level-4 (BSL-4) labs across the country. It also wanted one P3 research laboratory and a P2 lab in every one of its twenty-three provinces.

The shortcomings of qualified staff and China's relatively poor safety standards came to public notice in 2004, when the WHO reported several alarming cases of the SARS virus escaping from the Chinese Institute of Virology in Beijing, part of China's Centre for Disease Control. A twenty-six-year-old female post-graduate student and a thirty-one-year-old male postdoc were both infected, apparently in two separate incidents. The lab was closed, and its 200 staff were put in isolation in a hotel. The infected twenty-six-year-old travelled twice by train from Beijing to Anhui province, where she was nursed by her mother, a physician, who fell ill and died. The nurse in turn infected five third-generation cases, causing no deaths.

Antoine Danchin, an epidemiologist at Hong Kong University, said that the latest incidents were probably the result of lab accidents. 'Normally, it's not possible to contaminate people even under level-two confinement, if the security rules are obeyed, with the appropriate hoods, and so on', Danchin said. SARS work requires level three. 'So it suggests there has been some mishandling of something.'

'The lab might have all the right rules, but the people may not comply! For example, notebooks are not supposed to be taken out, a lot of things like that. A virus doesn't jump on people!' Danchin continued.[4]

A subsequent report stated that a batch of supposedly inactivate SARS virus was brought from a high-containment facility into a low-safety diarrhoea research lab, where the two were working. Apparently, the inactivation process—adding a mix of detergents to the virus—did not work properly. The director of the Centre for Disease Control and Prevention (CDC), Li Liming, was later made to resign, along with several lower-ranking officials.

China is, of course, far from the only country to report such incidents. In August 2003, a virology graduate student at the National University of Singapore fell ill. Although he had not worked directly with SARS, it was present in the laboratory where he worked. He recovered and produced no secondary cases. The second escape was in Taiwan in December 2003, when a SARS research scientist fell ill on a return flight after attending a medical meeting in Singapore. The scientist had handled leaking biohazard waste without gloves, a mask, or a gown. In response, the WHO convened a committee of experts to design new and more stringent lab safety regulations for SARS. The Chinese government did the same by issuing the Management Regulations on Laboratory Biosafety of Pathogenic Microorganisms (Order No. 424 of the State Council).

At this stage, many countries were lining up to offer their support, as China upgraded its capacity to monitor and deal with infectious diseases that threaten to cause a global pandemic. This was clearly in everyone's interests. France was keen to play a role. The Chinese leader Hu Jintao was on a state visit to Paris that year, and so he signed a memorandum of understanding on cooperation over preventing and fighting new infectious diseases. The French offered to support the Wuhan Institute of Virology, the country's oldest microbiology lab, and to provide equipment and training. More top-level political meetings and exchanges took place over the next four years, but very little actual progress was made to build it.

The problem was that many countries were uneasy with China's requests for the construction of the BSL-4 laboratory. It is dual-use technology, and China had never come clean about its biowarfare programme. France had built its first state of the art BSL-4 laboratory in Lyon only in 1999. How could the French be sure that, if they built something similar in China, the technology wouldn't be passed on to the military to make biological weapons? The United States opposed the transfer of this technology to China although, of course, it has many military BSL-4 military labs of its own. In 2004, the French had agreed to sell the Chinese four level-3 mobile labs, but later nobody could find out what had happened to them. Had they been handed over to the Chinese military?

In addition, China said it had plans to build five other BSL-4 labs, and that two of these were for the military. Why did China need so many labs? There are only seven amongst all the EU countries. Then, the Chinese also requested dozens of BSL-4 protective suits—why did they need so many? And didn't they have their own factory to make these things somewhere in north-west China? And why did the Chinese demand that the French provide samples of the most deadly viruses, such as Ebola?

The French security services and the military argued strongly against the project. Paris refused to supply samples of the Ebola virus, or any other deadly pathogens. Later, China obtained samples of the Ebola virus when it made the unusual and unprecedented aid effort in West Africa during the 2014 Ebola outbreak. So did China have any ulterior motives when it decided to play such a large role in this humanitarian intervention?

On the other hand, many French were keen to strengthen economic ties with China. The project was driven by a pharmaceutical billionaire, Alain Mérieux, whose family had founded Sanofi Pasteur. Mérieux's grandfather had been a student of Louis Pasteur and built up a successful vaccine business. Sanofi

Pasteur now claims to be the world's largest producer of vaccines, with 13,000 employees around the world, and has developed strong business interests in China. In 2017, for instance, it invested $94 million to build a dedicated influenza vaccine facility in Shenzhen. It provides more than five million doses of influenza vaccines in China every year. The company also has an agreement with the China National Pharmaceutical Group and Wuhan East Lake Hi-tech Development Zone to co-create a production base in the Biolake International Vaccine Park.

In 2004, the conglomerate became even bigger after it merged with another giant, Aventis. Its headquarters are in Lyon, which is where France's BSL-4 laboratory—the Jean Mérieux-Inserm Laboratory—was built in 1999. It was this laboratory that first identified the strain of the Ebola virus responsible for the outbreak in West Africa. The Mérieux Foundation website declares that it is proud of setting up 'a procedure for the urgent transport of samples taken in Africa to the BSL-4 laboratory in Lyon. This enabled local authorities without the resources to perform screening to pinpoint infectious hotspots, a key step in preventing the spread of highly contagious pathogens.' In 2005, the Mérieux Foundation had also set up the Christophe Mérieux Laboratory in Beijing in collaboration with the Chinese Academy of Medical Sciences to study acute viral respiratory infections and to help identify new viruses.

The French were now faced with a familiar dilemma. China wanted to acquire this advanced technology, and it dangled the prospect of obtaining a share in potentially the world's largest market. Every country was under pressure to cultivate ties with China, in case a rival gained an advantage. France had plunged into cooperating with China by building nuclear power stations, high-speed railways, passenger planes and cars. If France didn't voluntarily offer the technology, the chances were that the Chinese would steal it anyway.

Yet the French also knew that the Chinese strategy was to obtain the technology, copy it as quickly as possible, push out the foreign partner, control the domestic market and then start exporting abroad, usually by undercutting its original partner on price. The foreign company might then find itself losing its market dominance, as Nortel did. Yet for a long time, the belief was that the risk was worth taking because China was becoming a market economy and would surely then become a democracy and a genuine friend.

Wuhan was a key centre for French investment in China. Ties with Hubei province go back to 1966. There are over a hundred French companies there, led by the car giant Dongfeng Peugeot-Citroën Automobile Co, as well as Faurecia, Valeo, Plastic Omnium, EDF, L'Oréal, Pernod Ricard, Alstom and Total. Air France had six direct flights a week to Wuhan. Shi Zhengli had obtained her doctorate at the French University of Montpelier in 2000. She would later spend many months training at the Mérieux lab in Lyon.

An architectural firm in Lyon, RTV, was chosen to manage the project, and the Chinese selected an engineering giant, China IPPR Engineering Co Ltd, as its construction partner. The French provided the Chinese with some drawings, and the site at the Jiangxia Zhengdian Park was decided on, some 30km from the university campus. Work finally started in 2011, but there were more delays and disputes. Once the Chinese had the blueprints, Chinese suppliers moved in to undercut the French suppliers. The French engineering company, Technip, which was supposed to supervise the construction and to certify the quality, then withdrew, declaring it could not accept any legal responsibility for the work done by the Chinese. The Chinese might be supplying substandard parts and materials. Finally, the French shipped over some key equipment, such as airlock doors for the laboratory, but there were continuing disputes between the French experts and the Chinese contractors.

In March 2014, the Chinese leader Xi Jinping visited France and chose to take a look at the Mérieux lab in Lyon. There he declared: 'The BSL-4 laboratory construction in Wuhan is very important for Chinese public health and a good symbol of the France China Collaboration in public health.'

On 31 January 2015, the lab was finished and a small ceremony was held. The whole building cost around $44 million. The plan was that at least fifty French scientists would come over, work at the lab and share research. Relations with the French worsened, although it is not entirely clear why. Alain Mérieux, who until 2015 was the co-president of the joint supervisory commission in charge of the project, admitted in an interview on French radio that 'after 2016 there were no more meetings of the Franco-Chinese committee on infectious diseases'.

He went on: 'I am giving up the co-presidency of the BSL-4 because it is a Chinese tool. It belongs to them even though it was developed with the technical assistance of France.' (*'J'abandonne la coprésidence du P4 qui est un outil très chinois. Il leur appartient, même s'il a été développé avec l'assistance technique de la France.'*)

Even though the cooperation stopped, the pretence continued. The French Prime Minister Bernard Cazeneuve officially cut the ribbon in February 2017. By this time the French were completely out of the picture. None of the fifty French scientists ever went to Wuhan, and the money allocated for the exchanges was never spent. In the end, only one French scientist ever set foot in the completed lab; Renee Courcol, a microbiologist from Lille University Hospital, went there in May 2018 to assess the quality of the work and safety procedures to ensure that they met international standards. The US State Department claimed in its factsheet statement on 15 January 2021 that: 'The WIV has engaged in classified research, including laboratory animal experiments, on behalf of the Chinese military since at least 2017'. So the timing suggests that the Chinese got rid of the French just before the PLA started using the lab.

As the French connection faded, the WIV deepened its ties with the Galveston National Laboratory in Texas, with the Australian Animal Health Laboratory, Geelong, Victoria, and above all with the University of North Carolina. The latter specialized in coronavirus research into SARS and MERS including gain-of-function experiments, and when these were suspended in America, the UNC encouraged similar work to be done in Wuhan, where there were no such restrictions.

It sounds very much as if the French were embarrassed to admit in public that, in the end, the lab was built by a contractor with strong ties with the People's Liberation Army, that it could only be certified domestically, and that the whole ballyhooed cooperation project was a disaster. Renee Courcol has not given interviews, so we don't know what he found. After COVID-19 created a pandemic, the French would have been even more anxious to save face and escape censure for building the lab in the first place.

Following eighteen months of 'soft opening', the laboratory became fully operational in early 2019. It was only accredited to carry out research on three viruses—Ebola, Congo-Crimea haemorragic fever and Nipah. So it was not registered to conduct research into SARS or MERS—although these could be handled by a BSL-3 lab.

The situation was sufficiently alarming for US embassy staff to pay numerous visits to the lab between January and March 2018. Two of their cables (reports) were sensitive but unclassified and were seen by journalists. The first cable, on 19 January 2018, said: 'current productivity is limited by a shortage of the highly trained technicians and investigators required to safely operate a [Biosafety Level] 4 laboratory and lack of clarity in related Chinese government policies and guidelines'. On 27 March 2018,

Rick Switzer, Counselor of the Environment, Science, Technology and Health Section of the Embassy of the United States in China, visited, accompanied by the US Consul General in Wuhan, Jamison Fouss. The second memo, dated 19 April 2018, has more specific details about the lab's work. It noted that the research 'strongly suggests that SARS-like coronaviruses from bats can be transmitted to humans to cause SARS-like disease'.

'Most importantly', the cable states, 'the researchers also showed that various SARS-like coronaviruses can interact with ACE2, the human receptor identified for SARS-coronavirus. This finding strongly suggests that SARS-like coronaviruses from bats can be transmitted to humans to cause SARS-like diseases. From a public health perspective, this makes the continued surveillance of SARS-like coronaviruses in bats and study of the animal-human interface critical to future emerging coronavirus outbreak prediction and prevention.'

The memo also observed that the Wuhan Institute of Virology's English brochure highlighted a national security role, saying that it 'is an effective measure to improve China's availability in safeguarding national bio-safety if [a] possible biological warfare or terrorist attack happens'.

The expensive lab was built to accommodate 250 researchers and was apparently not being put to much use. There were just thirty-eight researchers listed at the WIV—thirty-four PhDs, two completing masters and another two completing bachelor degrees. Nearly all of them had studied abroad—fifteen in the US, and the rest in France, Denmark, Japan, Australia, Singapore, Netherlands and the UK. There were six from Wageningen University in the Netherlands.

The BSL-4 laboratory is an extremely sophisticated and complicated piece of engineering, a bit like a nuclear submarine. Nothing is allowed to escape untreated, and the procedures to enter and leave are elaborate. The air must be filtered and pressurized.

The entire building is suspended and divided into four floors, but the BSL-4 lab is contained in a stainless steel laser-welded box. To get in, personnel have to pass through a double-door autoclave with a dynamic sealing technology to ensure differential pressure levels among different functional areas.

Inside, staff have to wear a one-piece, positive-pressure suit ventilated by a life-support system protected by HEPA filtration. The HEPA filter was developed during the 1950s. It is constructed of fibreglass 'paper' that is pleated to maximize the surface area of the filter. These filters can remove 99.97 per cent of particles as small as 0.3 microns, which effectively means that they can remove the smallest viruses. The filters force particles in the air to circulate long enough for them to stick to the filter with tiny microfibres. Any air that leaves the lab has to pass through two of these filters.

Actually the COVID-19 virus is 0.125 microns—less than 0.3 microns—but due to 'Brownian motion', these tiny particles jiggle about in an erratic, zig-zag motion, ensuring that they are trapped by such fibres. This means that many are unconvinced that asking the public to wear masks does much good. It is possible that a special medical N95 mask works, as it has the right kind of fibres (provided it is replaced after each use), but not an every day cloth or paper face mask. On the other hand, viruses can stick to bigger things such as dust or water droplets, which can be trapped by more humble masks. As zillions of viruses are blown about, they could also enter people's houses carried on unseen specks of dust or water, infecting people who are housebound. This seemed to the case in New York, where it was noticed that many people who had stayed indoors became infected. And paper and cloth masks are themselves a source of these dust particles, so if people are shedding viruses, they could be transmitted in this way.

In the photographs published by newspapers everywhere, Shi Zhengli is shown wearing a white space suit such as those described above, with a fancy helmet and transparent visor, and the whole ensemble is attached to a flexible blue tube cord linking her to a life-support system. Like an astronaut, this gives her access to an emergency air tank and breathing air compressors triggered by an alarm system.

It is important that the air pressure within this space suit is kept at a higher level than the (negative) pressure in the lab. To ensure that the lab is kept at the right pressure, you enter through a portal with magnehelic gauges or pressure-monitoring devices to ensure that the air flows in the right direction. Alarms go off if the pressure drops. When staff want to leave the lab, they must walk through a chemical shower that washes the surface of the suit.

The door lock mechanism must be installed the right way and work perfectly, so that a door does not close unless the filters are working properly. Normally, the filters are replaced and tested with a mechanism using a clear plastic bag and glove sleeves housed in a device that ensures that nothing can escape during the changeover.

The BSL-4 lab also contains lab animals, small rodents kept in ventilated cage racks in a holding room. These racks are designed to minimize direct contamination through the air. They need special exhaust systems, as well a system to regulate temperature and humidity. The lab has two sections for animals and a dissecting room.

The wastewater from the chemical shower and vital toxic wastewater generated from jobs in the laboratory is centrally collected and piped to a sewage treatment station. This is on the ground floor, where the life support and power distribution protection equipment are also housed. Infectious solid wastes are first disinfected in a two-leaf high-pressure sterilization pot and are then incinerated.

The Americans weren't the only ones concerned by lab safety procedures. Professor Yuan Zhiming, head of biosafety at WIV, wrote an article for the *Journal of Biosafety and Biosecurity* confessing to concerns about high security laboratories in China. He said that maintenance costs were 'generally neglected', and that several of their top-level research centres lacked sufficient funds for 'routine yet vital processes'. He admitted that 'part-time researchers' performed the work of skilled staff, which 'makes it difficult to identify and mitigate potential safety hazards'. In a second article, co-authored with four colleagues, he wrote that their biosafety systems needed to be 'further improved and strengthened'.

In one known case, in December 2019, a lab accident caused sixty-five lab workers at the Lanzhou Veterinary Research Institute to be infected with brucellosis. Then in January 2020, a renowned Chinese scientist, Li Ning, was sentenced to twelve years in prison for selling experimental animals to local markets.

Further, the quality of the equipment made in China was clearly not good enough to meet French standards. This might include the steel box that a Chinese manufacturer had provided. There were (unconfirmed) reports from France that the staff used bleach in the decontamination showers, which corroded some of the stainless steel materials, and that the airlocks leaked and the sewage disposal system became blocked.

It is not clear how much work was actually done in the BSL-4 lab in the three years to November 2019. In order to conduct research into bat-related viruses like SARS, Shi Zhengli and her colleagues could have used the BSL-3 part of the building and worked under less onerous safety procedures. This is where the lab animals used in testing gain-of-function research would have been housed. Most work—including all published work using live bat coronaviruses that were not either SARS or MERS—was conducted under BSL-2 conditions. This would be consistent with both WHO and CDC recommendations.

BSL-2 provides only minimal protection against infection of laboratory researchers, and these regulations were almost certainly too lenient for work with bat coronaviruses. All such work should be carried out under BSL-3 conditions. Extremely high-risk gain-of-function (GoF) studies with bat SARS-related coronaviruses are supposed to be carried out at BSL-3 or BSL-4 facilities. The lab wasn't certified for BSL-4 until 2018, so it was BSL-2 for anything not involving human SARS or MERS. Any research on bats, mice, pangolins or other animals and their SARS-like or novel coronaviruses did not require BSL-3, and this is why Shi Zhengli used Bat SL-CoV-WIV1 as a backbone for making new viruses. Multiple published studies by Shi confirm that chimeric and infectious mutants were studied at BSL-2, and she confirmed herself that everything in that lab was done at BSL-2 until after COVID-19.

The only research that is known to have taken place in the BSL-4 lab dealt with Crimean-Congo haemorrhagic fever (CCHF). The disease was first reported in the Crimea in 1944, but in 1969 was found to afflict people in the Congo. It is deadly and is spread by a tick-borne virus (Nairovirus) in the family *Bunyaviridae* that lives in livestock. Every year, around 10,000 to 15,000 people are infected with it, and for half of them it is fatal. It is mostly found among herders in Europe, Central Asia and the Middle East, and in China it is restricted to herdsmen in Xinjiang province.

If a SARS or COVD virus did escape from a lab in China, it would more likely have escaped from a level-2 or 3 lab. In 2020, there were close to ninety such labs operating in China. The BSL-4 lab in Wuhan was a flagship operation and despite the criticisms of it, normally such national models are going to enjoy better access to staff and funding than any other lab far from the public view. A case in point is the lab run by the Wuhan Centre for Disease Control and Prevention, which, as we know, like all Chinese CDC centres was suffering a shortage of funding and qualified support staff. The lab is just three hundreds yards from

Wuhan's Huanan seafood market and is adjacent to the Union Hospital where the first group of doctors were infected during this epidemic.

A fifty-seven-year-old female shrimp seller at the market, who was identified as one of the first victims of coronavirus, visited the Union Hospital on 16 December. Wei was among the first twenty-seven patients to test positive for COVID-19 and one of twenty-four cases directly related to the market. At least fourteen doctors or nurses at the hospital caught the virus during the first phase. Between January and March, the hospital treated more than 5,200 hospitalised patients and more than 20,000 who had fever at outpatient clinics. It also dealt with more than 80,000 patients over an internet platform and two makeshift hospitals (so-called Fangcang hospitals), putting the Union Hospital at the eye of the storm.

We know that bat coronaviruses were studied in Wuhan CDC at biosafety level 2, which requires only minimal protection. An article by two academics, Botao Xiao and Lei Xiao, from respectively Guangzhou's South China University of Technology and the Huazhong University of Science and Techology in Wuhan, called 'The possible origins of 2019-CoV coronavirus', claims that the Wuhan Centre for Disease Control and Prevention kept disease-ridden animals in its laboratories, including 605 bats. It also mentions that bats once attacked a researcher and that 'blood of bat was on his skin'. A video from the Wuhan CDC shows that staffers were 'collecting bat coronaviruses with inadequate [personal protective equipment] and unsafe operational practices'. Two Chinese articles, from 2017 and 2019, describing the work of Wuhan CDC researcher Tian Junhua, show him capturing bats in a cave without protective measures, so that 'bat urine dripped from the top of his head like raindrops'. Tian Junhua has described quarantining himself for two weeks after a bat's blood got on his skin. He also quarantined himself after a bat urinated on him. Surgery was performed on the caged animals and the tissue samples were collected for DNA and RNA extraction and sequencing. The tissue samples and contaminated waste products were a source of pathogens. Botao Xiao told the *Wall Street Journal* in February 2020 that he had withdrawn his paper because it 'was not supported by direct proofs'.

The research of Tian Junhua involved capturing 155 bats including *Rhinolophus affinis* in Hubei province, and another 450 bats in Zhejiang province. He also mentions discovering a live tick from a bat. These parasites are known for their ability to pass infections through a host animal's blood. On the Researchgate website, Tian Junhua's name appears on thirty-nine papers authored by researchers at the Wuhan CDC, including a number concerning ticks. It is therefore quite plausible that the Wuhan CDC might have carelessly disposed of wastes or materials close to both the seafood wet market and the Union Hospital, or an infected tick might have escaped, as this might explain the origin of the first cluster of infections.

An epidemiological investigation by the Wuhan CDC revealed that the market definitely did not sell bats. In addition to fish and shellfish, it sold hedgehogs, badgers, snakes and birds (turtledoves) as well as animal carcasses and animal meat.[5]

It is therefore safe to assume that the only bats in Wuhan during this period were either at the CDC lab or the Wuhan Institute of Virology. We also know that there were cases when level-2 lab staff sold laboratory animals in markets. We also know that the overall level of safety procedures at labs around the country was not high.

A Chinese report, 'Biosafety threats of the rapidly established labs for SARS-CoV-2 tests in China', investigating safety in labs in China, in particular eighty-nine operating in Sichuan province, paints a worrying picture:[6]

The most severe risk was the lack of automatic doors at the main entrance or in core operation areas (28 out of 89; 31.5 per cent), especially in CDC (17/43; 39.5 per cent) and hospitals (11/36, 30.6 per cent). This risk, together with failure for keeping pressure in the core operation areas at 25 ± 5 Pa (11/70; 15.7 per cent), especially in labs in the third-party testing agencies (3/8; 37.5 per cent), may cause accidental exposure to biological agents from lab activities.

Another severe risk was failure for standard labelling of SARS-CoV-2 wastes (22/89; 24.7 per cent), which often occurred in non-hospital labs, i.e., in the third-party testing agencies (5/10; 50 per cent) and CDCs (12/43; 27.9 per cent); lacking regular monitoring of sterilization effects was a less severe risk (17/89; 19.1 per cent), but still increased potential risk for waste management, especially in CDCs (10/43; 23.3 per cent).

Two less severe but still serious risks existed in sample transfer, acceptance and management: failure to meet the UN2814 requirements for outer packaging of specimens to be transported (15/89; 16.9 per cent) and lack of double-locker management of specimens by two people (14/89; 15.7 per cent) (Table 3). Some other issues, although generally fine, may still run certain types of agencies into risk.

This is not a problem restricted to China alone. The report points out that:

According to the US governmental data on biosafety in the labs, during 2008–2012, there had been plenty of accidents (e.g., spills, record-keeping errors) occurring, with between 100 and 275 potential releases of pathogens each year in labs that handle select agents, although few lab workers were reported to be infected.

The labs in China mentioned in this report fall under the supervision of local governments and not the national Centre for Disease Control (CDC). And unlike its counterpart in America, China's CDC only advises the National Health Commission. It does not have the authority to announce outbreaks or take legal action to control them. After April 2018, these local governments, and indeed all government levels, report to the National Emergency Management Department, which manages natural and man-made disasters. The Party's Political and Legal Committee deals with what are called 'public security incidents'.

The Wuhan CDC lab was not the only lab in Wuhan that was carrying out risky experiments. Wuhan University and some hospitals such as Zhongnan Hospital and Renmin Hospital were using the CRISPR-Cas technology on both mice and humans in order to investigate diseases such as hepatitis B, HIV and sepsis. These researchers were using chimeric RNA to modify the genomes of mammalian cells.

At Wuhan University, there is an Institute of Model Animals, which is a centre for creating genetically modified animals. The institute is an animal bio-safety level 3 facility. 'So far, over 1000 genetically engineered animals, including mouse, rat, rabbit and monkey, have been generated, and the amount grows at a speed of approximately more than 200 new strains each year. Equipped with modern and advanced facilities for genetic engineering and management of small animals, the IMA also established a standard environment for monkey accommodation and experiments to facilitate clinic translation of scientific research', reads an article in the *European Heart Journal*.[7]

'China has a huge demand for animal disease models for its burgeoning biomedical research enterprise but the dedicated support is relatively inadequate. IMA of Wuhan University is currently one of the largest national model animal supporting platforms with a sophisticated professional service system. [...] Within the past 10 years, about 500 labs received genetically modified animals from this institute, and more than 600 scientists have benefited from IMA's service', the article continues.

There are therefore quite a few places in Wuhan in addition to the WIV that have been carrying out research into bats and other animals. This research can easily have created or facilitated the emergence of COVID-19. Dealing with live animals, as they did at the Wuhan CDC or the Institute of Model Animals, poses unique safety challenges. After all, monkeys can run about, bite and scratch, unlike a pathogen kept in a test tube in a top security lab. And there is also the fact that the city is also a centre for the production of anti-viral vaccines at enterprises such as the Wuhan Institute of Biological products, and boasts many other biotechnology firms—they too might be doing risky work that we don't know about.

Yet it is Shi Zhengli's work at the Wuhan Institute of Virology creating a mutant chimeric virus—the gain-of-function research—and then testing it on lab animals, that has garnered the most attention. Did her team create the virus in a lab through gain-of-function manipulation of cells in a petri dish, or did it emerge from gain-of-function research by passing a virus between lab animals? What exactly had she and her team been doing during the three years between the lab's opening and the arrival of the virus? The next chapter takes a closer look at what we know.

16

LOOKING FOR A GAS LEAK WITH A LIGHTED MATCH

In the three years between the lab opening and the sudden appearance of COVID-19, Shi Zhengli continued researching the bat viruses collected at the Wuhan Institute of Virology. We know that her research team also had the funding to continue the gain-of-function research which had been suspended at the University of North Carolina. Yet it is hard to know from the available evidence if this work created the SARS-COVID-19 virus.

Contrary to what one might have expected, she chose not to reveal her laboratory records and notes. These would have shed light on whether the virus came from nature or was artificially created, either by altering the genome or through animal-passage experiments with lab animals. On 3 January, China's National Health Commission ordered all biolabs in China to destroy not only the samples of the SARS-CoV-2 that they had isolated from those infected, but also the genetic sequencing of the virus' RNA strand. This has further muddied the water.

Given a global pandemic, China should have provided standard operating procedures both at the labs and during fieldwork, including risk assessments of individual experiments, experiment logs and fieldwork notebooks, training records, waste management logs, accident and infection records, facility maintenance and automated systems records, access logs, security camera footage and communications logs. In early May 2020, the WHO's representative in China, Gauden Galea, complained that China had refused repeated requests to give the WHO access to laboratory logs at the WIV, or those of the Wuhan CDC.

The funding organisation for her research, EcoHealth Alliance, has been equally reluctant to provide the US government with information. A report in the *Wall Street Journal* said that the US had sent a letter making a number of requests from EcoHealth Alliance.

'The NIH has received reports that the Wuhan Institute of Virology [...] has been conducting research at its facilities in China that poses serious bio-safety concerns', read the letter quoted by the *WSJ*, which was signed by Michael Lauer, the NIH deputy director for extramural research.

'We have concerns that WIV has not satisfied safety requirements under the award, and that EcoHealth Alliance hasn't satisfied its obligations to monitor its partner to ensure it has complied with regulations regarding the use of the grant money', said the letter quoted by the *WSJ*. Recipients of US government research grants are required to routinely monitor sub-recipients to ensure that they are using the money as intended.

The letter required EcoHealth Alliance to provide a sample of the sequenced coronavirus; to supply the Wuhan institute's response to the safety concerns described in the 2018 cable sent to the State Department; and to arrange for an inspection of the Wuhan Institute of Virology by an outside team that would examine the facility's lab and records 'with specific attention to addressing the question of whether WIV staff had SARS-CoV-2 in their possession prior to December 2019'.

It also wanted Ecohealth Alliance to explain the apparent disappearance of a scientist, Huang Yanlin, who worked in the Wuhan lab and is rumoured on some social media to be 'patient zero' of the pandemic. (The Wuhan institute said that the scientist in question was a graduate student who went to work elsewhere after receiving her master's degree.) Further, it asked about the purported restrictions at the Wuhan Institute, including 'diminished cell-phone traffic in October 2019, and the evidence that there may have been roadblocks surrounding the facility from October 14–19, 2019.'

Unless EcoHealth Alliance complied with the requests, its grant would be withdrawn. In response, Peter Daszak said that the conditions exceeded the scope of the grant and that his organisation didn't have access to this sort of information. He defended his organisation's activities by saying: 'Our work is part of protecting the U.S. citizen against diseases like Covid-19. It's just so short-sighted to drop that research'.

Daszak went on to organise a protest letter writing campaign against the government's request. One signatory, Harold E. Varmus, a former NIH director, said that the NIH's list of conditions 'is outrageous, especially when a grant has already been carefully evaluated by peer review and addresses one of the most important problems in the world right now—how viruses from animals spill over to human beings'.

Daszak told *Nature* magazine that: 'Conspiracy-theory outlets and politically motivated organizations have made Freedom of Information Act requests on our grants and all of our letters and e-mails to the NIH. [...] We don't want to hand those over to conspiracy theorists for them to publish and ruin and make a mockery of.'[1]

In the absence of any of the lab records and other information becoming available, one has to look at the scientific papers that Shi Zhengli published and then relate this to the genome of the virus. It therefore becomes a piece of detective work best understood (or obscured if you wish) by experts. The key issue they must explain is how a bat virus could change so much that it could infect human cells. The theory heavily promoted by Peter Daszak and his supporters is to argue that, since it is a natural virus, there must be an intermediary animal, and it is only a matter of time until it is identified. In the past, this has taken several years.

'We estimate that every single day, somebody in China or in South East Asia gets infected with a new bat coronavirus. Right now, somebody is walking around, and they might be developing the first signs of a cough from the next COVID. We fully intend to be an organization that helps to prevent the next pandemic. That is our mission', he said.

For those investigating the lab explanation, there are two areas of the COVID-19 genome that are critical. There are two critical parts of the genome that either appeared naturally or were artificially added. SARS-CoV-2 forces its way into host cells and takes control. The cells are reprogrammed and forced to produce viral genetic material and viral proteins—the building blocks of more viruses. The first part is done by the spike proteins which the virus uses to unlock the ACE2 receptors in the cell's membrane so it can enter the cell—this is like a combination code. The second is called the furin cleavage site, which enables the virus to replicate and spread to other cells once it has finished the 'breaking and entering'. These two things make COVID-19 twenty times more virulent to humans than SARS.

The furin polybasic cleavage site in COVID-19 stands out a mile, because it is not found in any other bat virus, not even RaTG13. The WIV alone collected 780 bat viruses. Even the original SARS virus does not contain this polybasic cleavage site.

It is an amino acid sequence of proline-arginine-arginine-alanine or 'PRRA'. The genomic nucleotide combination that codes for it, the repeated cytosine-guanine-guanine or CGG-CGG, is also extremely rare. This sequence of amino acids, PRRA, precedes an arginine-serine cleavage point, R–S.

It is unknown where the PRRA sequence comes from because it does not exist in any of the bat coronaviruses identified as close relatives of the COVID-19 virus. It is, of course, also possible that these amino acids could mutate naturally on their own, but the chances are one in a million or even ten million.

These furin polybasic cleavage sites are known to increase viral infectivity and pathogenicity. This is because they are sequences of amino acids that interact with human cell enzymes in order to 'cut' or 'cleave' parts of the viral structure. This is essential so that the virus particles are ready for entry into the next cell, that is, to infect them.

The receptor binding affinity of the spike protein of COVID-19 is also very unusual and striking. It is configured to bind to human cells and has been changed so much that it cannot bind easily to bat cells.

'COVID-19 virus is exquisitely adapted to infect humans. It was like it was designed to infect humans', according to Flinders University Professor Nikolai Petrovsky. 'The virus's ability to bind protein on human cells was far greater than its ability to bind the same protein in bats, which argues against bats being a direct source of the human virus.'

He and a team from Flinders University in Australia carried out computer modelling that showed that the SARS-CoV-2 virus also bound strongly to cells of pangolins, an exotic anteater illegally imported into China.[2]

So what it looks like is that Shi's team had taken a basic bat virus, and then grafted on the ACE2 receptor spike protein from somewhere else—such as, say, the Pangolin SARS virus—which is known for being able to bind onto human cells. Next they would have grafted on the furin cleavage amino acid sequence from another virus like the MERS virus, so as to make the virus more virulent. Now they would have a new virus combined from different bits of viruses that exist in nature. The technology to do this sort of thing has existed for at least fifteen years, and by 2019 was becoming quite routine.

We know from the terms of the Ecohealth Alliance grant to the WIV that this is exactly the sort of research that Shi was obliged to engage in:

Aim 1 was to investigate bat coronavirus and to 'sequence receptor binding domains (spike proteins) to identify viruses with the highest potential for spillover which we will include in our experimental investigations'.

Aim 3 concerned 'The key activity for bat coronavirus gain of function investigation [...] We will use S protein sequence data, infectious clone technology, *in vitro* and *in vivo* infection experiments, and analysis of receptor binding to test the hypothesis that divergence thresholds in S protein sequences predict spillover potential.'

What this means is that the *de novo* synthesis would be used to construct a series of novel chimeric viruses. The team would mix up recombinant hybrids using different spike proteins from each of a series of unpublished natural coronaviruses in an otherwise-constant genome of a bat coronavirus.

They would then test the ability of the resulting new viruses to infect human cells in culture, and to infect live laboratory animals. They wanted to find a direct correlation between the spike and the ability to infect human cells in culture and to infect laboratory animals. A novel virus encoding spike proteins with the highest receptor-binding affinity ought to have the greatest ability to infect human cells in culture, as well as laboratory animals.

The whole point of this gain-of-function research was to beat nature to the punch. To anticipate what can happen in nature in order to work on vaccines, or to prepare in some way before there would be an outbreak of a new disease. So far, this has not produced anything in the way of vaccines, but the research can supposedly be used to warn of potential looming viral outbreaks and signal preparedness.

From 2004 onwards, the WIV had published many dozens of partial or full genome sequences of coronaviruses in their collection. Daszak and Shi had published partial genetic sequences of 781 Chinese bat coronaviruses, more than one third of which had never been published previously. WIV also infected laboratory animals with bat coronaviruses, that is to say live viruses, as opposed to just fragments of RNA. Shi Zhengli's group had started to learn how to create new viruses—chimeric constructs—back in 2007, and they learned a great deal more from their collaboration with Ralph Baric's group at the University of North Carolina. This group had been engaged in this sort of research into infectious clone technology far longer.

In 2013, Dr Shi had published in *Nature* the discovery of two bat viruses very similar to SARS; one of them (WIV1) was able to grow in mammalian cells and to bind our ACE2 receptors. Since the capabilities of the second virus (SHC014) were less clear, the researchers asked Ralph Baric for help in understanding whether the spike of SHC014 already had what it takes to infect humans. To find out, Shi and Baric built a chimera: the spike of the bat virus was attached to a mouse-adapted SARS virus (called MA1 virus), obtained by Baric some years earlier. Tested on human cells, the chimera showed effects similar to those of SARS, thus demonstrating that this spike, too, could potentially attack humans. It did not have to adapt to the human receptor, it only needed the right genomic context, which in this case was provided by the MA1 virus already adapted to mice.

A 2017 paper attempted to prove that in theory, there could be some kind of bat virus recombination in nature, because they had done exactly that in their lab. In this paper, Shi and her colleagues concluded that after looking at all the bat viruses that had been collected over five years, none had the features that would allow it to infect people.

It concluded that therefore 'none of the currently known bat SARSr-CoVs is thought to be the direct ancestor of SARS-CoV'. It went on to declare:

> Despite the cumulative evidence for the emergence of SARS-CoV from bats, all bat SARSr-CoVs described so far are clearly distinct from SARS-CoV in the S gene and/or one or more accessory genes such as ORF3 and ORF8, suggesting they are likely not the direct ancestor of SARS-CoV. Thus a critical gap remains in our understanding of how and where SARS-CoV originated from bat reservoirs.[3]

For their theory to work, there had to be a spillover to an intermediate species, but that species had yet to be found: '[...] a critical gap remains in our understanding of how and where SARS-CoV originated from bat reservoirs', the authors wrote.

The WIV team believed that the original SARS virus had not come directly from a bat, but they didn't know or couldn't explain what the intermediary species was. This is the reason why some people still suspect that the SARS virus might also have been made in a lab.

The problem was that the part of the virus—the S protein that harpoons into a human cell—was too different from bat viruses. The S protein (the spike or corona) is functionally divided into two sub-units, denoted S1 and S2, which are responsible for receptor binding and cellular membrane fusion. In order to explain the transformation in nature of this part of the virus, the team conducted what they called 'virus infectivity experiments' by experimenting with different S proteins.

Then in Wuhan, Dr Shi went further:

> We constructed a group of infectious bacterial artificial chromosome (BAC) clones with the backbone of WIV1 and variants of S genes

from eight different bat SARSr-CoVs. To assess whether the three novel SARSr-CoVs can use human ACE2 as a cellular entry receptor, we conducted virus infectivity studies using HeLa cells with or without the expression of human ACE2. All viruses replicated efficiently in the human ACE2-expressing cells. The results were further confirmed by quantification of viral RNA using real-time RT-PCR.

Translated into normal language, they had cut and pasted some viruses in their laboratory in order to add the human ACE2 receptor protein and then made eight chimeric viruses, which they tried out on some human HeLa cells. HeLa are the name of the human cells commonly used to culture things in a lab. The WIV1 refers to an artificial virus, named after the Wuhan Institute of Virology, and created in 2013 by isolating a live horseshoe bat virus in VeroE6 monkey cells, which had ACE2 receptors from humans, civets and horseshoe bats. They used WIV1 as the backbone in the new experiment and it worked. These synthetic viruses could unlock the entry into a human cell and then replicate. It only worked with two of the eight live chimeric viruses, but these two strains definitely had the ability to bind to the human ACE2 receptor.[4]

After the COVID-19 genome was decoded and published, many virologists published papers in *Nature* magazine, the *Lancet* and elsewhere, and issued statements saying that they believed that the genome showed no indication of genetic manipulation, and, secondly, that even if it had been manipulated, there was no evidence that it escaped from a laboratory. Therefore it must have been created in an unknown host species where the viruses mutated or recombined naturally. Further, if one couldn't find traces of this cut-and-paste handiwork, then this 'proved' that COVID-19 was not man-made.

Yet other experts deny that it was ever possible to detect a history of cut-and-paste activity simply by sequencing the

COVID-19 virus. On the contrary, advances in genetic engineering technology make it easy and quick to cut and paste snippets of viruses so that no trace is left behind. Alterations to the bases in the RNA genome would be undetectable if you took the receptor-binding domain from one type of virus (like, say, MERS) and replaced it in another from a very similar virus. By 2019, such genetic engineering techniques were so advanced that they had become routine and could be done by a graduate student. After all, we know that it is easy to build a whole artificial version of, say, the polio virus in a laboratory.

There are two other ways that a laboratory such as WIV might turn a bat virus into one that infects humans that do not involve cut and paste. These are a passaging process using either live cells in a petri dish (*in vitro*), or 'passaging' between live animals (*in vivo*). Both are about artificially accelerating the process of mutation that takes place in nature, or might take place naturally. As these mutations are acquired randomly by selection, they would not show any sign of human intervention.

You would take a bat coronavirus that is not infectious to humans and then 'culture' it with cells that express human ACE2 receptor. Gene 'expression' is the technical phrase used in biology to describe the process by which the information encoded in a gene is used to direct the assembly of a protein molecule such as the ACE spike proteins. Such cells were created years ago to culture the SARS coronaviruses. In this way you can 'help' a bat virus to adapt to infect human cells via mutations in its spike protein. It would increase the strength of its ability to bind to human ACE2, and correspondingly reduce the strength of its binding to bat ACE2. These spike proteins are the bits sticking out of the crown shape of a coronavirus, after which it is named. This is what Shi's team had already done, according to the 2017 paper. But they could have accidentally done more. So if you have human cells in a culture which the viruses are infecting and there happened, by accident, to be not one but two viruses in that petri dish, they would be able to swap genetic information, and you can accidentally or deliberately create a whole third new virus that way.

This can be done quickly. SARS and MERS *in vitro* experiments have shown that significant mutations can be observed after only a few passages. For example, one paper reported that after only 600 passages there already was a 2.1 per cent difference in the genomic sequences of spike proteins between the original strain and its progeny.

It is much quicker to do it this way than with passaging using lab animals. The *in vitro* mutation speeds (i.e. per unit of time) are high, far higher for cell passaging than with lab animals. The second animal passage route would be to adapt a virus enough to infect an intermediate animal, like a mouse, and then to pass it between different generations of mice and watch it to see if or when it mutates into something that could infect people. This is the sort of experiment that Fouchier and Baric had conducted. It mimics a natural process, but accelerates it.

You would hope to show how a virus could change into something that was transmitted through the air—aerosol transmission. Otherwise, you would be left with the proposition that somewhere out there was a bat virus that could infect people, but only if one of these tiny bats bit someone (as does happen with rabies), or if someone came into prolonged exposure to a pile of bat excrement in some remote cave. This sort of event is evidently going to be rare, but not impossible.

We don't know exactly what sort of animal passage experiments the WIV was doing. They were in a kind of professional rivalry with Ralph Baric's lab, which had already done this with mice and SARS. It is conceivable that they were trying to outdo the Americans and, as we have seen in other fields of biotechnology, Chinese scientists are prone to ignore safeguards and rush ahead.

If that is the case, the Wuhan team would then have wanted to stop people thinking that the COVID-19 virus had emerged out of the lab experiments with chimeric viruses they revealed in 2017. They wanted people to think that it must have come from nature. So, rather than releasing the WIV lab records, which would have ended a great deal of this kind of speculation about chimeric viruses, they took a series of actions that look like a number of hasty efforts to kick over the traces and sow as much confusion as possible.

The authorities quickly ordered the destruction of all lab samples of the virus. The story was put about that the virus came from bats sold in the Huanan Seafood Wetmarket. Then, on 23 January 2020, just two weeks after China revealed the genome of the COVID-19 virus, Shi Zhengli unexpectedly announced the existence of a new virus—RaTG13—that had supposedly been discovered seven years earlier in the abandoned copper mine in Yunnan province at Tongguanzhen, Mojiang. Then they revealed the research about coronaviruses found in sick pangolins captured in 2019. Shi called it RaTG-13, Ra for *Rhinolophus affinis*, the Latin name of the Intermediate Horseshoe Bat, and 13 for 2013, the year she discovered it. It was collected from a *Rhinolophus affinis* bat in July 2013. Shi registered her new virus on 27 January 2020 with the National Center for Biotechnology Information (NCBI) of the US National Institutes of Health, the customary repository to register such information.

This RaTG13 is strikingly similar to COVID-19, much more so than all the other bat viruses. When the COVID-19 genome was sequenced and made publicly available on 10 January 2020, it was a riddle, because it did not resemble anything known. Now, here was a bat virus that was 96 per cent identical throughout the whole sequence of the viral genome.

If RaTG13 is a natural virus, then it is easy to believe that the Wuhan coronavirus must have come from nature and must share a recent common ancestor with RaTG13. By presenting the world with this new bat virus, she was able to put the theory of a natural virus hosted by these tiny bats back into the centre of the picture.

However, the whole story of the miners who died after working in the abandoned copper mine, and the discovery of this new virus, is a little odd. Shi originally reported that three of the miners died from pneumonia after removing slag from the mine, and that they had caught it from the fungus growing on bat guano. Nothing in the scant medical records suggests that they were infected or had antibodies to RaTG13, although they did reportedly have anti-bodies to SARS. Subsequent surveys of the rural population in Yunnan failed to turn up any conclusive evidence of bat viruses making local residents ill.

Yet while they were looking hard for this evidence in order to solve the SARS mystery, they had apparently discovered such a bat virus which was extremely intriguing—however, Shi and her team neglected to say anything about it for seven years. Later, Shi changed her story and said that in fact the new virus was sequenced in 2018. It also turned out that the name was changed from another virus identified in a 2016 paper, but was not cited. It was partially sequenced in 2016 and registered in GeneBank under accession number KP876546.

This was unusual and seems to be an attempt to obscure links to the dead miners. In response to complaints, Shi wrote an 'addendum' that *Nature* published. It confirmed that the virus was linked to the miners and that she and her colleagues collected eight more bat-borne SARS viruses from the same mine.

It was strange that the original paper masked any connection to the miners by saying that they died of a fungal infection. If Shi thought they had discovered a new virus that might have killed people, what did they do about it? And what happened to the genetic sequences of the other eight samples? Were any of these used as a backbone to create COVID-19?[5;6]

A lot of digging around by sceptics of her story uncovered a Master's thesis dealing with this disease: 'The Analysis of 6 Patients with Severe Pneumonia Caused by Unknown Viruses' by Li Xu, supervisor Prof. Qian Chuan Yun, published in 2014. Another doctoral thesis, 'Novel Virus Discovery in Bat and the Exploration of Receptor of Bat Coronavirus HKU9' by Canping Huang, also turned up, and the supervisor was George Gao (head of China's CDC). It was published in 2018. The two theses precisely describe the six patients as well as their symptoms, which are similar to those associated with COVID-19. So it looks like Shi and George Gao were not being transparent, since there clearly was a lot of research going on into this mysterious virus.

Shi Zhengli and colleagues have also removed from the web a database of other bat viruses: the Wildlife-borne Viral Pathogen Database, which contains sequences of about 20,000 samples collected over the years, some of which were unpublished. The dataset has been removed from the web; there is only one page left, which can be reached through the Internet Archive Wayback Machine.

Another problem is that Shi's team have not actually produced a sample of the real virus. Apparently only one sample of RaTG13 was ever collected. So no one else can independently verify its existence. No other lab has a sample of it, and no one else has ever sequenced it. What Shi did was upload a database of the virus. This consists of a string of letters alternating between the four nucleotides, A, U, G, and C. A coronavirus contains fewer than 30,000 different nucleotides.

If Dr Shi wanted to invent the RaTG13, then it wouldn't have been hard to do. She only had to type in some alterations to a small part of the data that relate to the receptor-binding domain where the ACE2 receptor spike proteins and the furin site are located. The spike protein is only about 1,300 amino acids long.

The furin polybasic cleavage site is also a shortish sequence of amino acids. All that was needed was to spend a few hours typing in the genetic sequence, a string of letters alternating between the four nucleotides, A, U, G, and C and changing a few things here and there, a few nucleotides, so they looked like the sort of random mutations that occur in nature.

Did she make some mistakes in doing this that give away the deceit? As viruses evolve, they mutate, and one of the four nucleotides is randomly replaced by another. Most of these random mutations do not produce changes in the amino acids that make up the protein, and these mutations are called 'synonymous' since the three-nucleotide 'codon'—part of the messenger RNA—still codes for the same amino acid despite the change. So nothing changes.

Then there are mutations (non-synonymous) that do change the resulting amino acid and therefore the resulting protein. In nature, the ratio of synonymous to non-synonymous is approximately 5:1. Dr Shi may have typed far too many non-synonymous changes at the beginning, then, one third of the way through the sequence, made too few non-synonymous changes, to look like it was natural. Over the entire genome there is a 5:1 ratio; in some places it is 2:1 but elsewhere it is 44:1.

On the other hand, if the RaTG13 is not a forgery, then where is the intermediate species? What the Wuhan team and Daszak wanted to show was that an animal host had been infected by two coronaviruses at the same time and created a new virus that could and did infect humans. This would explain the 'natural' evolution of both SARS and now COVID-19.

The SARS intermediate host was initially thought to be civet cats, but this explanation eventually turned out to be inconclusive. In fact the WIV team discounted this theory themselves. This time, with the COVID-19 outbreak, scientific papers describing the coronaviruses found in pangolins were published in *Nature* and elsewhere. These papers, which started appearing in February, revealed a virus that, although it was only 90 per cent identical to COVID-19, had an almost identical receptor binding domain—ACE2—with the difference of only a single amino acid. These viruses were found in samples taken from a handful of sick pangolins that the Guangdong customs officers seized in 2019. Therefore, a bat virus and a pangolin virus could have met some time ago and mutated to create a new virus with this ACE2 spike, after which a bat with this new virus infected a Yunnan farmer, who then travelled directly to Wuhan and started the outbreak. Or someone like Dr Shi could have deliberately cut out this segment from the pangolin strain and used it to replace the receptor-binding domain in RaTG13, as they are pretty much identical.[7]

Eventually, this connection to the diseased pangolins was discounted. 'While it has been suggested by some Chinese scientists that the COVID-19 virus might have been transmitted to humans from pangolins, currently available data does not support this idea', Professor Petrovsky concluded. Likewise, the Palm civets captured from the wild were found to test negative for the SARS virus, so they are evidently not a natural reservoir.

The same conclusion was reached by Ralph Baric, who said in an interview in mid-March that no one had identified the reservoir species of COVID-19, but that it was certainly not pangolins:

> They have not identified the actual reservoir species. Reports show that pangolins are potentially the intermediate host, but pangolin viruses are 88–98% identical to SARS-CoV-2. In comparison, civet and racoon dog strains of SARS coronaviruses were 99.8% identical to SARS-CoV from 2003. In other words, we are talking about a handful of mutations between civet strains, racoon dog strains and human strains in 2003. Pangolins [strains of CoV2] have over 3000 nucleotide changes, no way they are the reservoir species. Absolutely not.[8]

The second challenge was to explain where the new furin site came from. This small but very special stretch of four amino acids in COVID-19 could either have been inserted or come from a bat or an intermediate species. How easy is it to insert this without leaving a trace? It can be done artificially by using the 'seamless' ligation method, which means creating segments with new restriction sites that disappear after the complementary ends are joined. The Baric group used this method in 2002 to create a synthetic clone of a murine coronavirus, a type of virus that infects mice. In 2003 the Baric team did it again to make a synthetic clone of SARS: 'To rapidly assemble consensus clones, we used class IIS restriction endonucleases that cut at asymmetric sites and leave asymmetric ends. These enzymes generate strand-specific unique overhangs that allow the seamless ligation of two cDNAs with the concomitant loss of the restriction site.'[9]

Since then, this sort of thing has become routine, with the use of a 'seamless assembly kit' offered by many companies advertising on the internet, such as Thermo-Fisher Scientific. The work can be done in half an hour, as the company's publicity material explains:

> The GeneArt Seamless Cloning and Assembly Enzyme mix, the GeneArt Seamless Cloning and Assembly Kit, and the GeneArt Seamless PLUS Cloning and Assembly kit enable cloning of DNA fragments into virtually any linearized vector, without extra sequences, or restriction endonuclearease digestion and ligation. The proprietary enzyme mix recognizes and precisely assembles the DNA fragments sharing at least 15-base pair (bp) end homology created by PCR amplification in a simple -30 minute room temperature reaction. The DNA Oligo Designer guides users through experimental design.

The fact that it can be done does not prove that it was done. Many coronaviruses have naturally occurring furin sites, which are quite diverse and emerge from random mutations. This was the case when the Middle East Respiratory Syndrome (MERS) virus jumped into humans. So Dr Shi could simply have cut and pasted in the MERS virus furin site to make COVID-19.

In May 2020, Chinese scientists released a paper in *Cell Biology* that claimed they had discovered a new strain of a SARS-like coronavirus called RmYN02, in samples taken from bats in Yunnan province: 'Since the discovery of SARS-CoV-2 there have been a number of unfounded suggestions that the virus has a laboratory origin', said senior author Weifeng Shi, director and professor at the Institute of Pathogen Biology at Shandong First Medical University in China. 'In particular, it has been proposed the S1/S2 insertion is highly unusual and perhaps indicative of laboratory manipulation. Our paper shows very clearly that these events occur naturally in wildlife. This provides strong evidence against SARS-CoV-2 being a laboratory escape.' The bat samples were taken in May 2019, but the RNA from the swab was sent for sequencing in early January 2020. 'Our findings suggest that these insertion events that initially appeared to be very unusual can, in fact, occur naturally in animal betacoronaviruses', Weifeng Shi said.[10]

Another line of argument has been developed to suggest that the whole RaTG13 virus had been concocted to divert attention from the fact that, excluding that virus, the next most similar bat viruses to COVID-19 that have been identified were discovered by military researchers in the Zhoushan Islands, which lie about a hundred miles East of Shanghai. Samples taken from 334 bats from the species *Rhinolophus pusillus* between 2015 and 2017 helped identify two new viruses, ZXC21 and ZC45. They then infected suckling pigs, which fell ill. The scientists involved concluded that the bats are a natural reservoir of SARS viruses.[11]

One has to wonder why the PLA General Logistics Command and Institute of Medicine, Nanjing Command, was so interested in collecting bat viruses, which is research that was otherwise the specialisation of the WIV. Are the scientists who published this paper working on biowarfare? Was one of these viruses used as the backbone to make COVID-19 part of a military-sponsored project? This is the theory put forward by Dr Yan Li-Meng in several papers.[12]

Dr Yan, a Chinese-born scientist, had been working at the famous Hong Kong University Institute of Public Health set up by Malik Peiris, and later sought refuge in the United States after claiming that mainland China had warned the Hong Kong scientists to keep quiet about what they knew. But Dr Yan's allegations were met with a chorus of both criticism and derision from American virology experts. Her reports did not really convince anyone that these bat viruses, ZC45 or ZXC21 from the Zhoushan Islands, are particularly significant in the story of understanding the origin of COVID-19.

So twelve months after COVID-19 first appeared in Wuhan, no one has found any convincing animal candidates that could be a natural host for COVID-19, or put forward an explanation of how a bat virus could have naturally mutated so it could not only infect humans but also become easily transmissible between them. So much is unknown about viruses in general, and so many viruses in wild animals such as bats have still to be identified, that this may just mean that, even if it takes a while, researchers will eventually find an explanation. Yet, even with MERS, there's no real explanation of how a bat virus would infect a camel so it would infect a human being. Just as there is no real explanation about how the SARS virus was transmitted, since it is not present in civet cats in the wild.

A lot of circumstantial evidence suggests that it could easily have been created in a lab and then escaped, but there is no proof of this. Yet it certainly looks as though Dr Shi and others are making a lot of clumsy efforts to hide something. Her explanations are self-contradictory. She told one story to *Nature* and another blaming the miners' death on a fungus to

Scientific American and *Science* magazine.[13] Is it possible that the Chinese government has been deliberately destroying evidence, and that it knew the real origin of the virus quite early on? It is the case that the absence of evidence (of COVID-19 being manmade) is not evidence of absence. The next chapters look at the course of events to try to understand why the government behaved as it did.

17

SECRECY STOPPED CHINA'S DISEASE CONTROL CENTRE FROM DOING ITS JOB

In the months leading up to the lockdown of Wuhan, the Chinese government could have contained the outbreak. We know that it must have been sufficiently widespread in Wuhan in November 2019 to infect people who carried it overseas. This implies a pool of infected people larger, far larger than the handful of cases recorded by Wuhan hospitals in December. There were forty-four officially recorded hospital patients in late December, and a total of 200 cases in 2019. It has been established that patients in Italy, France, the UK and the United States whose blood samples were taken in December 2019 had antibodies that affect the virus attachment and the entry of the virus. In most cases, these overseas patients had not been in Wuhan. By extension, it also strongly suggests that the outbreak started well before the cases recorded by the Wuhan hospitals in early December.

As soon as the first cases of a new virus were confirmed, the Chinese government had only to work backwards and track down where each of the carriers had been and with whom they had been in contact. It took China only twenty-four hours to identify 100 people who had been in contact with a person infected with the MERS virus, which arrived in China in 2015. So China could easily have traced all the contacts of the first 200 patients. It has a very powerful surveillance apparatus, an absence of privacy protections and the manpower to monitor the movements of its citizens. It can probably do this sort of track and trace better than almost any other country.

It is surely the case that it has in fact done so. The identity of the first person in the transmission chain must therefore be known to the Chinese government. If this is so, then the Chinese government has chosen not to share that information. If it did not carry out a track and trace operation, then it has also decided that for some reason it is not obliged to explain why it did not carry out this essential and routine work.

Imagine if it had done so and traced the origin of the virus back to a laboratory in Wuhan: then all those involved would be criminally liable. Those who had sponsored this research would be to blame, too. Everyone connected with this, including the World Health Organisation and EcoHealth Alliance, would have to share responsibility. The repercussions would be huge, reaching all across the biotechnology industry. It would start a political earthquake, bigger than Chernobyl. So a great many people have a vested interest in shutting down any investigation into this possibility.

The Chinese government initially adopted a narrative that linked the outbreak to people working with wild animals sold in the Wuhan seafood market. This was the story that was presented to explain SARS in 2003, and it was readily accepted. China claimed to have learned the lessons from SARS, to have banned the sale of endangered species and set up an early warning system through the Chinese Centre for Disease Control. So the outbreak of the new disease would still be China's fault. A year after the outbreak, no illegal wildlife traders have been identified or punished. China should also have to acknowledge the failures of its early warning system run by the CDC. This has not happened either. Instead, it moved away from linking COVID-19 to the sale of wild animals at the seafood market, perhaps to avoid any kind of responsibility.

The (Chinese) Centre for Disease Control was set up in the wake of the SARS epidemic, modelled on the US system, and comes under the control of China's National Health Commission, a cabinet level body. At the time the CDC was run by (George) Gao Fu, an able and open-minded scientist who had initially trained as a veterinarian and studied at Oxford (in 1991) and at Harvard (in 1999) with support from the Wellcome Trust. Like other scientists, he was lured back to China by the offer of a top job, that of the director-general of the Institute of Microbiology at the Chinese Academy of Sciences, and possibly large bonuses. A glowing profile by *China Daily* reported that in 2013, when the MERS virus was a threat, Gao's team took only weeks to find out how it invades cells, thus providing the insights for developing a vaccine and an effective therapeutic agent. In the same year, *China Daily* reported that, when H7N9 bird flu hit China, Gao's team figured out that poultry farms were the source of the avian influenza A(H7N9) virus.

Gao speaks good English and has an outgoing personality, which made developing international contacts very easy. In September 2014 he led a sixty-three-member China Mobile Laboratory Testing Team to Sierra Leone to help combat the Ebola outbreak. 'Gao's team discovered how the Ebola virus enters cells and infects humans, making a breakthrough in the battle against the virus. The research, published by the scientific journal *Cell*, provides a theoretical basis for the prevention and control of Ebola and offers a new direction for drug development', reported *China Daily*.

'People like us who study infectious diseases are always on the front line of natural disasters, because the plague always comes after the disaster, and our duty is to prevent it', Gao was quoted as saying. Gao took over the CDC in 2017 and was a considerable asset, as the Chinese government wanted to use the CDC to help raise China's profile abroad and bolster its Belt and Road Initiative. The CDC was given new office buildings in a suburb of Beijing.

According to Song Hao, who was Gao's doctoral student from 2011 and is now a member of Gao's team, Gao follows the news of all viruses in the world and is a stickler for detail.

'That's why we can react so fast when a virus starts to spread, because we begin researching the virus from the moment it appears', Song was quoted as saying. Gao wrote a successful book together with viral immunology specialist Liu Huan called *Influenza Virus—An unavoidable enemy*, which recounts the history and spread of the influenza virus.

By the winter of 2019, the CDC had trained hundreds of staff in outbreak response techniques and had set up a national, real time reporting system for infectious disease. It was started in 2004, and in 2008 the WHO helped upgrade it. Doctors are required to log any case of unexplained pneumonia as soon as it is discovered. The system would then send automated alerts to local and national disease-control officials. By 2013, it had reduced the average reporting time from five days to four hours.

'I can confidently say there won't be another SARS incident', Dr Gao said in a speech a year earlier. 'Because our country's infectious-diseases surveillance network is very well-established, when a virus comes, we can stop it.'

In a lengthy speech in September 2015, at a workshop organised by the (US) National Academies of Sciences, Engineering and Sciences, Gao boasted about the efficiency of the Chinese system now, the Party's effectiveness at coordinating things under the direct authority of a vice premier, and the reliability of reporting by an extensive network of the local CDC office.[1]

He explained, too, how in just forty-eight hours, they had traced over 100 people who had come into contact with a person who had entered China infected with MERS. In the following years, Gao gave many speeches in which he emphasised that, when it came to dealing with public health emergencies, it was best to involve the public, to be open and to encourage voluntary public participation. That way, people could take precautions for themselves and would not be panicked by the spread of rumours.

Yet this system failed in Wuhan. The hospital staff didn't enter the details of the first patients into the data system, because the doctors and nurses took orders from the hospital administrators, who in turn awaited permission from the local Party officials. The Wuhan Party leadership had to implement the strict regulations on the dissemination of any information relating to infectious diseases, which were introduced after SARS. Hospital administrators were well aware of this.[2]

One can imagine, too, that the Wuhan leadership knew that there was a severe winter flu going around and that patients were already crowding the hospitals. And if they made it public that there was a new and mysterious virus, anyone sick with winter flu would flock to the hospitals. The situation would get quickly out of hand. It might be better to keep the news from spreading.

The CDC system should have been reporting the existence of cases of people who had fever, fatigue, coughing and aching limbs, but who had all tested negative for influenza. In some Wuhan hospitals doctors resorted to giving patients chest scans, and after discovering severe lung damage, they sent samples to laboratories run by private companies. By 20 December, there were at least sixty infected patients.

One report in *China News Weekly* said that a lowly official Wang Wenyong of the local Jianghan District disease control office started the ball rolling after receiving a report from the Hubei Provincial Hospital of Integrated Chinese and Western Medicine (Hubei Xinhua Hospital) about patients with unexplained pneumonia. He went to other hospitals and found more cases, and then pushed the information up to the next level in the bureaucracy. The earliest known test was done by Vision Medicals, based in the city of Guangzhou, from a sample taken on 24 December from a patient who had fallen sick on 18 December. It shared the genome with Wuhan officials and the Chinese Academy of Sciences on 27 December. Some reports say it was later asked to destroy these samples, because they revealed when the outbreak started.

If the system had been working, then information about these alarming cases of an unknown pneumonia should have been seen by George Gao in Beijing, who would then have informed the China National Health Commission. It would have been reported further, to the state council, which would have coordinated actions with other ministries. The first step would have been to set up an emergency response team, and that would have passed instructions down to the Wuhan government. Instead, hospital doctors notified their superiors in the hospital administrations of their concerns. The Wuhan government then issued two internal notices on 30 December warning about cases of a mysterious pneumonia.

One notice requested the Wuhan Central Hospital and Wuhan Union Hospital to search for unexplained pneumonia cases linking to the seafood market. The authorities had apparently heard from these hospitals that there were about twenty-five cases over the past four weeks, and understood that twenty of them were related to the seafood market. Around 1:30 pm that afternoon, the Wuhan Municipal Health Commission announced twenty-seven cases of pneumonia related to a seafood market. It said their investigations found no clear human-to-human transmission.

Both hospitals are close to the market and the Wuhan CDC. The other directive ordered an immediate clean-up of the market. The west side of the market, where most of the animal cages were, was reported to be especially unsavoury, with 'rubbish piled everywhere, a damp floor and poor ventilation'. The authorities ordered it to be cleaned and disinfected. A local company, Jiangwei Disinfection, immediately arrived to sterilize the area.

At the same time, the authorities quickly shut down a WeChat group with about 100 members used by hospital staff. Messages posted by several doctors, including ophthalmologist Dr Li Wenliang, warned colleagues about the danger of a new SARS-like virus. These doctors didn't contact the media or the CDC. Instead, copies of the two administrative orders were leaked on China's social media platforms. This is how George Gao heard about the outbreak. He checked the alerts on his mobile phone before going to bed on 30 December. The WHO staff in Beijing heard about the outbreak in the same way, at around 11 in the morning.

According to Shi Zhengli's account, the CDC sent her samples from seven patients on 30 December at 7 pm with an urgent request to analyse them. She was in Shanghai and quickly took a train back to Wuhan to start the work. This seems to have been before George Gao in Beijing heard of the outbreak. So perhaps it was in fact the provincial government that sent her samples. Her team set about carrying out PCR tests and also sent samples to two other institutes to get a full sequence, rather than using their own sequencing machine.

George Gao then contacted the Wuhan CDC and asked them to go immediately to the seafood market and take samples. It is not clear if they arrived in time to take samples from the caged animals, but an official from the Jiangwei Disinfection company has said that he saw officials from the local CDC office sampling and removing some of the dead and live animals. There were no pangolins, civets or bats in the market. The officials got their team to take about seventy to eighty specimens of faeces and fur from the dead animals, mainly dogs and rabbits.

When a CDC team from Beijing arrived on 1 January, led by Li Qun, head of its Public Health Emergency Centre, the whole market had already been closed and sterilised. This meant that this team could only take samples from stalls, sewers, surfaces, tools and other surroundings, but not from any animals. Later, however, the CDC claimed it did take samples from farms supplying 'wild' animals to these markets.

Three weeks later, Gao said that the market had been closed before his team could conduct any research. On 22 January, a news report said scientists had found the coronavirus in fifteen samples taken at the market, but it is unclear if the virus was shed by humans or by animals. And if it came from animals, then which animals? Dr Gao had at one point seemed confident that the source of the infections was a bamboo rat, a creature bred in local farms as a delicacy and sold at the market.

In January he twice claimed that the virus came from wild animals sold at the Huanan market. At a press conference on 22 January, Gao explained that the virus likely first infected people through contact with wild animals and the environment that the wild animals were in. Then, the virus began mutating and became capable of human-to-human transmission. 'The original source of the virus is wild animals that were sold at the [Huanan] seafood market', Gao stated firmly.

Another source claims that the CDC's report showed that of 585 environment samples from different areas of the market, thirty-three tested positive for the virus. The positive samples came from shops located throughout the market, as well as surfaces, walls, and tools used in connection with the animals. Animals and the environment of farms that supplied livestock to the market were also evaluated, with all 139 samples testing negative. Although Chinese officials said they were tracing the suppliers of the wild meat in the market, no information on those people or the animals they handled has been published. Without evidence of a wild animal source of infection, the story died.

Then in March, George Gao changed his line. He told the journal *Science* that the virus may not have originated at the market. Maybe, he said, it could be a place where the virus was 'amplified', meaning it began elsewhere but spread wildly there. Then he told a local TV station that the animal samples from the market did not contain the virus. There was no longer a real link between the trade in wild animals and the new virus. Since a market attracts a lot of visitors, it meant that even if samples taken from surfaces at the market indicated the presence of the virus, this would not help to trace its origin. The cases could all have been caused by one super spreader.

CDC officials reportedly told the WHO experts that they would eventually be able to create an epidemiological map of the market showing details of which animals were where, and which patients visited which section of the market, but no such map has ever been released.

Only twenty-seven of the first forty-one confirmed cases had been 'exposed' to the market, and only one of the four initial cases in the first two weeks of December. In other words, 80 per cent of the first cases had nothing to do with the market.

The other theory—that the virus came from the WIV lab—had to be quashed. Shi Zhengli did her best to do this. She said that she looked at the sequences of the virus and compared them with her own bat virus data, and found nothing. As she told *Scientific American* in an interview, none of the sequences matched those of the viruses her team had sampled from bat caves. 'That really took a load off my mind. I had not slept a wink for days', she reportedly said. She also 'frantically went through her own lab's records from the past few years to check for any mishandling of experimental materials, especially during disposal', and concluded that an accident was out of the question, too.

We are supposed to take her word for it. Later, in February, she would muddy this story and discover a new and previously unreported bat virus RaTG13, which was close to the COVID-19 virus. This kept the animal theory alive, but not so as to assign any responsibility to the lab.

Over the first half of the year, the official story changed to suggest that in fact many of the early cases were people who were unconnected with the seafood market. These first cases were people who neither worked there nor had been near it. So the notion was left floating in the air that bats in a remote cave in Yunnan had infected an unknown person, either directly in some unknown way, or through some unknown intermediate mammal. Then this unknown infected person had gone directly to Wuhan without infecting anyone else on the way but had then infected an unknown person in Wuhan who had started an epidemic.

It would obviously take Chinese scientists a very long time to clear up so many unknowns, but in the meantime, the Chinese government could push the notion that it was not in any way responsible. It left no one to finger for the blame, except perhaps this or that local party official who had acted too slowly to stop the epidemic at the start.

In-depth reporting by journalists from both the *Wall Street Journal* and the Associated Press presents a narrative that gives the impression that the actions taken during this critical period, when the spread of the virus could have been stopped, were largely taken by the local Party leadership in Wuhan.[3]

They apparently made decisions without consulting the Hubei provincial party leaders, let alone the higher-ups in Beijing. And they tried unsuccessfully to contain the growing crisis in order to save face and to ensure that their political meetings carried on undistracted by this emerging crisis. Local leaders had just hosted the Military World Games and were hoping that their city would soon be given new status on a par with Beijing and Shanghai. This would automatically entitle the Wuhan Party Secretary to a seat on the politburo. The city was also either preparing for or holding the annual meeting where hundreds of top officials from across the province came together to agree the following year's targets. The idea was also planted that the impact of these reckless independent actions was further compounded by bureaucratic confusion between different ministries and competing lines of authority.

American journalists tend to see things in China through the prism of their own political system. America has a federal system of independent states, so turf wars between federal and state officials, or the alphabet of different branches of the government in Washington, form a staple plot device in a great many Hollywood movies. China's political system may on paper appear to be similar, but it isn't.

All Party officials are hugely disciplined members of one very centralised organisation. The Party has its own highly secretive communications system. Chinese officials may carry titles common in Western democracies such as mayor, governor, minister or president. They don't mean much, because they exist only for outward appearances, a nod to the norms of the rest of the world. No mayor or governor answers to a local electorate, nor are they subject to oversight by any independent judiciary or scrutiny by any local legislative body. In the Chinese political system there is no separation of powers. The loyalty of officials is solely to the Party.

The security system is quite different, too. China is a police state, in which the actions of anyone of any significance are liable to be under surveillance by a network of informers. China's KGB is not a byword like in the Soviet Union, but it operates in just the same way. No official would take any action on their own initiative, because they would fear—rightly—that they were under surveillance. Yet many Westerners also assume that Party officials who transgress fear being purged, either shot or sent to the GULAG, just as they were in Stalin's time during the Great Terror of the 1930s. This is quite mistaken.

Chinese party officials know that if there is a disaster but something goes wrong, they are safe so long as they can show that all along they have 'observed party discipline', as it is called in China. The system will protect them. When it was revealed that tens of thousands of school children had died during the 2008 Sichuan earthquake when their shoddily built schools collapsed, only one very minor official was sent to jail. Or when many hundreds of thousands of peasants contracted HIV/Aids from blood plasma donations, not a single senior official was held responsible.

In the days of imperial China, when communications were slow and uncertain, a provincial governor might have been forced to act before seeking and obtaining instructions from the emperor. Yet in a time of instant communication by mobile phone, it is hard to believe that the Wuhan Party secretary acted on his own initiative. It is possible, of course, but highly unlikely. If the outbreak started in November but only came to the ears of top Wuhan party leaders in late December, then the idea that they conspired to keep the news from reaching the ears of their superiors in Beijing for almost a month is very hard to believe. If there had been a lab leak at the WIV in October, then Wuhan officials kept the whole thing secret from October to mid-January—three-and-a-half months.

On 27 January, the deputy party secretary of Wuhan, Zhou Xianwang, gave a sorry-but-not-sorry apology during an interview with CCTV, the state broadcaster. He said his hands were tied by rules that required Beijing's approval before releasing sensitive information, and that the initial management of the epidemic and the speed at which information was shared with the public was 'not good enough'.

'As a [member of] local government, after I got the information, I must ask for authorisation before I could disclose it. Many people didn't understand this at the time', he said. 'We locked down the city to cut the spread of the virus, but it's likely we'll leave a bad reputation in history [...] As long as it helps contain the spread of virus, I'm willing to resign as a form of apology. Wuhan's party chief, Ma Guoqiang, and I will take whatever the responsibility it contains.'

In the event Beijing replaced Wuhan's Party secretary, Ma Guoqiang, and Hubei's provincial Party secretary, Jiang Chaoliang, in mid-February. This was a political reshuffle, not a punishment. They were not accused of breaching party discipline, of acting unilaterally or of delaying measures that would have prevented the virus from spreading around the world. On the contrary, when the Wuhan lockdown ended, China's leader Xi Jinping declared that the victory over the virus was a triumph that had been accomplished thanks to China's special political system. Under the strong leadership of the CPC Central Committee, China had effectively curbed the spread of the virus and 'protected people's lives and health to the greatest extent'. Xi said: 'The laws of science were followed in making decisions, treating patients, conducting technological research and governing society'.

Even after George Gao found out about the outbreak, the CDC could not persuade local hospitals to start using its online reporting system. On 3 January, it was the National Health Commission that issued an internal Party instruction ordering a news blackout. Hospitals were explicitly told not to use the CDC system. Any laboratories that had tested samples were ordered to destroy them or hand them over to the government. No one was allowed to publish any independent research on the virus. As the rules stated: 'No organisation or individual shall make public any medical information on the disease with the outside world'.

From 4 January, no one was allowed to report any new cases, and for the next two weeks, no new cases were reported either inside or outside China. China would not say that there were human-to-human infections.

In Beijing, Dr Gao was reportedly so exasperated that, in a call with his American counterpart, he came close to tears. It must have been horribly humiliating for Gao who had gone around the world bragging how great China's disease surveillance systems were, and how much better than those of supposedly backward countries in Africa. It would have looked to anyone familiar with working with China as though Dr Gao had been manipulated and used in an effort to show foreigners that China was being open and cooperative. He appeared to have only been given some token authority, while all the time the CCP reserved the real information for itself and excluded him from any real decision-making.

The Chinese government's efforts to manage the flow of information failed, so it was repeatedly forced on the back foot by events. The Wuhan Central Hospital had sent a sample from a forty-one-year-old male vendor who worked at the Seafood Market for analysis at the Fudan University in Shanghai, which has a Public Health Clinic Centre with a BSL-3 lab. There, they immediately set about sequencing the genome without knowing much about the outbreak. In the early hours of 5 January, they recognized a virus that was very similar to SARS, and that it had a spike protein which allowed it to bind to human respiratory tracts.

The leader of the team, Zhang Yongshen, notified the National Health Commission, and without seeking permission, he uploaded the genome to the US National Center for Biotechnology Information (NCBI). A few days later, the *Wall Street Journal* broke the news that China was dealing with a new coronavirus. This forced the Chinese government to officially confirm it for the first time on 9 January.

Two days later, Zhang received a phone call from a colleague at the University of Sydney, Edward Holmes, who asked permission to publish it online. When Holmes posted it on the *Virological.org* website, it caused shock waves around the world. The next day the NHC officially shared the genome with the rest of the world.

Dr Holmes said that he knew of the notice from 3 January banning any public release. 'We decided to go ahead because this was an issue of such global importance that it just had to be done.' As a result, the Shanghai laboratory was shut down on 12 January for 'rectification' and did not re-open for three weeks.

Once the genome was available, many experts could easily see that the virus infected the respiratory tracts like a cold or a flu, and hence one had to assume that there was a high risk of rapid human-to-human transmission.

Zhang says he called Dr Zhao Su, head of respiratory medicine at Wuhan Central Hospital, to request the clinical data about the patient whose sample he had analysed. He then travelled to Wuhan, where he spoke to top public health officials over dinner on 8 January. 'I had two judgements: first that it was a SARS-like virus; second, that the virus transmits by the respiratory tract. And so, I had two suggestions: that we should take some emergency public measures to protect against this disease; also, clinics should develop antiviral treatments.'

In the meantime, the National Health Commission released the genome—not the one it obtained from Shanghai or the CDC, but rather the one from the WIV. Only with the publication of the genome could companies start designing test kits. The WIV team led by Shi Zhengli notified the WHO and uploaded the genome on 12 January—just after it was posted by Edward Holmes in Australia.

It doesn't take more than a day to sequence the genome of a virus and compare it to others. In fact Shi told some reporters she had sequenced the genome in a matter of days. It had already been done quickly by a private company in Guangzhou in December. The CDC had sequenced it on 3 January, Wuhan University by 7 January, Fudan University lab in Shanghai by 5 January, and Hong Kong researchers around the same time.

For still unexplained reasons, the Party apparently did nothing for two weeks but sit on the information. This inaction was probably not the fault of Wuhan officials. Meanwhile, the chain of infections expanded exponentially.

Experts in Taiwan spotted social media posts from Wuhan on 31 December and immediately took action, starting on-board health inspections of passengers from Wuhan to Taiwan. On the same day, it became the first country to ask the WHO about human-to-human transmission. The text mentions the reports of 'at least seven atypical pneumonia cases' and notes that patients were being 'isolated for treatment'. This clearly suggested that there was a possibility of human-to-human transmission, since this would not have been necessary if the disease had not been infectious.

In Hong Kong, the place that had always served as a sentinel for diseases coming out of China, the first case of a patient from Wuhan was registered as early as 2 January. By 6 January, Hong Kong had twenty-one patients in isolation words, none of whom had visited the seafood market. Hong Kong raised its response level to serious. It is also striking that there were no cases recorded in Hong Kong during the previous year which suggests that the virus was indeed not circulating beyond Wuhan before then.

Ho Pak-Leung, head of the University of Hong Kong's Centre for human infection, warned as early as 4 January that it was highly possible that the illness was spreading from human to human. The Hong Kong scientists came under pressure from the Chinese authorities to keep quiet, according to Chinese virologist Yan Li-Meng, who also reported that she was asked by her supervisor at the university, Dr Leo Poon, to look into an odd cluster of cases. She claims that Professor Malik Peiris also knew that it was dangerously transmissible, but was reluctant to speak out.

On 8 January, Thai airport officials pulled aside a woman from a flight from Wuhan who had a runny nose, a sore throat, and a high temperature. Chulalongkor University Professor Supaporn Wacharapluesadee's team found that she was infected with a new coronavirus. Wacharapluesadee reported it to the Thai government and spent the next days searching for matching sequences. As the Chinese government hadn't published any sequences, she found nothing.

On 9 January, a sixty-one-year-old man with the virus passed away in Wuhan, the first known death. The death wasn't made public until 11 January.

On 12 January, Professor Yuen Kwok-yung of the Hong Kong University Infectious Diseases Department warned health officials in China of suspected human-to-human transmission. Then, on 13 January, Thailand announced its first coronavirus case, a fifty-one-year-old woman from Wuhan who had visited local fresh food markets but not the seafood market.

Next, a group of experts from Taiwan, Hong Kong and Macau arrived on a fact-finding visit between 13 and 15 January. No new cases had been announced for ten days, so it looked as though the outbreak was over. Yet Chuang Yin-ching of Taiwan's Centre for Disease Control said that a Beijing official admitted that 'limited human to human transmission cannot be excluded', but insisted that no community outbreak had occurred. He thought that Wuhan officials were 'trying to hide something', because, when repeatedly asked about transmissibility, the answer was always unclear. Finally, he says, an official admitted that there were two family clusters among the confirmed cases, one involving a husband and his physically disabled wife. 'The possibility of his wife [going] to the seafood market is zero so we can pretty much be sure that the husband transmitted it to his wife', says Chuang.

On 18 January, another team arrived in Wuhan, including Dr Gao from the CDC in Beijing, Dr Zhang from Shanghai, and Dr Zhong Nanshan. The latter was a graduate of Edinburgh University and St. Barts, who ran the Guangzhou Institute of Respiratory Diseases and had won fame for treating the first SARS patients, at great personal risk. On arrival, local officials appeared furtive and anxious. The team toured hospitals, questioning staff, and heard that fourteen medical workers had been infected by a single patient. This was proof, alarming proof, of human-to-human transmission.

Yet between 5 and 18 January, the Wuhan authorities did not report any new cases. It was only on 20 January that the Chinese media first reported the possibility that a new virus was capable of being transmitted between people, but this was not officially confirmed until 22 January.

The report by the team of five Chinese scientists who went to Wuhan appeared to have tipped the balance and persuaded the Beijing Party leadership to declare a pandemic. 'We already had some suspected clusters, but by then we had some clear cluster cases [...] I think, for that, there is no doubt [that the virus can be spread between humans]', George Gao explained their thinking in an April interview with China Global Television Network, a state broadcaster directed at overseas audiences:

> Of course, we discussed human-to-human transmission, but then we also realized it is a very efficient human-to-human transmission, not just there is human-to-human transmission. We know that it is human-to-human transmission; the only problem is its seriousness, how serious [it is]. So, for the special senior advisory group members, we saw how serious it could be. So, once we got there [Wuhan], we talked to a lot of people. We already have some suspected clusters, but by then, we had some clear cluster cases already there.
>
> So, I think for that, there's no doubt. So, we had this press conference on the evening of January 19. Dr Zhong Nanshan and every-

body said, five of us were there, I said in the press conference that this virus, because the origin of the virus, everybody thought it's from the animal, has already finished its "jump". I called it a "jump", from animal to humans and said it had already finished the stage of limited human-to-human transmission. By January 20, we claimed the virus finished those three steps, and it was already becoming efficient human-to-human transmission.

From then on Wuhan was placed under a complete lockdown, which lasted for the following seventy-six days. It is obvious that the Chinese could have acted much faster, as quickly as the Taiwanese had done. Had they declared an emergency in Wuhan and put it under lockdown at the end of December, then a global pandemic would have been avoided. If the figures are to be believed, there were still only a few hundred cases of COVID-19 in Wuhan in December, but by 12 January, there were over 15,000. Wuhan is a key transport hub, and millions of people pass through it every week.

It is still hard to understand the delay of a month (if not longer). It might simply be that, just like in the fictional town of Amityville in the film *Jaws*, where the mayor doesn't want to close the beaches on the Fourth of July holiday, and the compliant medical examiner certifies the first shark victim as a death caused by a boating accident, it was bad for business.

Or it might it be that they waited to see more proof of the virus' pathogenicity to emerge? This makes some sense. Doctors, virologists or officials might have been cautious too, because they had cried wolf rather too often, repeatedly warning that this or that swine flu or avian flu had jumped to humans and was about to start a new Spanish flu pandemic—only for the crisis to subside after a handful of cases.

Even if some of what happened in November and December can only be guessed at, there is little doubt that secrecy, which is such a major feature of China's political system, is partly to blame. The Chinese officials may well have been acting to hide a lab accident or a secret weapons programme, in which case they might have thought the secrecy justified. But they probably would have acted like this regardless. Whatever the true origin, they would have kept the outbreak secret for as long as they possibly could, because the CCP considers secrecy a higher good than public health, or indeed almost anything else. The tougher secrecy laws introduced after SARS to deal with public health emergencies are not really any different to those applied to information about every other aspect of life in China. It is true that it helps local officials duck scrutiny if they mess up, but the real purpose is to ensure that the Party claims credit for what it wants and avoids blame for current failures and past crimes. This secrecy is no secret. It is part of an openly declared political programme to continue a one party dictatorship, and to defeat the emergence of an open society.

The science of virology and medicine flourishes best in an open society, where knowledge is immediately shared and pooled. If news of a suspected new virus such as SARS or COVID-19 had been immediately released, many people around the world would have collaborated and quickly sounded the alarm about viral human-to-human transmission. People would have taken matters into their own hands and avoided Wuhan. Foreign countries would have halted flights from Wuhan.

On the other hand, it is also important to note a paradox. China's secrecy also encouraged many individuals and organisations to enthusiastically support China no matter what it did. They believed that supporting and flattering China was the only way to obtain a minimal amount of cooperation, and so they attacked anyone in their own countries who ventured to criticise or pressure China. It would be even worse if you offended China, they reasoned. It also meant that disbelieving whatever China said left you open to accusations that you were believing in unproven conspiracies. The next chapters look at how that worked out.

18

'IT'S ALL FAKE'

CONFUSION AND DECEPTION IN WUHAN

In January, as the Chinese authorities and WHO experts issued soothing words, the world saw images of Wuhan hospitals crowded with patients, people dying in corridors, and body bags being bundled into ambulances. A new and deadly virus was spreading uncontrollably.

The reality was a little different. Throughout January, thousands of people did wait in hospitals, queuing for up to eight hours, but they were waiting to be tested, not treated. There weren't enough test kits, and without a positive test, no one could get treatment. Getting a positive COVID-19 test was so difficult to get, people said, it was like winning the lottery. If a sick person didn't have a positive test result, there was no chance of being admitted. The tests were often faulty, resulting in false negatives. Anyone without a test, or with a false negative, was sent home, to infect others.

Reports suggest that some people tested negative up to six times even when they were clearly infected by the virus. This is what happened to Dr Li Wenliang, the ophthalmologist who alerted others to the outbreak and was reprimanded by Chinese authorities. Wenliang developed a cough and fever after unknowingly treating an infected patient. He tested negative for coronavirus five times before finally receiving a positive result. Only then could he be hospitalised in his own hospital, Wuhan Central. On 30 January the doctor posted: 'Today nucleic acid testing came back with a positive result, the dust has settled, finally diagnosed', according to the BBC. By then it was too late. Dr Li passed away on 7 February.

The authorities decided that they could only consider a patient a confirmed case if he or she tested positive for the virus by taking a nucleic-acid test. With limited hospital beds, authorities gave preference to patients testing positive for coronavirus. The nucleic-acid test—using nasal or throat mucus collected with cotton swabs—was favoured because it can be performed by nurses and other regular hospital staff.

The Chinese CDC was unable to act decisively at the start because there was a massive shortage of testing kits, and the ones that it did have were no good. This meant it was unable to monitor the disease. The flawed testing system prevented scientists and officials from seeing how fast the virus was spreading. With few and faulty kits, only one in nineteen infected people was tested and found positive as of 31 January, according to an estimate by Imperial College in London. The average time from onset of illness to diagnosis was as long as twenty-three days. So China's official totals were lagging three weeks behind reality.

Shi Zhengli had come up with a test by 3 January, but the CDC barred her from obtaining more samples and testing them. According to a detailed report by the Associated Press, based on interviews with forty sources, China didn't want to set up an open collaboration mechanism for creating new tests. Instead, there was a secret evaluation of test kits on 10 January. After 12 January, the National Health Commission urged medical staff around the country to only use test kits from these three small Shanghai companies: GeneoDx Biotech, Huirui Biotechnology and BioGerm Medical Technology. Two days later, China's top health official, Ma Xiaowei, held an internal teleconference to order secret preparations for a pandemic. After that, the CDC started distributing CDC-sanctioned kits and relaxed the requirements needed to confirm cases. BioGerm began taking orders from provincial CDC staff across the country over WeChat.

The three obscure Shanghai companies chosen all had personal ties with the CDC—they had 'gone through the back door', as the Chinese say. In other words, Huiri, BioGerm and GeneoDx had paid the CDC for information and distribution rights. According to the Associated Press, they had paid one million RMB each. At the same time, the NHC tried to prevent other scientists and organisations from testing for the virus with their own homemade kits. Tan Wenjie, a CDC official originally in charge of training, was put in charge of developing test kits. He ensured that the three companies quickly received samples of the virus so they could sequence it.[1]

Next, Tan came up with test designs, and these were only given to these three Shanghai companies in a secret selection process. Other companies tried to get samples and create their own test recipes, but the CDC stymied these efforts.

CDC staff were told that, instead of testing and reporting cases by themselves, they had to send patient samples to designated labs in Beijing for full sequencing, a complicated and time-consuming procedure. Otherwise, the cases would not be counted in the national coronavirus tally. 'It was absolutely abnormal', a CDC lab technician said. 'They were totally trying to make it harder for us to report any confirmed cases.'

Wuhan hospitals also had to send virus samples just to these central labs. This further contributed to making testing requirements to confirm coronavirus cases much more complicated. The hospitals could only use the endorsed tests kits made by the three Shanghai companies. When the test kits arrived, it turned out that many didn't work properly, producing inconclusive test results or false negatives. Then the CDC hindered technicians from using tests kits from more established companies, even those that would be more accurate.

GeneoDx had fewer than one hundred employees at the time, compared to competitors who had thousands. It was a subsidiary of the giant SinoPharm Group, which had previously used imported kits and foreign technology to expand its business instead of developing its own products.

In October 2019, it had organised an internal CDC training programme on emerging respiratory diseases on behalf of Tan Wenjie, the CDC official who was then in charge of training. In November 2019, the company won a contract to sell test kits to the CDC. The next month it won a contract to sell test kits to Tan's institute.

The founder of BioGerm, Zhao Baihui, had left her job as the chief technician of Shanghai's CDC microbiology labs in 2017. In fact she had started the company while she was still officially working at the CDC in charge of purchasing. Over five years, she had sold kits to her own workplace using an intermediary. Next, she won contracts with Shanghai customs, where her husband worked, and another with the Shanghai CDC offices.

The third company was Huirui, whose founder, Li Hui, was a long-time associate of Tan Wenjie, the CDC official in charge of test kits. The two of them had co-authored a paper on coronavirus tests in 2012 and 'jointly developed' a test kit with the Shanghai CDC for the MERS outbreak in 2015.

After the first kits started arriving in Wuhan hospitals on 16 January, the kits supplied by GeneoDx kept showing inconclusive results, and eventually people stopped using them. Huirui kits performed just as badly. Only the BioGerm kits worked.

They were more dependable because they used chemicals from Invitrogen, a subsidiary of the US biotech giant Thermo Fisher. Huirui and GeneoDx used their own mixes of chemicals. In the meantime, bigger companies such as Chinese genetics giant BGI and Tianlong developed their own kits, which were more effective, but these weren't endorsed by the CDC. Other cities in Hubei didn't get any kits until 22 January.

By the end of the month, China's National Medical Products Administration approved test kits from seven companies, including BioGerm and GeneoDx, but not Huirui. After Wuhan was placed under lockdown, it became physically difficult to move the kits into Wuhan. On 26 January, the authorities set up a fast-track channel, but even so, in early February Wuhan was still struggling to meet demand.

This meant that many feverish residents, even though they had clear symptoms of a viral infection, had no choice but to try to recover on their own at home with the help of relatives. Sometimes they tested positive on later tests. Even when performed correctly, the throat-swab test is not very helpful, because it only picks up infections in the upper airways, but many patients had a viral infection in their chest. This can be investigated by inserting an endoscope (that is, a camera) into the lungs, but this is a difficult operation requiring a lot of expertise. Another option is to take lung scans, but these don't prove the presence of a coronavirus infection. It wasn't known if the new virus tends to infect the lower part of the lungs more often, as is the case with SARS, but it was common enough.

The lab tests analyse nucleic acids, that is, RNA, taken from either saliva or mucus in the nasal passages, and see if they match coronavirus strains. The RNA is converted to DNA and then bits are amplified using PCR (polymerise chain reaction) with COVID-19 specific primers. If a patient is actively infected with the virus, then its RNA material will show up. The computerised tomography screening method (CT scans) can show if fluid has entered the lungs, but it can't prove that this is due to a COVID-19 infection. It could be viral pneumonia, for instance, or bacterial pneumonia. Not all people infected with the COVID-19 virus have abnormal CT lung scans.

In the closing months of 2019, Hubei was in the midst of an unusual winter flu epidemic. There were twenty times the normal flu cases being reported in the towns of Yichang and Xianning. Wuhan was the third worst infected city. A large number of flu cases, including in Wuhan, were diagnosed as 'unknown cause'. There is no knowing how many of these might have been COVID-19 cases.

Since it was so difficult and time consuming to establish if a patient was infected, the hospitals struggled to deal with sick people queuing for a test or waiting to hear the result. Many had to keep coming back again and again. In the meantime, they stayed at home and infected other family members.

The hospitals and labs lacked qualified and trained staff, and those that were available soon became overworked. Very few patients were admitted for treatment, and even if they were hospitalized in an isolation ward, the medical staff had little idea how to treat them. The last thing the hospitals wanted to do was to become overloaded with cases. They didn't have enough beds or protective clothing. At the same time, many families couldn't afford hospital treatment, which often has to be paid for in advance. If there was no positive test result, then a few days' hospital treatment could cost 10,000 RMB—equal to a month's wages for a low-income family. However, if someone did test positive, then they were entitled to government subsidies.

It is quite hard, therefore, to make much sense of the statistics that China reported. Without a test result, doctors marked down patients as 'suspected' or 'clinically diagnosed'. It was only in mid-February that the Chinese started adding 'clinically diagnosed' cases to its total. On 12 February, China released data showing 15,000 newly confirmed cases of infections, mostly in Hubei, more than five times the number of cases in the previous day's report. The Chinese magazine *Caixin* reported that this jump was due to Chinese officials revising the diagnostic criteria for confirming infections. The new criteria allowed doctors in Hubei to use clinical CT screening alone to confirm infections, instead of waiting for confirmation from the lab test.

If a patient died, the only real way to identify the main cause of death was to perform an autopsy, an expensive and time-consuming process that, in these circumstances, would have to be done with maximum precautions. If there was no autopsy, then it was entirely at the discretion of the hospital to record which of the patients had died of the new virus. There are precedents, such as during the Great Leap Forward famine (1958–62), when doctors were ordered not to record deaths from starvation. It is quite common in China for both officials and businessmen to keep two sets of accounts, one for public show, the other for internal use.

After the Wuhan lockdown ended, China claimed that it only experienced 5,117 cases and 4,641 official deaths from COVID-19 for the whole country of nearly 1.4 billion. The low official figures that China reported, especially in the first weeks, influenced the attitude of other governments, who then assumed it was not very contagious and unlikely to spread rapidly to their countries. This idea was reinforced by the WHO as well as by the Chinese government.

According to internal documents obtained by CNN from sources in the Hubei CDC, the authorities in China deliberately sought to hide what was going on. They declared that there were only forty-four cases in 2019, but had actually recorded 200. On 10 February, they declared 2,478 new cases, but the leaked data shows that on the same date Hubei actually logged

5,918 cases. Another report records the deaths of six healthcare workers by 10 February, but these were never publicly disclosed. On 17 February, Hubei reported ninety-three deaths, but the actual toll was 196. Then on 7 March, Hubei reported a cumulative death toll of 2,986—but documents showed that it actually stood at 3,456.[2]

The Chinese government quarantined the entire city of Wuhan on 23 January, just before Chinese New Year. In the zodiac calendar, it was the start of the Year of the Rat. The lunar holiday festivities start on 24 January and last fifteen days, culminating with the Lantern Festival. In the countryside, it is a season when no farm work is done. People mostly just sit around at home, visit relatives, and eat large banquets such as dumplings. In the old days, they would attend temple fairs or the opera house. These days, hundreds of millions of peasants have left their villages to work in factories or on building sites, where they are usually housed ten to a room in dormitories. Some may not have left their home province, but vast numbers need to travel across the country on planes, long-distance trains and coaches. The cost and difficulty of getting home means that many factories decide to close down for a whole month to make this difficult journey worthwhile for their staff. It is often the only time of the year when families can spend time together, since the wife and husband may be working in places far apart. Their parents are left to do some farming and look after the grandchildren.

In the run-up to the Spring Festival, people were in a mad rush to travel home in time, and they crowded into shops to buy gifts and to stock up on food for the celebrations. Millions were leaving Wuhan and its industrial suburbs to get back to see their families in villages and small towns around Hubei. As Wuhan is a major transportation hub in the centre of the country, huge numbers would also have passed through by train, bus or car, on their way to somewhere else. Speaking to reporters a few days after the city was put under quarantine, the mayor estimated that five million people had already left.

Travel data from the Chinese tech giant Baidu shows that in the fortnight before the lockdown, nearly 70 per cent of trips out of Wuhan were within Hubei province. As the Associated Press reported, another 14 per cent of trips were to neighbouring Henan, Hunan, Anhui and Jiangxi provinces. About 2 per cent travelled south, to Guangdong province, and the rest fanned out across China. The cities outside Hubei province that were listed as the top destinations were Chongqing, Beijing and Shanghai.[3]

Baidu gathers travel data based on more than 120 billion daily location requests from its map app and other apps that use Baidu's location services. Only data from users who agree to share their location is recorded and the company says data is masked to protect privacy. Baidu's publicly available data shows proportional travel, not absolute numbers of recorded trips, and does not include trips by people who don't use mobile phones or apps that rely on Baidu's popular location services.

At 2 am on 23 January, authorities issued a notice informing residents of Wuhan that from 10 am, all public transport, including buses, railways, flights and ferry services would be suspended. The last trains left Wuhan the morning of 23 January, and about 300,000 people were reported to have left Wuhan by train alone before the 10 am lockdown. It cut off a surge of outbound travel that had begun three days earlier, Baidu data shows. Nearby cities rushed to impose travel restrictions of their own. From 23 to 26 January, the fifteen cities that Baidu data shows received the most travellers from Wuhan—a combined 70 per cent—all imposed some level of travel restrictions. Other nations quickly followed suit, including the United States, Australia, Singapore, New Zealand and the Philippines, all of which sharply restricted entry for people coming from China. Others, like Italy and Indonesia, barred flights.

In recent years, wealthier Chinese have started flying abroad to take their Chinese New Year holiday in a beach resort or a tourist city. The top ten global destinations are Thailand, Japan, Hong Kong, Taiwan, South Korea, the United States, Malaysia, Singapore, Vietnam and Australia. It is reckoned that before the lockdown, around half a million people may have taken flights out of Wuhan.

One interesting anomaly is that the data from Zhejiang province, which is not normally a top destination from Wuhan, also recorded a very high number of cases. About 200,000 people went back to Zhejiang for Chinese New Year, and the first official case reported was on 21 January. There is probably a strong link between infections in Zhejiang and Italy. The worst affected city in Zhejiang was Wenzhou, which was eventually placed under a particularly tough lockdown. Wenzhou is famous for its small private companies making shoes, haberdashery, apparel and accessories. Most of the 320,000 Chinese living in Italy come from Wenzhou, and mostly live in the Milan region and around Prato (an estimated 50,000, or a third of the population). They run businesses importing cheap fabric from China and quickly turning them into high fashion garments and sometimes handbags, which can then be sold with a 'made in Italy' label. They live and work in workshops, putting in fifteen-hour days. Most of them are illegal immigrants, so there is an incentive to avoid recording deaths and burials even of those with proper papers.

The connections with Milan are so strong that there are direct flights between Wenzhou and Milan. It is thought likely that someone from Wenzhou, a super spreader, brought the virus to Milan and the nearby city of Bergamo, which quickly became the most infected city in Italy, and indeed in Europe. Footage of the dying patients in overwhelmed hospitals in Lombardy and the mounting death toll—over 3,000—shocked viewers around the world. Military trucks had to transport bodies to a neighbouring region for cremation.

The spread of the virus may well have been accelerated by the unusual success of the local soccer team, Atalanta. Despite being a small city of just 120,000, the team staged an improbable success when it reached its first ever Champion's League knock-out match against Spain's Valencia. As their home venue was being renovated, 44,000 supporters banded together to travel to Milan and cheer their team on at Milan's famous Stadio San Siro. After they defeated Valencia 4–1, they all celebrated the unlikely, giant-killing triumph together, but unwittingly setting in motion a rapid chain of infections. Valencia fans brought the virus back to Spain.

Within ten days of Wuhan's quarantine, the virus had spread to more than two dozen countries; nine of the ten countries with the most flight connections to at-risk mainland cities also had the highest numbers of confirmed cases, mostly afflicting people who had been in China. It was therefore not surprising that the first case of the virus outside China was reported on 13 January in Thailand, the most popular holiday destination for that time of year.

In other ways, the coincidence of the dates of the New Year Holiday made the management of the crisis a little easier. The Chinese government could simply extend the holiday and keep people at home with their families, rather than have them encounter strangers on public transport or at work places. In Wuhan, they locked down for seventy-six days, after which the highway tollroads reopened, and flights and train services once again began leaving the city. Residents could leave provided they were able to prove they were virus-free. To begin with, people were allowed out to shop for food, but by mid-February, nobody was allowed to leave their residential compounds.

On 1 February, ten days after Wuhan's lockdown, the health authorities launched a more intrusive testing and quarantine system. The government ordered anyone who tested positive into temporary field hospitals, called *Fangcang*. These were created in stadiums and convention centres. It gave the doctors and nurses the opportunity to triage patients. Some were kept behind for further monitoring, and others were immediately sent for intensive care. Severe and critical cases made it to hospitals with intensive care units. Sometimes, those who tested positive and had symptoms were sent to stay in special hotels—in particular, close contacts of confirmed or suspected cases were despatched to live in hotels or college dorms.

The city opened three *Fangcang* shelter hospitals on 5 February 2020, which provided an extra 4,000 beds. Over the following weeks, Wuhan opened an additional thirteen *Fangcang* shelter hospitals, providing 9,000 more beds. The first of these closed on 1 March 2020, and by 10 March, all *Fangcang* shelter hospitals had been suspended. At the peak, about 12,000 patients were being cared for.

The media reported that an extra 40,000 medical professionals were sent to Wuhan, mostly army medical staff. Two new hospitals were built, Huoshenshan Hospital next to the Wuhan Workers' Sanatorium, and Leishenshan Hospital, next to the village which housed the athletes who attended the Wuhan Military Games—both within a fortnight, which was achieved by employing shifts working round the clock. The hospitals were modelled on the Xiaotangshan Hospital in a suburb of Beijing, which had been built in seven days during the 2003 SARS epidemic. These new hospitals were each supposed to house 1,000 patients and were staffed by PLA medical personnel. China also put up sixteen temporary hospitals, mostly by converting stadiums and convention centres.

The wearing of masks became compulsory, and the state ordered factories making cars or electronics to switch to manufacturing masks. This quadrupled mask production to over 100 million a day. China, which was the largest PPE exporter before the pandemic, now made almost half the world's supply of face masks, protective gowns, gloves and goggles. In January and February, its exports fell by 15 per cent as the government prevented consignments from leaving the country.

In January 2020, the Wuhan Institute of Virology filed for a patent covering the use of remdesivir, an experimental antiviral drug for the treatment of COVID-19, which had been produced by Gilead Sciences, a California-based pharmaceutical company, as a treatment for Ebola. Gilead had filed patent applications at several patent offices, including in China. The decision to claim rights over an unproven use of the drug was heavily criticised. The WIV's first *in vitro* studies suggesting that both remdesivir and an antimalarial drug called chloroquine could effectively inhibit COVID-19 were published in early February 2020. The Suzhou-based company BrightGene Bio-Medical Technology synthesised remdesivir's active ingredient without first obtaining permission from the patent holder. Though the company claimed it was interested in setting up a voluntary licensing agreement with Gilead at some point in the future, it also stated that its work did not infringe on the company's patent rights, because the final product was not being sold on the market.

The state expanded its already powerful surveillance system. Alibaba's payments app, AliPay, created a health code status that flashed red, yellow or green based on self-reported health data and travel history. Before anyone could enter a shop or use public transport, the app had to show a green code. Many buildings were equipped with a camera that scans everyone's infrared signal at the entrance. Mapping services directed people to the nearest hospital handling coronavirus cases. Mobile phone messages instructed people to go for testing or to stay at home. Towards the end, the state allowed some people to leave their residential compounds on a limited basis, and residents with green 'health codes' and documents from their employers were gradually able to return to work. The health code allowed other people to check the colours of other residents when their ID numbers were entered. Malls and restaurants required visitors to scan a QR code, so that all movements could be recorded. The official state news agency, *Xinhua*, told citizens that those who violated virus prevention and control measures could be subject to three years in prison, and up to seven for particularly serious cases, in accordance with China's criminal code.

The central government helped make it possible to order food and goods for home delivery. Many people didn't leave their flats for six weeks. Couriers dropped off meals and packages at the entrance of the apartment compound. Meituan-Dianping, one of the main food-delivery apps, even attached the temperature reading of the cook and the courier on their delivery bags. The government media reported how the state released 300,000 tons of pork from its strategic pork reserves to keep prices down. It diverted and requisitioned trucks once used to deliver electronic goods to ensure that there was enough transport available to deliver vegetables to everybody who needed them.

Many places in Hubei and the rest of the country issued an order allowing only one person from each household to go outside for provisions once every two days, except for medical reasons, or to work at shops or pharmacies. The neighbourhood control system sprang back into life. Everywhere there were guards sitting outside residential compounds recording movements with pen and paper on top of the electronic surveillance. Sometimes, this was monitored through the allocation of exit vouchers. In most of the residential units or villages, only one entrance and exit point were kept open and each household was only permitted so many entrances and exits. Many places effectively ordered a night-time curfew. At all times people entering and leaving were required to wear masks and have their temperatures taken. The extensive system of facial recognition monitoring cameras was rendered useless because everyone wore masks. There are some 350 million surveillance cameras operating in China. Soon, a Wuhan company, Hanwang Technology Ltd, announced that it had developed new software that could identify people 95 per cent of the time even when they were wearing a full facial mask.

In Beijing and other cities the quarantine lasted for two months. Anyone who entered Beijing was required to self-quarantine for fourteen days, enforced by the new residential security guards. Anyone who returned from outside the city might have a sticker posted on their apartment, implicitly encouraging neighbours to check that they weren't out and about. After mid-March, everyone flying into Beijing from abroad had to quarantine in designated hotels at their own expense. Subsequently, the country suspended entry of nearly all foreigners, a restriction that was not lifted until the last weeks of the year.

Wuhan came close to declaring a victory on 10 March, when President Xi made a trip to Wuhan. On the same day, the city announced the closure of all sixteen temporary hospitals. And in late March, Hubei announced that it would allow residents of Wuhan to leave, so long as they tested negative. China reported just twenty new confirmed cases on 10 March, seventeen of them in Hubei province, and the other three in Beijing, Guangdong and Hong Kong.

'Hubei and Wuhan have been the decisive battleground in this struggle to contain the epidemic', Xi said. 'Through hard work, there has been a promising turn in epidemic containment in Hubei and Wuhan, and we've achieved important interim results.'

But he warned: 'This is a critical moment, and you must clench your teeth and hang on. Don't drop your guard, don't relax. Pay attention to every detail of prevention and control.' China's leader said the coronavirus had been 'basically curbed' in Wuhan and the surrounding Hubei province, and declared that China had succeeded in stabilizing the situation and in 'turning the tide'.

He called Wuhan a 'city of heroes', and he walked around waving to people looking out of their apartment windows. Photos on social media claimed to show two policemen entering these apartments before Xi arrived and giving orders not to make trouble. A week earlier, residents had stood on their balconies to heckle the vice premier Sun Chunlan as she inspected a residential compound to look at delivery arrangements. 'Fake! It's all fake!' they shouted.

Xi also visited Huoshenshan, one of the hospitals that was rapidly constructed to tackle the outbreak. He was shown on TV wearing an N95 mask in a large room flanked by military and party officials. He stood several feet away from a large digital screen, and spoke to a coronavirus patient through video chat. 'Now what you must do is fortify your faith. We will definitely win this battle. Wuhan must be victorious, Hubei must be victorious, and all of China must be victorious', he said, pumping a clenched fist. He also spoke to medical workers through the screen. Medical workers are 'the most beautiful angels' and 'messengers of light and hope'. The frontline medical workers have taken on the most arduous missions, and they are 'the most admirable people in the new era' who deserve the highest commendations, President Xi said.

'There's no way to describe the kind of anger in our hearts', said a Wuhan resident, a businessman living close to the compound Xi was inspecting, who spoke to the *Los Angeles Times* on condition of anonymity. He couldn't verify what was happening in the neighbouring compound, he said, because, like most other Wuhan residents, he'd been unable to leave his apartment for more than forty days.[4]

'I have many relatives and friends around me who were infected. Many elderly people, my friends, aunts and uncles, have died.

Entire families have gone extinct', he told the *Los Angeles Times*. 'All this is because of the doctors who were silenced and punished after speaking up. That allowed this virus to transmit to the whole world. But we Wuhan people have suffered the most.'

The source complained that food prices had shot up since the crisis started although the government said that there was a national effort to deliver extra supplies of essentials to those trapped in the city. When residents tried to complain or to organize their own efforts to help their neighbours, the police threatened them. When he had tried to organize volunteer efforts from neighbouring Hunan province, the state security had called him and told him to stop speaking up. 'I tell them, you should first take care of the alone, the poor, the elderly... They die at home and nobody knows,' the source said. The source also disparaged Xi Jinping's visit as a 'performance' and said: 'He's living in a world of total separation from the people.'

The official data released from Wuhan showed that the number of cases peaked in a sharp spike between 8 and 16 February with 4,000 cases. According to the National Health Commission, nearly 58,000 people were discharged from hospitals in Hubei Province and 2,579 people had died, out of a population of 11 million. This figure was raised to 3,869 in mid-April.

From mid-March, the number of new infections in Wuhan stayed below a dozen patients a day. The official figures also show that very few people under the age of fifty died in Wuhan, just as has happened elsewhere. A local doctor working at a quarantine facility told *Kyodo News* that the data on the number of coronavirus patients in Wuhan was manipulated in time for President Xi Jinping's visit. The authorities suddenly released a lot of symptomatic patients from quarantine and stopped some of the testing in order to show that Xi's policies were working and successfully bringing the outbreak under control. The National Health Commission rules require patients provide two negative tests and CT scan for pneumonia before discharging a patient. Yet before the visit the doctor said patients were released just on the say so of a "specialist" from the epidemic prevention and control authority. After the rules were relaxed "a mass release" of infected patients began, the Japanese news agency reported. The testing of suspected cases was also changed to make it easier to discharge patients.[5]

The authorities changed the definitions for determining a case of virus death at least three times, and the official figures are hard to understand. They seemed unbelievably small. Around 64,000 Chinese die every year from traffic accidents. A study published in the *Lancet* found a mean average of 88,000 influenza-associated excess respiratory deaths for the whole of China. A million people die from smoking related deaths per year. Three million from cancer.[6]

American researchers tried to come up with more realistic figures by examining the activity of crematoriums in Wuhan. They found that the city may have been burning between 800 and 2,000 bodies every day by the second week of February, when the official death toll for the whole of China was only around 700. They found reports of eighty-six Wuhan crematoriums operating twenty-four hours a day at full capacity, raising suspicions that the number of people dying was more than just hundreds. Funeral homes were also buying thousands of urns for ashes, giving an estimate of around 36,000 people who died in Wuhan by mid-March. The official number for all China at the time was 2,524. The study was carried out by the University of Washington, Ohio State University, and the US communications company AT&T. It was led by Dr Mai He, a pathologist at Washington, and was based mostly on media reports rather than on scientific data. It was published on medRXiv.

The study calculated that all crematoriums in Wuhan—of which they found seven, with eighty-six furnaces between them—would normally burn around 136 bodies per day and would operate for four hours. But in February, operating hours were scaled up to twenty-four hours a day, and crematorium staff were drafted in from other cities. This increased rate of burning—combined with measures that cut the cremation time in half, to one hour per person—brought the numbers up to between 680 to 2,000 extra bodies per day. By 23 March, 36,720 people could have died and been cremated in Wuhan, the researchers calculated. Their figure lined up with reports of funeral homes in the city buying up urns. A report from *Newsweek* in late March, the study said, revealed that a single crematorium had bought 5,000 extra urns. This would have been enough to handle the remains of all Wuhan's coronavirus victims (2,524) twice over, and more than enough to handle all the COVID-19 deaths reported by that date in the whole of China (3,277). Applied city-wide—multiplying those 5,000 extra urns for each of the seven crematoriums—the increasing demand for urns suggested the death toll was significantly higher than data let on. The estimates of 35–36,000, the researchers said, did not take into account the fact that forty mobile crematoriums had been set up in the city during the epidemic. Those mobile services were capable of destroying up to five tonnes of 'medical waste' every day, they said, and concluded that 'the calculations here could be significant underestimates'.

Two separate studies that involved antibody testing for COVID-19 suggest that more than 3 per cent of people in Wuhan—a city of 11 million—may have previously had infections, possibly with no or very mild symptoms. One team of Chinese scientists tested 17,368 people in Wuhan—where the first cases were reported in December—and other cities in China from 9 March to 10 April, aiming to assess how prevalent the disease had been. The antibody tests check the blood for immune-system markers that indicate that a person has been infected by the virus and fought it off. The proportion of people with antibodies is considerably higher than that of confirmed cases, suggesting that many people here were infected without realizing it, developed mild or no symptoms, and could now be immune.

The bad news is that the number of those with antibodies still falls far short of herd immunity—levels above 50 per cent are typically needed for the virus to be suppressed. And there could still be thousands of unidentified asymptomatic cases. Wuhan's Zhongnan Hospital found that 2.4 per cent of its employees and 2 to 3 per cent of recent patients and other visitors, including people tested before returning to work, had developed antibodies, according to senior doctors there. It involved testing 3,600 healthy employees, including security guards and cleaners as well as doctors and nurses. They also tested about 5,000 visitors, including people who were required to take the tests before being allowed to return to work or leave Wuhan. Only two of the hospital workers were found to still be infected with the virus, and both were asymptomatic. The results showing that more than 2 per cent of both groups had antibodies suggest that the virus might have spread much further than indicated by China's official figures: Wuhan accounts for 50,008 confirmed cases, or about 0.45 per cent of its population, according to the local government.

Doctors in Wuhan have reported several cases in which people who became sick with the virus recovered and tested negative, only to test positive again later. While some suspect that this may be due to flawed test results, others remain concerned about the potential for reinfection. Of 143,056 people tested before going back to work between 29 March and 10 April, the local government says that 113—or 0.08 per cent—were found to be still carrying the virus. Almost all of them were asymptomatic.

However, as the next chapter explains, the public's perception of the death toll in Wuhan is something quite different from the actual figures.

19

CHINA AND THE WORLD HEALTH
ORGANISATION

The WHO first heard about what was going on in Wuhan on 31 December from an email alert from software which scours the internet and flags reports on disease outbreaks. The next day, it asked the Chinese government for more information. Under WHO regulations, members are obliged to respond in twenty-four to forty-eight hours. China did respond two days later, and reported that there were forty-four cases linked to an unknown pneumonia and no deaths in Wuhan.

It took another month for the WHO to declare a global pandemic, which it did on 30 January, and by that time the virus had spread across China and the rest of the world. The number of cases increased by a factor of 100 or possibly 200. WHO experts were slow to accept that the virus could be airborne and encouraged international travel as usual. Throughout the period, it praised China for its speedy response and its commitment to transparency.

Behind the scenes, its officials based in Geneva and its regional offices were very frustrated. They quickly realised that China was not being transparent, that the threat was serious, and that many Chinese scientists wanted to be more open. Yet China hid what was going on and would only cooperate on its own terms. China's priority was to remain in full control, and perhaps it wanted to buy time in order to shirk its responsibility and avoid blame.

The WHO could have shamed China by going public, but the institution had by then already been compromised by the numerous concessions it had already made to Beijing. These had ratcheted up over the past fifteen years. The WHO relies on the good will of member states because it has no enforcement powers and cannot independently investigate epidemics in any particular country. It calculated that if it continued to acquiesce, it would at least get some cooperation from China and retain a role. As China was the origin of so many veterinary and animal diseases, the WHO was desperate to avoid the risk of being shut out of China.

If the WHO had been more confrontational, it could have triggered the far worse situation of not getting any information at all, according to Ali Mokdad, a professor at the Institute of Health and Evaluation at the University of Washington, quoted by the Associated Press.[1]

'If the WHO had pushed too hard, it could even have kicked WHO out of China', concurred another expert, Adam Kamradt-Scott, a global health professor at the University of Sydney.

As it turned out, events in China followed a pattern familiar to those with a long experience of the country. It would start with a summit meeting between a top Chinese leader and the head of some organisation such as a UN agency or a multinational company. There would be pledges of open cooperation, friendship and mutual cooperation. The foreign dignitary would be feted and praised as an old friend of China. Yet then the executive staff posted to implement the project would arrive in China and struggle to get their job done according to the normal procedures followed everywhere else in the world.

If the foreign executive kicked up a fuss, he would often be replaced. His superior would suspect that it must be the executive's fault that things had not worked out, since he himself had received such a warm reception. Most executives, for whom this was only a temporary posting anyway, would choose to make a steady retreat and accede to China's demands. UN staffers and business executives posted to Beijing would wryly refer to this as becoming 'house trained'.

Sometimes matters did reach crisis point. There would be some incident where China would be openly accused of breaching international laws or norms. These often related to large World Bank projects, international sports events like the Olympics, breaches of labour standards or incidents of political repression where clearly something more had to be done. China might then reluctantly agree to show foreign journalists around, or possibly foreign diplomats, or even agree to host an investigation by a panel of international experts. Then China would ensure it would carefully vet and control the participants, determine who could be interviewed, what travel was permitted, and so on. The CCP has been successfully stage-managing this sort of thing since the 1950s. The techniques were largely borrowed from the Soviet Union, when during the 1930s Stalin invited 30,000 foreign intellectuals to inspect the achievements of his first five-year plan. Visitors would be shepherded around a model farm, factory, or prison and often meet officials who dressed up as prisoners or peasants to fool the visitors who, anxious not to offend their hosts, invariably put aside any doubts or misgivings.

After China emerged out of its self-imposed isolation, it went through a phase of becoming much more accommodating as it sought access to international capital from multilateral institutions and global companies, as well as to learn from the outside world. Relations with the World Bank were so important that it became by far and away the Bank's largest and most prized customer. As such the World Bank made an exception of China and permitted Beijing to flout regulations, such as those requiring public consultation on large infrastructure projects, rules for open procurement, or treatment of minorities. It endorsed China's dubious statistics, which the World Bank presented as its own. This gave China's manipulated data a patina of credibility that they might otherwise not merit. It showered praise on China, but it also managed to get a great deal done, because China often heeded its advice.

In recent years, however, Beijing's relations with multilateral organisations have changed. It has set out to bend UN institutions to its will by dint of its sheer size and by the number of officials and professionals it could get appointed to leading positions. Beijing pushed its civil servants, or those of clients and partners, to the helm of UN institutions that set global standards for air travel, telecommunications and agriculture. Gaining influence at the UN has helped China to stifle international scrutiny of its behaviour both at home and abroad. In March, Beijing won a seat on a five-member panel that selects UN rapporteurs on human-rights abuses which had previously targeted Beijing for imprisoning more than a million Uighurs in camps in Xinjiang. Out of the UN's fifteen specialized agencies and groups, Chinese representatives now lead four, and only a concerted campaign by the US and partners defeated a Chinese effort to take over the leadership of a fifth, the World Intellectual Property Organization, known as WIPO.

No other nation has its citizens running more than one UN agency. It puts Beijing in a strong position to shape international norms and standards. For instance, the Chinese secretary-general of the International Telecommunication Union backed Huawei Technologies Co. in its fight with the US, and pushed for a new internet protocol that Western governments say would allow more surveillance and censorship. China has also co-opted the

UN to join China's Belt and Road Initiative. The UN Secretary-General Antonio Guterres has said that the Belt and Road Initiative is 'intrinsically linked' to the UN's sustainable development goals. All fifteen of the UN agencies as well as the World Bank and the International Monetary Fund have signed up for it.

China has increasingly wielded its clout at the World Trade Organization, leading its critics to claim that its mercantilist policies, its abuse of intellectual property rights, its complicated system of subsidies, its huge CO_2 emissions and its unmerited status as a developing country are undermining the global trading system. China is, of course, large enough to strike out on its own and to set up a rival system. This is what it did with the internet when it set up its Great Firewall and developed its own social media and mobile phone platforms. It could conceivably, too, move away from a global trading system based on the US Dollar and effectively split the world and create its own RMB-based field of influence.

As the COVID-19 crisis deepened, the WHO rapidly became another front in a much bigger battle for global influence fought between two elephants—Washington and Beijing. The Europeans and others opted to say little in public. When faced with a prospect of offending China or meeting the expectations of its largest donors, the WHO struggled and ultimately failed to walk the fine line.

The WHO chose to portray China in the best possible light in the hopes of securing more information. It repeatedly thanked the Chinese government for sharing the genome 'immediately', and declared that its work and commitment to transparency were 'very impressive, and beyond words'. Yet amongst themselves they took a different view.

The genome of the virus was decided on 2 January. A delay of just a few days in releasing genetic sequences can be critical, and as they waited, WHO staffers debated on how to press China for more information and detailed patient data without angering the Chinese state. On 8 January, the *Wall Street Journal* reported that scientists had identified a new coronavirus from pneumonia patients in Wuhan, pre-empting and embarrassing Chinese officials and WHO officials. Dr Tom Grein, chief of WHO's acute events management team, was quoted by the Associated Press as saying in internal reports that the agency looked 'doubly, incredibly stupid'. Maria van Kerkhove, an American epidemiologist, said that the WHO was already late and told colleagues that it was critical to push China.

In the second week of January, the WHO's chief of emergencies, Dr Michael Ryan, told colleagues that it was time to 'shift gears' and apply more pressure on China, fearing a repeat of SARS: 'This is exactly the same scenario, endlessly trying to get updates from China about what is going on', he said according to documents seen by the Associated Press. 'The WHO barely got out of that one with its neck intact given the issues that arose from transparency in southern China.'

'The fact is we're two or three weeks into an event, we don't have a laboratory diagnosis, we don't have an age, sex or geographical distribution, we don't have an epi curve', Ryan complained, referring to the standard graphic of outbreaks scientists use to show how an epidemic is progressing.

Ryan said the best way to 'protect China' from possible action by other countries was for the WHO to do its own independent analysis with data from the Chinese government on whether the virus could easily spread between people. China simply was not cooperating in the same way some other countries had in the past.

'This would not happen in Congo and did not happen in Congo and other places', he was quoted as saying, referring to the 2018 Ebola crisis. 'We need to see the data [...] It's absolutely important at this point.'

'We are going on very minimal information,' admitted Maria Van Kerkhove in one internal meeting. 'It's clearly not enough for you to do proper planning.' They desperately needed to know how efficiently it spread between people.

'We are currently at the stage where yes, they've giving it to us 15 minutes before it appears on CCTV', said chief China representative Dr Gauden Galea. 'We have informally and formally been requesting more epidemiological information but when asked for specifics we could get nothing.'[2]

The WHO officials heard many reports suggesting the worst. Beijing officials were reportedly so alarmed that they considered locking the capital down.

Ryan grumbled that, since China was providing the minimal information as required by international law, the WHO couldn't do much. He also noted that the previous September, the WHO had issued an unusual rebuke to Tanzania for not providing enough details about an Ebola outbreak. 'We have to be consistent', Ryan said. 'The danger now is that despite our good intent [...] especially if something does happen, there will be a lot of finger-pointing at WHO.'

Ryan noted that China could make a huge 'contribution' to the world by sharing the genetic material immediately, because otherwise 'other countries will have to reinvent the wheel over the coming days.'

The WHO is required to quickly share information and alerts with member countries. Yet China insisted that it first be consulted and agree what information could be shared with other countries. It was difficult to get live samples of the virus and transfers were delayed by the bureaucratic hold ups involved in negotiating a Material Transfer Agreement. The most frustrating period came after the genome was sequenced. The infectious disease expert John Mackenzie, who served on the WHO emergency committee, praised the speed in sequencing it, but once the central authorities got involved, detailed data trickled to a halt.

'There certainly was a kind of blank period', Mackenzie said. 'There had to be human to human transmission. You know, it's staring at you in the face [...] I would have thought they would have been much more open at that stage.'

The Associated Press reported in April 2020, based on internal documents, that top Chinese officials had determined that they were facing a pandemic from a new coronavirus on 13 January well before warning the public. The National Health Commission sat on the data even as the number of patients in Wuhan tripled to 3,000 people. On 14 January, China's top official ordered the country to prepare for a pandemic, calling the outbreak the 'most severe challenge since SARS in 2003'. Chinese CDC staff began screening, isolating and testing for cases, turning up hundreds across the country. They internally declared a level-one emergency, the highest level possible, but to the outside, Chinese officials continued to say that the chance of sustained transmission between humans was low.[3]

In public WHO officials didn't know what to say. Van Kerkhove stated in a press briefing that it 'it is certainly possible there is limited human-to-human transmission.' But hours later on 14 January, the WHO seemed to backtrack, and tweeted that 'preliminary investigations conducted by the Chinese authorities have found no clear evidence of human-to-human transmissions'.

A top official in WHO's Asia office, Dr Liu Yunguo, who had studied medicine in Wuhan, flew to Beijing to make direct, informal contact with Chinese officials. A former fellow student working in Wuhan told him that pneumonia patients were flooding the city's hospitals. Liu pushed for more experts to be allowed to visit the city, and they finally got permission to send a small team, led by Galea, to Wuhan for two days. They were not allowed to go to the market, but they could go to the largest hospital for infectious diseases, where they heard about a worrying cluster of cases among more than a dozen doctors and nurses. Yet they were not given any 'transmission trees' showing that the cases were connected. No one explained how widely it was spreading and who was most at risk. Galea said that the Chinese talked openly and consistently about human-to-human transmission and that there was a debate about whether or not it was sustained. He reported to colleagues in Manila and Geneva that China's key request to the WHO was for help 'in communicating this to the public, without causing panic'.

Public confirmation of the human-to-human transmission did not emerge from the health ministry until 19 January. The next day Zhong Nanshan, the famous virologist and leader of the expert team returning from Wuhan, declared publicly for the first time that the new virus was spreading between people.

On 22 January, the WHO convened an independent committee to determine whether to declare a global health emergency. After two inconclusive meetings in which the experts' opinion was split, they decided against it—just as Chinese officials ordered Wuhan sealed in the biggest quarantine in history. China presented data to the committee, portraying the situation as under control.

In Geneva, China's ambassador lobbied the committee to reject the resolution and warned that his country would view a declaration of an emergency as an unfriendly act and a vote of no confidence. Half the committee voted against declaring an emergency. A German intelligence report claimed that President Xi Jinping had personally asked WHO Director General Tedros Adhanom Ghebreyesus to withhold information about human-to-human transmission and to delay a pandemic warning.

The next day, Tedros described the spread of the new coronavirus as 'limited'. Tedros publicly praised both Xi and China's pneumonia surveillance system: 'It was that system that caught this event', he said during a news conference.

Dr Tedros, an engaging man who calls leaders and diplomats 'my brother', had taken over in 2017 after the WHO's botched response to an Ebola outbreak in West Africa. He trained as a microbiologist before becoming health minister and then foreign minister of Ethiopia. Tedros had started out as a member of the Dergue, the Marxist military Junta that ruled Ethiopia 1974–87 and who were strong admirers of Mao, although they were allied with the Soviet Union. More recently, China has channelled billions of dollars into Ethiopia. Washington turned against him, claiming that he was in China's pocket and owed his job to intense lobbying by China.

Tedros' attitude to China was contrasted with that of his predecessor, Gro Harlem Brundtland, who, after China hid the SARS outbreak for months and ignored WHO requests for information, did finally come out with criticism and attempted to coax China into cooperating. Tedros tried to flatter the Chinese leader into being more cooperative by repeatedly and ostentatiously praising Xi. At one point, Tedros said that China had agreed to share samples that had been taken early on at the seafood market as well as from patients, but nothing came of this.

On 28 January, Tedros and other top experts, including Ryan, made an extraordinary trip to Beijing for an audience with president Xi. It was a highly unusual move. The men were photographed seated on the usual armchairs in the Great Hall of the Peoples in front of a huge mural, but sitting far apart from each other. On his return to Geneva the next day, Tedros praised Xi's leadership, saying he was 'very encouraged and impressed by the president's detailed knowledge of the outbreak'. The WHO chief added that China was 'completely committed to transparency, both internally and externally'.

'We should have actually expressed our respect and gratitude to China for what it's doing. It has already done incredible things to limit the transmission of the virus to other countries', he said. Tedros would later say that Beijing set 'a new standard for outbreak response'.

'I will praise China again and again because its actions actually helped in reducing the spread of the coronavirus to other countries [...] We should tell the truth', he said.

Tedros's staff had prepared a list of requests for information, and while Xi did not really welcome the suggestion that China needed help, he consented to let a WHO mission evaluate the situation 'objectively, fairly, calmly, and rationally [...] The epidemic is the devil, and we cannot let the devil hide.'

On 30 January, the WHO finally declared an international health emergency. Once again Tedros heaped praise and thanked China, saying nothing about the earlier lack of cooperation. Nearly every member of the WHO committee voted for it, apart from the Chinese delegate. The WHO resolution insisted that the WHO mission should 'review and support efforts to investigate the animal source' theory. A week later two WHO experts arrived in Beijing to negotiate the mission, and it turned out there was no question of securing a visit to Wuhan, let alone a visit to the WIV lab. The mission ranked finding animal hosts as one of its top tasks. It would also avoid investigating China's earlier response to the crisis.

Once in China, the mission managed to persuade the Chinese to let them go to Wuhan. It was under lockdown, but they boarded a special train with three Chinese scientists. They stayed for about a day and visited two hospitals. They did not go to the market.

The next task was to write a report about their mission. This involved a group of twenty-five people who took three days to parse every word. The Chinese members wanted to take out anything critical of China and insisted on personally crediting Xi Jinping for directing the prevention and control response.

'It was an absolute whitewash', said Lawrence O. Gostin, Professor of global health law at Georgetown University, quoted by the Associated Press. The report asked the Chinese government to prioritize a 'rigorous investigation' of the virus.[4]

At first, President Trump had followed the same tack as Tedros and tried to flatter the Chinese leader into being more open.

'China has been working very hard to contain the Coronavirus. The United States greatly appreciates their efforts and transparency. It will all work out well. In particular, on behalf of the American People, I want to thank President Xi!', President Trump tweeted on 24 January. Yet his attitude shifted as China continued its effort to block any genuine investigation into the source of the outbreak and to insist that it was not responsible in any way. Trump became convinced that the WHO's reluctance to confront China at the start had been a mistake. Although the United States provides roughly 15 per cent of the WHO budget, the WHO seemed to elevate China's interests over those of others.

'They seem to be very China centric. That's a nice way of saying it', Trump told reporters. The American NIH withdrew its funding from EcoHealth Alliance, frustrated by its reluctance to share information about its collaboration with the WIV.

At a WHO briefing on 4 February, Tedros continued to discourage travel bans two days after Trump imposed a travel ban on people coming from China. 'We reiterate our call to all countries not to impose restrictions that unnecessarily interfere with international travel and trade. Such restrictions can have the effect of increasing fear and stigma, with little public health benefit.'

Throughout February, Beijing asked the US, Italy, India, Australia and its South East neighbours not to impose travel restrictions on China, even though Beijing was stopping internal movement inside the country.

The Chinese government also stymied efforts to get to the bottom of how the pandemic started, and instead began to issue more statements alleging that the virus could have come from anywhere, such as the US. In March, the Chinese even dropped the seafood market theory when Gao told the journal *Science* that he now thought the virus may not have originated in the market.

By May, the US government could no longer hide its disgust at the way the WHO was behaving and announced it was leaving the organisation and withdrawing its funding. 'We will be today terminating our relationship with the World Health Organization and redirecting those funds to other worldwide and deserving urgent global public health needs', President Trump said. 'The world needs answers from China on the virus.'

'The world is now suffering as a result of the malfeasance of the Chinese government', Trump continued. 'China's cover up of the Wuhan virus allowed the disease to spread all over the world, instigating a global pandemic that has cost more than 100,000 American lives, and over a million lives worldwide.'

The Chinese government denied this. 'Since the beginning of the outbreak, we have been continuously sharing information on the epidemic with the WHO and the international community in an open and transparent and responsible manner', said Liu Mingzhui, an official with the National Health Commission's international department at a press conference on 15 May.

In the White House, Trump raised the possibility of stripping China of its 'sovereign immunity', so it could be sued for damages, or of cancelling US debt to China. In the end the Trump administration couldn't find an easy way to punish China, nor to hold it to account. It did persuade the WHO to agree to an independent investigation into the WHO's handling of the outbreak and the source of the virus. The WHO agreed to this and soon appointed the former New Zealand Prime Minister Helen Clark and Ellen Johnson Sirleaf, who as president of Liberia had experience of dealing with an Ebola outbreak.

Washington made other demands. It called on Tedros to ask China to provide live virus samples and to stop censoring Chinese doctors and journalists. It also wanted Tedros to say that countries were right to consider travel restrictions during the pandemic, and to study and revisit its travel guidance. It asked the WHO to dispatch a team to Taiwan to study its successful pandemic response. The Trump administration also asked Tedros to ensure that countries like the United States, that contribute heavily to the WHO, are proportionally represented on the organisation's staff.

Some of these demands were difficult if not impossible for Tedros to comply with. For instance, China insists on excluding Taiwan from the WHO and other international organisations and the WHO officials can do nothing about it, this being up to member states. Yet the WHO allowed China to set the terms of the investigation into the origins of the virus, a sign of its control over the organisation. Beijing consented to the investigation, but the terms of reference document were never shown to the Americans. The WHO also allowed China to vet the scientists taking part in the probe. The White House wanted its own experts to take the lead. A WHO spokesman said that it was 'customary' for a host nation to agree to any investigatory teams deployed in their country.

The ten-member team was been recruited from the United States, Russia, Australia, Sudan, Denmark, The Netherlands, Germany, Japan, Vietnam and the United Kingdom. It included Peter Daszak of EcoHealth Alliance, who drafted a statement to the *Lancet*, then persuaded twenty-six other prominent scientists to sign it, condemning 'conspiracy theories suggesting that COVID-19 does not have a natural origin'. The signatories include six of the twelve experts appointed to the *Lancet* commission's task force investigating the virus origins, which is headed by Daszak. The release of emails by a freedom of information request reveal the strong efforts made in February and March by Ralph Baric and Peter Daszak to persuade American government scientists to reject any investigation into their work with the WIV.

This plan for the investigation, which was published on 5 November, includes interviews with early cases from Wuhan; mapping of the animals and products sold at the Huanan market; reviews of old hospital records; evaluation of trends in pneumonia and influenza syndromes in months before the outbreak; and testing of sewage and blood samples collected before December 2019. The WHO team will do most of the work remotely, consulting the results and documents provided by their Chinese counterparts. A visit to China 'at the appropriate time' was also planned. The Wuhan Institute of Virology is not mentioned in the document.

'The terms of reference for investigating the SARS-CoV-2 virus origins was not negotiated in a transparent way with member states', the US government said in a statement. 'Member states only received TOR [terms of reference] a few days ago. And it seems to be inconsistent with the mandate provided by the World Health Assembly's member states.' This refers to the WHA resolution mandating the virus quest, which was approved in May.

To some others it also looked as though the investigation was being set up to produce another whitewash. 'A lot of time has been lost and there is still no evidence of an effective independent investigation starting into the origins of COVID-19', complained Nikolai Petrovsky, professor of medicine at Flinders University.

Richard Ebright, the professor of chemical biology at Rutgers University and critic of Daszak, said that he should be disqualified because of his ties to the Wuhan lab, and that his inclusion suggested that both inquiries would be 'crude whitewashes'.

David Relman, Professor of microbiology and immunology at California's Stanford University School of Medicine, in the journal of the National Academy of Sciences condemned both the WHO and the *Lancet* inquiries for being 'cloaked in secrecy'. He demanded that conflicts of interest must be 'addressed' to ensure credibility.

'Rather than resorting to hunches and finger-pointing, each scenario must be systematically and objectively analysed using the best available science-based approaches', he wrote. 'The "origin story" is missing many key details, including a plausible and suitably detailed recent evolutionary history of the virus, the identity and provenance of its most recent ancestors, and surprisingly, the place, time, and mechanism of transmission of the first human infection.'[5]

The investigative mission went ahead after some delays in early 2021 but at the time of writing, its report has not been published and no new information has been forthcoming that sheds any fresh light on the origins of the virus.

20

PANIC AND DISSENT IN WUHAN

On 25 January, a nurse in Wuhan appeared on social media dressed in mask and full protective gear to 'tell the whole truth' and said that 90,000 people had been infected by the coronavirus and the medical system couldn't cope. 'There are no supplies [...] We are all in imminent danger', she said. 'If there is a second mutation really horrible things will happen. Do not go outside. Do not eat outside.'

A number of 'citizen journalists' like Chinese lawyer Chen Qiushi aired videos on YouTube showing chaotic scenes in Wuhan hospitals with sick people queuing, screaming, or lying helplessly in corridors, and bodies in yellow bags being taken away. Other videos appeared showing a man lying in the street, apparently dead but wearing a mask. Some videos showed officials pushing residents to the ground for not wearing a face mask, beating a man for selling vegetables in the street, or forcing their way into people's homes. Many videos appeared showing people being dragged away by their ankles and arms on the street or carried out of their flats. Some showed doors in residential blocks being welded shut.

The final video of whistleblower doctor Li Wenliang speaking in his bed through his mask was aired after he died, and suggested that no one was safe. Even the best doctors in the top hospital could do nothing to save the life of a healthy young man.

The picture of events in Wuhan that emerged completely contradicted the government account. Then the authorities suddenly veered from saying there was nothing to worry about to implementing the most severe and total lockdown imaginable. Everyone around the world saw eerie drone-shot images of deserted streets, motorways, bridges, airports and railway stations, shrouded in grey river mist. It was almost as if everyone had died or at least vanished. A ghost town created by a mystery disease.

Clearly something unimaginably catastrophic was happening, and now the panicked government was doing everything possible to hide it by censoring the truth. Foreign journalists struggled to gain access to Wuhan. Western governments battled to pull their citizens out of Wuhan, apparently fearing that otherwise they might all die.

The harder the Chinese government battled to censor information circulating on Chinese social media, the more implausible the official information became. The government figures were simply too low to be credible, but the Party made a big effort to create the impression that it was working valiantly to deal with a situation but also that it was under control. A Party that has 90 million members can draw on the efforts of hundreds of thousands of people to flood social media with supportive comments, or to share content that reinforces the Party's message. Some universities are rumoured to have recruited students and teachers to help out. Party members are also in controlling positions in top internet companies in China.

The authorities also struggled to keep information and opinions from the outside world from reaching citizens in China, and to prevent information from citizens such as the unidentified Wuhan nurse from reaching the outside world. Chinese authorities started censoring news of the virus from search engines from 31 December, deleting terms including 'SARS variation', 'Wuhan Seafood market' and 'Wuhan Unknown Pneumonia'. An investigation by The Citizen Lab, an interdisciplinary laboratory based at the Munk School of Global Affairs and Public Policy, University of Toronto, reported that by March, the Chinese messenger app WeChat was successfully blocking out references to international groups like the WHO and the Red Cross, as well as references to outbreaks in other countries. In particular, the social media companies blocked information regarding critical comments made by leaders of countries like the United States and Australia. One directive said that it was necessary to avoid 'giving the false impression that our fight against the epidemic relies on foreign donations', and that news outlets should downplay reports on donations and purchases of medical supplies from abroad.[1]

It was in an awkward situation. The Party had to raise sufficient alarm and fear in order to mobilise the population and to justify the extreme measures. Yet it had to prevent the frustration and hysteria becoming a focal point for those who would use it to rally support against the Communist Party and to demand free speech and other political reforms. A number of daring critics like Chen Qiushi, the thirty-seven-year-old lawyer Zhang Zhan, the businessman Fang Bin, and Li Zehua, who aired videos and commentaries highlighting the gap between the official narrative and reality, were simply taken from their homes and did not reappear for months. Some were eventually released, but others, like Zhang Zhan, were given prison sentences. While in prison, she went on hunger strike and was force-fed. Her lawyer Zhang Keke described on social media that Zhang had a feeding tube attached to her nose and mouth and her hands were tied to prevent her from removing the device, and that she suffered from a constant headache and pain in her stomach and throat. She then appeared briefly in court when she was given a four-year prison sentence on the charge of 'picking quarrels and provoking trouble'.

Wang Zhonglin, the city's newly appointed Chinese Communist Party chief, had called for a 'gratitude education campaign', under which Wuhan citizens would be taught to express their thanks to Xi and the party for their efforts in tackling the illness. 'Is gratitude something you can teach? If you can, it must be a fake gratitude', Zhang asked in her video. She then went on the streets of Wuhan asking residents if they really felt grateful.

The country's Communist leaders were shaken by a nationwide outcry which saw the hashtag #wewantfreedomofspeech shared two million times in the space of hours. A day before Dr Li's death, lawyer Chen Qiushi—whose videos of chaotic scenes in Wuhan hospitals with coronavirus victims lying in corridors had been shared with an audience of more than 400,000 YouTube and 250,000 Twitter followers—went missing. His family was told the following day that he was being held in medical quarantine at an undisclosed location. Before his disappearance, Mr Chen realised that police were closing in on him and told his followers ominously: 'As long as I am alive, I will speak about what I have seen and what I have heard. I am not afraid of dying. Why should I be afraid of you, Communist Party?' He vanished days later.

Three weeks later, Li Zehua, twenty-five—a reporter with Chinese state TV who went rogue to report on the death toll in Wuhan—live-streamed his own arrest when plain-clothes police officers arrived at his flat. Mr Li made a point of telling viewers he was healthy and well before he was taken away. Earlier that day Mr Li, who filmed a series of videos showing desperate scenes of communities running low on food in virus-riddled areas of Wuhan, gave viewers a running commentary on how he was chased by police after visiting the Wuhan Institute of Virology.

A billionaire property tycoon, Ren Zhiqiang, sixty-nine, vanished in March after calling President Xi Jinping a clown for mishandling the virus outbreak. Weeks after his arrest, Beijing officials announced that Mr Ren was being detained for 'serious violations' of the law and Communist Party regulations.

The law professor Xu Zhangrun was put under house arrest in Beijing and had his internet access cut off after writing a searing critique of Xi Jinping's handling of the crisis which included the prediction: 'This may well be the last piece I write'.

An interview with Dr Ai Fen, whose text message prompted her colleagues, including whistle-blower Li Wenliang, to raise the alarm, was quickly withdrawn. The ER doctor criticised the management of Wuhan Central Hospital for dismissing the early warnings of the coronavirus. Chinese magazine *Renwu* quickly retracted the article after publishing it online on 10 March.

More than 5,100 people in China were arrested for sharing information in the first weeks of the outbreak. Dissidents were labelled as sick, so the government could place them in medical quarantine. Hundreds of ordinary citizens were detained and fined over innocuous online messages about hospital queues, mask shortages, and the death of relatives.

Then WeChat started to block coronavirus-related content on 1 January and expanded the scope of censorship as the outbreak grew. But it wasn't until 7 January that the Chinese authorities announced they had identified a new virus.

The outpouring of grief after the death of Dr Li was one of the most difficult moments. 'A healthy society should not only have one kind of voice', he told a magazine shortly before his death. The government's regulations controlling the news were leaked onto Weibo, the Chinese version of Twitter. Thousands of people flooded Dr Li's Weibo account with comments. The authorities allowed expressions of grief for a while, but after a few days the online memorials began to be removed. By the end of February, this wave of emotion had disappeared and was replaced by reassuring messages. Gradually the doctor was turned into an official hero and martyr.

When China first started censoring the information, it tried to downplay the similarities with the 2003 SARS outbreak. Later, the state news media were ordered to emphasize the work carried out by heroic medical workers in Wuhan and the achievements of Communist Party members. At the peak of the epidemic, they were directed to avoid words like 'incurable', 'fatal', and 'lockdown'.

Chinese people with experience of how the government deals with dissidents and troublemakers, as well as how it manipulates information in its propaganda, grasped that they were being fed false information. Yet they had no way of knowing what the real situation was. So even if they didn't believe the government, they were still scared enough to obey the government emergency orders, largely without question.

To make sure that they realised there was no choice, China released footage of drones hovering above pedestrians and ordering them to wear masks. Videos on Chinese social media also showed how people were punished for breaking strict virus lockdown rules by being paraded through towns, tied to poles and in some cases beaten to the ground. Even at the best of times, the space to passively oppose the orders, or to actively assemble and stage an anti-government protest, is very limited in China.

One permitted critical voice that was sort of tolerated belonged to Wang Fang, a sixty-four-year-old writer and resident of Wuhan. She wrote in a widely followed online diary about life in the locked-down metropolis under the name of Fang Fang. 'Dear internet censors, you should let Wuhan people speak', she wrote.

The blog was uploaded to Chinese social media on a daily basis, but her million plus followers had to stay up late to read her posts before they were deleted by the authorities in the early morning.

Wang admitted that before the lockdown, she had reassured her friends who mentioned rumours of a novel virus because she thought that 'The government would never dare to try to conceal something so huge'. When there was 'a critical event' like this pandemic, she believed that the government would err on the side of transparency and common sense. Later her attitude changed. She felt that official statements claiming that the coronavirus was 'not contagious between people' and 'controllable and preventable', as well as the bureaucratic inaction in the early days, 'have transformed Wuhan into a city of blood and tears filled with endless misery'.

As the lockdown continued, she became ever more caustic: 'The government should put an end to its arrogance and humbly express gratitude to its master—the millions of people in Wuhan'.

'This outbreak has [...] exposed the rudimentary level of so many Chinese officials, and it has exposed the diseases running rampant through the very fabric of our society', she wrote.

One night she uploaded a post saying that if anybody were to take responsibility for the handling of the coronavirus, 'the party secretary and the director of the Central Hospital of Wuhan should be the first to go'.

'The battle against the coronavirus will continue without you', she wrote to the secretary and director. 'Nobody will be troubled if you're gone.'

When viewed from overseas, the reporting in January by the official Chinese media gave the impression that the Chinese government was hiding a great deal both about the origins of the virus and the extent of the outbreak. The YouTube reports that came out of China in late January and February only reinforced that message. Everyone believed something truly terrible was happening. In this sense it started off not unlike Chernobyl, when Moscow had lied about the catastrophe and tried to hide it.

Yet the response of some governments, such as the UK's, was muted in January and February. They trusted the WHO. The British government was reassured by its experts that they were well prepared. However, Britain had readied itself to deal with the usual flu viruses that regularly come out of China. It assumed that a SARS coronavirus could be contained before it spread abroad, because with SARS the cases could be detected early and the sick isolated quickly. Yet with COVID-19, when the virus infected people, the time lag of two weeks before they showed any symptoms meant that people could travel abroad and infect quite a few people before they fell sick.

The complacency only turned to alarm when people saw the reporting of Italian hospitals, especially those dealing with the Bergamo outbreak. TV reporters who walked into a handful of small hospitals in Bergamo, Cremona and the small town of Codogno (15,000 inhabitants) filmed doctors struggling to find enough beds, equipment and medicines while working out the right way to treat the ill. It was clear they were badly frightened by this unknown disease.

The first confirmed cases were a Chinese couple who had arrived in Milan before travelling around and falling ill in Rome. A week later, an Italian man repatriated from Wuhan became the third case. On 31 January, Italy stopped flights to and from China, and by early March, it had to put the Lombardy region and then the whole of Italy under a lockdown. The outbreak was seeded at the 19 February football match. Over the course of three weeks, 1,135 people needed intensive care in Lombardy, but the region has only 800 intensive care beds. Italy has relatively few intensive care beds compared to most countries, and many patients are treated at home by their local doctors. Yet they could have been taken to hospitals in other parts of Italy and treated in ICU there. The Italians chose not to do this, and instead moved patients to private hospitals or treated patients at home.

The harrowing scenes from these small hospitals in Italy planted the idea that, since the Wuhan hospitals became overwhelmed and the Italian health service couldn't cope, then the UK's National Health Service would also be overwhelmed. As so little was known, it was assumed that no one had any immunity and that everyone of all ages and sexes was equally at risk.

When President Xi declared on 10 March that the severe lockdown in Wuhan had succeeded both in ending the medical crisis in Wuhan and stopping the virus from spreading across China, this was taken as proof that lockdowns are the best cure for COVID-19. This in turn may have been inspired by China's actions when dealing with SARS in 2003, when a similar lockdown was imposed and the disease apparently disappeared for good. In fact, both the wearing of masks and the imposing of lockdowns dates back to the bubonic plague outbreak in Manchuria in the last days of the Qing dynasty.

As far as we know, the Chinese government did not seek the advice of WHO experts before doing this, and the WHO has never recommended lockdowns in its entire seventy-year history of dealing with diseases. Its collective wisdom is summarised in a document released in October 2019, 'Non-pharmaceutical public health measures for mitigating the risk and impact of epidemic and pandemic influenza'. It explicitly ruled out, under all circumstances, the following: contact tracing; quarantine of exposed individuals; entry and exit screening; border closure. 'Border closures may be considered only by small island nations in severe pandemics and epidemics, but must be weighed against potentially serious economic consequences', it said. And it warned that travel restrictions 'may only delay the introduction of infections for a short period'.

'In all influenza epidemics and pandemics, recommending that those who are ill isolate themselves at home should reduce transmission. Facilitating this should be a particular priority. In more severe pandemics, measures to increase social distancing in schools, workplaces and public areas would further reduce transmission', it said. Although it recommends hand washing, it points out there is not really any evidence that it works with influenza. The same goes for wearing face masks in community settings.

The WHO did not reject China's approach, but neither did it openly endorse it. Instead, when asked directly, WHO experts tried to be diplomatic:

'I will say it again. We in the World Health Organization do not advocate lockdowns as the *primary* means of control of this virus', Dr David Nabarro, an Imperial College scientist, told the British journalist Andrew Neil. 'The only time we believe a lockdown is justified is to buy you time to reorganize, regroup, rebalance your resources, protect your health workers who are exhausted, but by and large, we'd rather not do it.[2]

'This is a terrible, ghastly global catastrophe, actually. And so, we really do appeal to all world leaders: stop using lockdown as your primary control method. Develop better systems for doing it.'

Dr Nabarro said that 'lockdowns just have one consequence that you must never, ever belittle, and that is making poor people an awful lot poorer [...] Look what's happened to smallholder farmers all over the world. Look what's happening to poverty levels. It seems that we may well have a doubling of world poverty by next year. We may well have at least a doubling of child malnutrition.'

Dr Maria van Kerkhove also voiced opposition to lockdowns, describing them as a 'blunt, sheer force instrument' that bought countries time to build the public health infrastructure needed to tackle COVID-19. She added that the economic, health and social costs of lockdown have been 'massive'.

'Lockdowns are not something that WHO recommended, but they needed to be used in a number of countries because the outbreaks were growing so quickly', Dr van Kerkhove said. 'But we're hopeful that countries will not need to implement national lockdowns again.'

Instead Dr van Kerkhove urged countries to make use of the tools currently available to adopt a 'tailored, specific, localised' approach to contain new clusters of infections.[3]

The compulsory wearing of masks by all members of the public is also a policy derived from the Chinese government and is not a policy of the WHO. It had only recommended wearing a mask for people who know they are sick and want to go out, and for caregivers and medical personnel. Then in June 2020, it clarified its recommendations by recommending surgical masks specifically for those working in a clinical area of a health facility.

It also said that:

> In areas with community transmission, the WHO now advises that members of the general public aged 60 and older and those with underlying conditions should wear a medical mask in situations where physical distancing is not possible: The general public should wear non-medical masks where there is widespread transmission and when physical distancing is difficult, such as on public transport, in shops or in other confined or crowded environments. Additionally, the WHO has released new guidance on cloth masks, recommending that they consist of at least three layers of different materials: an inner layer being an absorbent material like cotton, a middle layer of non-woven materials such as polypropylene (for the filter) and an outer layer, which is a non absorbent material such as a polyester or a polyester blend.

In short, the WHO experts have never really endorsed any aspect of Xi's strategy in Wuhan, neither the lockdown, nor the compulsory wearing of masks. It was an unproven and experimental method whose results were affirmed by Party propaganda. Still many countries rushed to copy China's methods in Wuhan, certain that they had been extremely successful and had also made the government look efficient and in control. Politicians envied the obedience compelled by the Chinese state, the resources it could deploy, and thought that if they could emulate it, then success and approbation would be sure to follow.

Yet in May, New York governor Andrew Cuomo expressed surprise that two thirds of admissions to hospital came from people who had been self-isolating at home.

'This is a surprise: Overwhelmingly, the people were at home'. He added: 'We thought maybe they were taking public transportation, and we've taken special precautions on public transportation, but actually no, because these people were literally at home', he said. It suggested that the virus may spread in unexpected ways, perhaps even by being blown about by the air, and that perhaps the fuss about masks and hand washing might be overdone. But there was no follow-up research, so lockdown and masks remained the best tools available.[4]

China's apparent success in Wuhan was not supported by any independently verified information, and what was made available is not easy to interpret. We can't know if the outbreak just died away naturally, like the winter flu does every year. Nor is it obvious how well Wuhan hospitals performed in treating the sick and saving lives. Or how many people died because they could not receive medical treatment during the lockdown. Or how many people were driven into poverty in Wuhan during the seventy-four-day lockdown.

Most of all, it never became clear how many people actually caught the virus in Wuhan, and who exactly was vulnerable. The most important fact about the virus, that really only those over sixty years of age were vulnerable, did not emerge from the data shared by the Chinese. Nor by the WHO. This may be because Xi's government wanted to convey a simple message that they had fought the virus and won, and then it was time to move on. A book, *A Great Power's Battle Against Epidemic*, was quickly published and designed to demonstrate the 'strategic foresight and outstanding leadership ability' of Xi. It was soon withdrawn in the face of widespread ridicule.[5]

A study by China's CDC, released in December 2020, puts the number of cases at 4.4 per cent of the population of 11 million; that is 480,000, rather than the official figure of 50,000. This was the finding of a survey of more than 34,000 people across the country conducted in April. If the modest number of 3,000 or so COVID-19 deaths from nearly half a million cases were true, then it appears that the lockdown was overkill, especially as the reported deaths are heavily concentrated among the elderly. It suggests that there were an awful lot of mild cases, something that was not apparent in the reporting in February and March.

This report also said that only 0.44 per cent of the population in central Hubei province outside of Wuhan exhibited antibodies for the virus, suggesting that the lockdown prevented the spread of the disease. It is clearly striking that the virus did not really spread to the rest of China, as might have been expected from the large number of people who left Wuhan or passed through before 27 January. As we know from other countries, it only requires a small number of people to seed a rapid chain of infections. Yet apparently this didn't happen in China, although it did in America and in Europe, and elsewhere. It might be thanks to the tough lockdown, but it is so strange that there *might* be other explanations.

The available Chinese data and those of every country show a similar pattern of a sharp spike, lasting ten to twelve days, when the number of cases shoots up and then subsides just as quickly. In Wuhan, the number of cases had peaked at the end of the first week in February. These patients must have become infected a fortnight earlier—so around 25–27 January, just when the lockdown started. Therefore it is not clear that the lockdown altered or even influenced the trajectory of the disease, at least in Wuhan. The number of cases was falling as the lockdown started.

Yet this is not what one might expect, since locking people indoors with their families, some of whom were already infected, should accelerate the disease's spread, at least initially. Yet it continued falling. Perhaps the opening of the large *Fangcang* hospitals, which started testing and isolating more patients, is the explanation. But they did not start operating for another two weeks. Rather, it seems that the virus infection rate followed its own somewhat mysterious pattern. New cases had plummeted by 11 February, although they would not show up in data for another two weeks.

The pattern was similar for the UK. The infections spiked during a twelve-day period in mid-April and the lockdown started in the last week in March. The peak of infections was 18 March, five days before the lockdown. The peak of deaths was 8 April, far too soon to have been affected by the lockdown. So the lockdown started a fortnight too late to influence the course of the disease. A similar pattern emerges around the world, whether or not a government enforces a severe lockdown. For example, the infection wave in Brazil, where there was no lockdown, is identical to the trajectory in Chile, which implemented a severe national lockdown. Sweden's infection and death rates were similar to the UK's, although it had no lockdown.

Could it be that the pattern of the disease might have little to do with government actions, and instead is more readily explained, like influenza, as a seasonal disease? It starts spreading in late autumn and dies down by April, only to reappear in another variant the following November. In Italy, for instance, where images of army trucks carrying the bodies of COVID-19 victims out of the overwhelmed city of Bergamo became emblematic, virus infections only slowed to a trickle with the start of summer.

The impact on public opinion of the reported success of China's actions was bolstered by success stories of governments in neighbouring countries—Taiwan, South Korea, Japan, Vietnam,

Hong Kong and Thailand. These are all countries where people have long been accustomed to wearing face masks. Their governments could rely on a disciplined, law-abiding citizenry. Plus the governments also proved to be much faster and more efficient at track and trace. On the other hand, none of these countries, apart from Thailand, resorted to a national lockdown.

Let's take Taiwan as an example. Its Central Epidemic Command Centre, which was set up after SARS, swung into action on 20 January. It used a real-time alert system that linked individual health records with immigration data and mobile phone data. So the government could immediately access a patient's travel history, occupation and contact history, and identify clusters at mass gatherings. This allowed it to quickly test a small but critical number of people instead of trying mass testing. It enabled the state to triangulate the location of quarantined individuals and anyone they came into contact with. It tracked them in real time and retrospectively for up to a month. People were given free access to testing, and anyone in quarantine was paid US $35 per day and given a care package including fourteen surgical masks, detailed instructions on quarantine, free online access to exercise videos and to films. Visitors to Taiwan were kept in quarantine for a fortnight. Taiwan did not introduce a national lockdown, but saw the usual spike in cases for a few weeks starting in mid-March. In all, it recorded only 800 cases and seven deaths.

Vietnam also did very well and avoided declaring a national lockdown. It shut its border with China in late January and tackled the threat with targeted lockdowns and quarantining. Yet Vietnam is a much poorer country with a population five times the size of Taiwan's. It did not have real-time data and a monitoring system equal to Taiwan's, but recorded no fatalities.

Some experts are examining other reasons that might explain why the death toll from COVID-19 has been lower in Asia. Even allowing for different testing policies and counting methods, and questions over full disclosure of cases, the stark differences across the world are puzzling. There could be differences in genetics and immune system responses, separate virus strains and regional contrasts in obesity levels and general health, which might explain the differences. We know that the 1918 flu pandemic did not affect people in China very much. And there are genetic differences, such as the one that makes people in China less tolerant of dairy products.

Some research shows that, since the virus mutated after it left East Asia, the initial strain may have been somehow adapted to the East Asian population and needed to change to overcome resistance outside the region. A team of scientists at Los Alamos National Laboratory has also argued that a more highly contagious strain of the virus has taken hold in Europe and spread in the United States.[6]

The Nobel laureate Tasuku Honjo, a Japanese physician-scientist and immunologist, said that people with Asian and European ancestry have enormous differences in the human leukocyte antigen (HLA) haplotype, genes that control the immune system's response to a virus. He thought that this might help explain why death rates are so low in Asia.

Another Japanese scientist, Tatsuhiko Kodama of the University of Tokyo, told the *Washington Post* that preliminary studies show that Japanese people's immune systems tend to react to the novel coronavirus as though they had previous exposure, and notes that there is a centuries-long history of coronaviruses emerging from East Asia. 'The enigma of lower death rates in East Asia can be explained by the presence of immunity', he said. Japan had so few cases that it never went into lockdown.[7]

Then there is the possibility that the Bacille Calmette-Guérin anti-tuberculosis vaccination (BCG) has something to do with it, because it boosts the immune system. It is given to everyone in

East Asia, but is not so common in Europe and America. 'Our hypothesis is that BCG, plus infection or exposure to TB, would be protective', Tsuyoshi Miyakawa of Fujita Health University told the *Washington Post*.

Another factor distinguishing East Asia from other parts of the world are differences in people's microbiomes, the trillions of bacteria that reside in a person's gut and play a huge role in immune response. People in different countries, eating different foods, may have a microbiome better or worse equipped to cope with the virus threat.

There's something else that is obvious on the outside. East Asia has far fewer overweight people. Only four in a hundred Japanese are obese and in South Korea the numbers are only slightly higher. Those who are overweight and those with diabetes are much more vulnerable to COVID-19. In Western Europe, one in five is obese, and in the US it is more than one in three. The fact that so few are overweight in Japan is a strong indicator that the elderly population in Japan is much healthier, and so their immune systems will be better at dealing with the virus. Elderly people who are overweight or diabetic account for a large part of the deaths in Europe.

John Bell, a professor of medicine at the University of Oxford, told the *Daily Telegraph* that nations like Vietnam avoided a flood of cases without a total lockdown because its citizens were not as immunologically 'naïve' as first assumed. This could mean that the regular existence of other SARS-like viruses had resulted in more natural resistance to such pathogens. Professor Guy Thwaites, the director of the Oxford University Clinical Research Unit in Ho Chi Minh City, credited Vietnam's success to its government. 'In Vietnam they responded very quickly, they were able to track the first people coming into the country with it [... They were] all isolated, contacts all isolated', he told the *Daily Telegraph*. 'They quarantined more than 200,000 people over a period of four months, even with relatively small numbers of cases.'[8]

'The possibility that in some rural areas there is a higher level of pre-existing immunity is something that we are actively studying', Professor Antonio Bertoletti, a specialist in infectious diseases at the Duke-NUS Medical School, told the *Daily Telegraph*. Bertoletti's research team found that there exists virus-specific T cell immunity in people who recovered from COVID-19 and SARS, but also in some who have never been infected by either virus. T cells, along with antibodies, are a major tool of the human immune system. They fight viral infections by directly hunting down and killing infected cells. Previous exposure to coronaviruses would leave a legacy of such T cells, and indeed they have been found in people who recovered from SARS seventeen years ago, but also in half of those who did not get either SARS or COVID-19. This means that a lot of people already have immunity to COVID-19.

'It is possible that such a level of pre-existing immunity can be one of the causes that enables the majority of infected people to control the virus without severe illness', Bertoletti said. Asymptomatic patients probably also have a good level of T cell immunity.

This might very well be the case in Wuhan and the rest of China too. It would explain why the disease did not readily spread beyond Wuhan as might be expected. It might also explain why China was able to stop the original SARS outbreak. It is not a subject about which Chinese researchers have said very much in public, perhaps because it would detract from the Party's accomplishments. Instead, the Chinese government seems more interested in promoting research to show that the virus came from outside China.

When it closed down a Beijing seafood market in June 2020, the Chinese government blamed the outbreak on imported frozen foods and imposed a local lockdown. The coronavirus, it seemed, had found its way into the mainland on fish packets at a stall in a wet market. It started a boycott of Norwegian salmon imports. Next, cold chain facilities in the northern port city of Tianjin were shuttered when a thirty-eight-year-old frozen food worker who tested positive for the virus was linked to a 28.1 tonne shipment of frozen German pork knuckles. Chinese authorities reported that two dock workers in Qingdao also caught the virus from the packaging of frozen cod.

Chinese state media have cited the presence of the coronavirus on imported frozen food packaging, as well as scientific papers claiming that the coronavirus was circulating in Europe earlier than previously believed, as evidence that China may not have been its place of origin. All other kinds of research into the virus have been put under strict central control.

'COVID19 did not start in central China's Wuhan but may come through imported frozen food and packaging', read a Facebook post by the *People's Daily*. China has stepped up inspections and made a spate of announcements that the virus was found on chilled food packaging. 'When and where did the virus start circulating? Tracing the virus cannot answer all questions, but it is very likely that the virus had co-existed in multiple places before being spotted in Wuhan', the *People's Daily* quoted Zeng Guang, the former chief epidemiologist of China's Center for Disease Control. He also claimed the fact that it was detected first in Wuhan showed the strength of China's infectious disease prevention system.

In March, a foreign ministry spokesman suggested that the US army brought the virus to Wuhan. State Councillor Wang Yi has also said that it was unclear whether the virus originated in China, while the foreign ministry has stated that the origin is a scientific matter and has rebuked countries that point to China as the source, including the United States and Australia.

'Although China was the first to report cases, it doesn't necessarily mean that the virus originated in China', foreign ministry spokesman Zhao Lijian told a briefing. 'Origin tracing is an ongoing process that may involve multiple countries and regions.'

Zeng and the Chinese state media have cited a paper published by Italy's National Cancer Institute which said that COVID-19 antibodies had been found in samples of cancer patients taken there in October last year. Another paper published earlier this year claimed to have found traces of SARS-Cov-2 in the sewage system of Barcelona in samples taken in March 2019. 'Strong claims supported by flimsy evidence get widely reported without the necessary scrutiny and consideration of a wider body of available evidence', Francois Balloux, a geneticist at University College London, commented on Twitter. He said that even if the virus was present in Italy in September, it doesn't necessarily mean that it originated there.

Reports of COVID-19 circulating in Italy in autumn 2019, based on samples from a cancer unit, seem 'weak', Professor Jonathan Stoye, a virologist at the Francis Crick Institute in London told the *Observer*. 'The serological data [from Italy] can most likely be explained by cross-reactive antibodies directed against other coronaviruses.' In other words, antibodies found in the cases in Italy had been triggered in individuals who had been infected by different coronaviruses, not those responsible for COVID-19.[9]

China tightened restrictions, requiring 'full coverage' testing and disinfection of imported food products, following a smattering of positive samples detected on beef, pork and seafood. The country has suspended imports of ninety-nine suppliers from twenty countries. Outside China, scientists say that chances of infection from frozen food are low. Testing cold-chain foods and packaging probably just detects dead fragments of the virus. 'People should not fear food, food packaging or delivery of food',

Mike Ryan, head of the WHO's emergencies programme said in August. 'There is no evidence the food chain is participating in transmission of this virus.'

At least ten cities across China say they have found traces of COVID-19 on the packaging of frozen food imports, and usually the discovery has prompted a dramatic lockdown of the city in question. It seems designed to bolster a theory that the original outbreak in Wuhan's fish market was imported, too. Meanwhile Taiwan, which imports some $11 billion of agricultural goods a year, has gone over 200 days without a single case of COVID-19.

Chinese scientists have reportedly submitted a paper to the *Lancet* claiming that 'Wuhan is not the place where human-to-human SARS-CoV-2 transmission first happened', and instead proposing that the first case may have been in the Indian subcontinent.

The Chinese government awarded a scientist, Bi Yuhai, a 1.5 million RMB grant to research the origins of the virus. He had earlier co-authored a paper suggesting that an outbreak in the Beijing seafood market came from frozen salmon.

According to internal documents seen by the Associated Press, China has put all such research into the virus under closer supervision. Any publication of research on the coronavirus must be approved by high-level government officials at the Ministry of Science and Technology. The orders come from President Xi Jinping. As a result, very little has been made public, research has been stifled, and so has cooperation with international scientists.

'They only select people they can trust, those that they can control', a public health expert who works regularly with the Chinese CDC told the Associated Press, declining to be identified out of fear of retribution. 'Military teams and others are working hard on this, but whether it gets published all depends on the outcome.'[10]

The government is handing out hundreds of thousands of dollars in grants to scientists researching the virus' origins in southern China and who are affiliated with the military, the Associated Press reported. Some Chinese scientists claim that little has been shared simply because nothing of significance has been discovered. 'We've been looking, but we haven't found it', Zhang Yongzhen, the famous Chinese virologist, told the Associated Press.

The internal documents show that various government bodies also sponsored studies on the possible role of the South East Asian pangolin, a scaly anteater once prized in traditional Chinese medicine, as an intermediary animal host. Within the span of three days in February, Chinese scientists put out four separate papers related to COVID-19 in the pangolins from Malaysia seized by customs officials in Guangdong. Blood samples should show evidence of COVID-19's presence in the rare mammals, but nothing has been found. The WHO has said that more than 500 species of other animals, including cats, ferrets and hamsters, are being studied as possible intermediary hosts for COVID-19.

The Chinese government is also controlling the re-testing of old flu samples, which ought to help identify the first people infected. This was done in America, where the CDC officials examined roughly 11,000 early samples collected under the flu surveillance programme after 1 January. In Italy, researchers did something similar and found a boy who had fallen ill in November 2019 and later tested positive for the coronavirus. In China, scientists have only published retrospective testing data from two Wuhan flu surveillance hospitals, although there are at least eighteen in Hubei and 500 across the country. This means just 520 samples out of the 330,000 collected in a year.

China is hiding the information. Internal data obtained by the Associated Press shows that by 6 February, the Hubei CDC had tested over 100 samples in Huanggang, a city south east of Wuhan. But the results have not been made public. The little information that has dribbled out suggests that the virus was circulating well outside Wuhan in 2019—a finding that could raise awkward questions for Chinese officials about their early handling of the outbreak. Chinese researchers found that a child over 100km from Wuhan had the virus on 2 January, suggesting that it was spreading widely in December. But earlier samples weren't tested, according to a scientist with direct knowledge of the study. 'There was a very deliberate choice of the time period to study, because going too early could have been too sensitive'.

21

CONCLUSIONS

We may never find patient zero, evidence of a laboratory leak, or the exact nature of the experiments that Dr Shi and others were doing in Wuhan. It is possible that after years of research, Chinese scientists will say that no intermediate animal host has been found to explain the origins of the virus. Many of those being asked to find answers have very strong conflicts of interest and a personal stake in seeing the origins of COVID-19 left as a mystery requiring further study.

The Chinese government backed away from the initial belief that the virus was spread by animals kept at the seafood market, since that would mean accepting liability. Instead, it is trying to conjure up evidence that the virus came from abroad.

The twin investigations into the origins of the virus and the behaviour of the WHO may put China in a bad light, but how many leaders around the world are really determined to hold China to account? It's simply too powerful. Besides, there is a deeper problem, which goes beyond diplomacy, and that is the science.

There are many things that we still don't understand about viruses, especially the ones that have caused epidemics. Even a hundred years later, we don't know where the Spanish flu came from, why it preferentially attacked younger people rather than older, or why people in East Asia were far less susceptible than others. Despite studying influenza intensely for more than fifty years, we don't know how to treat it or why, outside the tropics, it is a seasonal winter disease. Nor do we know why many diseases seem to disappear, sometimes for decades, and then re-emerge.

On the other hand, can it really just be pure coincidence that a new coronavirus very close to SARS but specially adapted to infecting humans has appeared in such close proximity to the only laboratory in the world that specialised in investigating and experimenting with the SARS virus? That is very hard to accept.

The collective judgement of the WHO experts has also been exposed as far from satisfactory. The WHO has been criticised for its handling of the swine flu epidemic and the last Ebola epidemic. Now its handling of COVID-19 has led some governments to question its usefulness. The Trump administration wanted to abandon it for something else. China has treated it as a mild irritant and mostly ignored its recommendations. Beijing has preferred to go its own way to develop vaccines and inoculate its population.

The effectiveness of its pandemic advice has been called into questioned by many countries that opted to shut their borders and locked down their populations for months on end. No one can say with certainty if these policies have actually altered the curve of infections. COVID-19 may turn out to be a seasonal infection like another coronavirus, the common cold. The effectiveness of those who are infected wearing masks is also open to question. The virus is not a living thing so it can exist for long periods outside any host. It is so small, too, that it is hard to block it, or to destroy it with sanitizers. It is probably transmitted through the air in droplets, but it may also simply be blown about by the wind, perhaps over longer distances than we imagine. Then there are unresolved questions about whether some people are super spreaders, or if they are more prone to shed viruses at one time rather than another.

Most of all, we don't really understand why the virus has proved to be so lethal to the elderly but relatively harmless to the young—the complete opposite of the Spanish flu. Nor do we know how many people have an immune system that can easily defeat the virus, or why this should be.

Still, the COVID-19 pandemic has brought new breakthroughs in the Cinderella of the pharmaceutical industry—vaccines. The mRNA vaccine is a new type of vaccine that it is much quicker and easier to develop, and that works in a different way. Instead of putting a weakened or inactivated germ into our bodies, it instructs a cell on how to make a protein that triggers an immune response. A number of companies have built platforms that could be used to create a vaccine for any infectious disease simply by inserting the right mRNA sequence for that disease. Such mRNA vaccines are being tested for other infectious agents, such as Ebola, Zika virus and influenza. Cancer cells make proteins that also can be targeted by mRNA vaccines: indeed, recent progress has been reported with melanoma. And theoretically, mRNA technology could produce proteins missing in certain diseases, such as cystic fibrosis.

Instead of taking ten or fifteen years to develop a new vaccine, it can be done in just a week. The Pfizer, AstraZeneca and Moderna vaccines have been shown to provoke both an antibody and T-cell response. Antibodies are proteins that bind to the body's foreign invaders and tell the immune system it needs to take action. T-cells are a type of white blood cell that hunt down infected cells in the body and destroy them.

China has least five COVID-19 vaccines from four producers, all of which use conventional methods. They include the Beijing Biological Products Institute; CanSino Biologics, based in Tianjin, in partnership with the Chinese Academy of Military

Medical Sciences; Anhui Zhifei Longcom Biopharmaceutical; and China National Biotec Group, partly based in Wuhan. Three of them use the whole inactivated virus, an approach that dates back to the first successful flu vaccine in the 1930s. The first vaccine, by CanSino Biologics, appeared within two months of the lockdown in Wuhan. The army virologist Chen Wei, a major general, stood in front of a Chinese Communist Party flag and received injections. As they had few cases in China, and many people distrust domestic vaccine makers, the vaccine producers have had to ask other countries, in the Arab world and in Latin America, for help in carrying out trials.

If the mRNA vaccines turn out to be a success, it is likely that they will replace the conventional vaccine makers. The AstraZeneca vaccine is cheaper than anything made in China. The new type of vaccines are quicker and more economical to produce, and one shot could provide immunity for quite a few diseases.

This would also be a setback for China, as it has been trying to use the vaccine trials, and the offer of free or low-cost vaccines, to bolster its image around the world. The biotech industry in the UK, Germany and America will have taken a major technological advance. On the other hand, a lot of the test kits and medical equipment that China sold abroad has turned out to be useless, and this has harmed China's image.

The inability to quickly explain why the virus originated in Wuhan is another major handicap. The involvement of the Chinese military in developing new viruses to wage biowarfare is an unresolved question. It is not an outlandish right-wing conspiracy theory to consider this a possibility.

China has been open about double-digit increases in its military budget for the last two decades. It has been an enormous effort to build a modern military to rival that of the United States, involving the large-scale theft of military blueprints and considerable manufacturing investment. It has ranged from high-performance computing to hypersonic missiles, new nuclear missiles, satellites, rail guns, stealth fighter jets, stealth drones, unmanned vehicles, missile defence systems and much more. A Chinese spy, Su Bin, was sentenced to forty-three months in prison for stealing the blueprints for the Lockheed Martin Raptor F-22. China used them to build its J-20 Stealth fighter, according to information released by Edward Snowden. Take the Chinese navy as an example. It will have more than 430 major surface combatants and almost 100 submarines by 2030. The growth of the People's Liberation Army Navy (PLAN) over the past decade and a half has been unprecedented. It far exceeds the build up in any other nation's navy in the era after the Second World War. China is building multiple carrier strike groups, a credible submarine-launch ballistic missile capability and blue sea strike capabilities. Its official defense budget in 2019 was $178 billion, but others put it at more like $455 billion, if one uses purchasing power parity. It is equal to the US military budget.

With this kind of money being spent, and an obvious effort to capture and reproduce every kind of military technology, it would be surprising if China hadn't invested a small amount to build a modern bio weapons system. It is a relatively low-cost investment compared to building a stealth fighter jet, and is much easier to hide. The technology is entirely dual use and can be housed in a conventional factory or lab. It doesn't require a cavern hollowed out in a volcano, like a James Bond set with thousands of guards milling around. Funding research into the collection of dangerous viruses and exploring how to make them more lethal or virulent is no more costly or challenging than the research China's biotech companies are already doing by gene editing livestock and plants.

In fact, the EcoHealth Alliance's research—its hunt for new and dangerous viruses—is heavily financed by the Pentagon. From 2013–20, some $39 million of its research was provided by contracts, grants and sub-contracts from the Department of Defense. A further $64,700,000 came from USAID under the State Department. There is no reason why China should not be doing the same and spending similar amounts. Defensive research against biowarfare threats is legal and permitted under the Biological Weapons Convention. China is not obliged to inform the rest of the world about the details of such research. Hence, there is no reason to exclude the possibility that the PLA had a strong motive to encourage Dr Shi's research, and may well have been doing similar experiments in labs that are unknown to the outside world. This is not the same as saying that COVID-19 was deliberately designed as a military weapon, but the know-how to find an unknown and dangerous bat virus and then make it more viral and lethal would be exactly what you would expect a military programme to focus on.

At the same time, we know that in the past, such military research has led to accidents, laboratory leaks and numerous deaths. There are documented attempts by Soviet scientists to find the 1918 pandemic H1N1 strain in old ice houses where victims were buried, and studies were performed attempting to create radiation-resistant and aerosolized influenza viruses. There was, for example, the release of anthrax spores in Sverdlovsk in 1979.

An accident at a virology research laboratory that was looking at the 1950 flu virus either in China or Russia may have started the H1N1 Russian Flu epidemic in 1977/8. In 1991, in the last days of the Soviet Union, researchers suggested that the virus was 'potentially frozen' in nature until its re-emergence.

In 2008, it was suggested that the epidemic was 'probably' the result of an influenza vaccine trial. Chi-Ming Chu, the director of the Chinese Academy of Medical Sciences, told Peter Palese, an American microbiologist at Mount Sinai School of Medicine in New York, that it had happened '[as] the result of vaccine trials in the Far East involving the challenge of several thousand military recruits with live H1N1 virus'. This might have been an ineffectively attenuated vaccine or a laboratory-cultivated strain.[1]

There is no doubt that China is throwing all its resources into dominating the biotechnology sector with its vast commercial potential to change whole industries such as health, agricultural and fisheries, and perhaps others such as energy or waste disposal. In its eagerness to outdo its rivals, China has pressured individuals and companies to steal know-how and to take foolish risks. Its record on safety and standards is poor. In this context, it is quite conceivable that it encouraged researchers to build a new chimeric virus that escaped from a laboratory in or near Wuhan.

No government of a country like the former USSR or China is ever likely to put up its hand and accept responsibility for creating a new virus, allowing it to escape and unleashing a global pandemic. They would be liable for reparations on a huge scale. For the Chinese, it would be like the reparations they were forced to pay after the Boxer Rebellion, when in 1900 the Empress Dowager Cixi stood by and allowed Boxer troops to attack and kill foreigners and to besiege the Legation quarter in Beijing. Eight nations sent troops to relieve the forty-day siege. Under a treaty, the Boxer Protocol, China agreed to execute government officials who supported the Boxers, to allow foreign troops to be stationed in Beijing and to pay 450million taels of silver to the eight powers. This is $10 billion at 2018 silver prices, and since it was more than the government's annual tax revenues, China had to pay it off over the next thirty-nine years, by allowing foreigners to supervise the customs service. When the foreign troops arrived in Beijing, the Empress Dowager disguised herself and fled the Forbidden City dressed as a peasant and riding an ox cart.

The national shame might spell the end of the Chinese Communist Party's seventy-year rule. It would start a political earthquake which would begin in China but spread around the world. All kinds of secrets that had lain hidden would emerge as the archives would open, and people would begin to speak freely. It would upend the world order. After the 1989 Tiananmen Massacre, which brought an end to the nationwide pro-democracy protests that seemed close to overthrowing Party rule, many Western governments, including that of President Bush, seemed deeply reluctant to take any steps to allow that to happen. They feared that the result would be 'chaos'.

One country that did call for a genuine investigation into the origins of COVID-19 was Australia. Its prime minister, Scott Morrison, put forward a plan to overhaul the WHO and give its investigators the same powers as weapons inspectors, enabling it to forcibly enter a country if it was necessary to investigate a disease outbreak. It would have similar powers of unfettered access to data and medical information, even without the express consent of the nation's government. He also called for an international review of wildlife markets, which, he argued, pose a big risk to human health and food production. Chair of Australia's Joint Parliamentary Committee on Intelligence and Security Andrew Hastie said after the cover-up and disinformation campaign from China, the world needed transparency and an inquiry.

'The world's nations must do all they can to understand the origins of COVID-19', Morrison said in an address to the United Nations General Assembly in September. 'This virus has inflicted a calamity on our world and its peoples. We must do all we can to understand what happened for no other purpose than to prevent it from happening again.'

Morrison pitched the proposal to President Donald Trump, German Chancellor Angela Merkel and French President Emmanuel Macron. Under its 1948 Charter, international officials must be invited by the host nation before they can be allowed to investigate, and any one of its 194 member states has the power to veto any reform of these rules. Given the barriers to reforming the WHO, the Australians suggested that a new world health oversight body might be the right alternative. The United Nations could establish a commission of inquiry but China could simply use its veto to block such a proposal. After the 1986 Chernobyl nuclear disaster and the Soviet cover-up, the international community quickly responded with the adoption of two treaties. One made it mandatory for a country to notify others once a nuclear accident that had cross-border impacts had occurred, and the other dealt with the capacity of other countries to assist in responding to the accident. The Convention on Early Notification of a Nuclear Accident was negotiated five months after the Chernobyl accident and became operative a month later. The Convention on Assistance in the Case of a Nuclear Accident or Radiological Emergency facilitated prompt assistance and support in the event of nuclear accidents or radiological emergencies. It requires signatory states to notify the IAEA of their available experts, equipment, and materials for providing assistance.

These treaties did not seek to apportion responsibility for Chernobyl, but just made it a bit easier to respond to future nuclear accidents.

Morrison's proposals apparently went nowhere. President Trump decided to leave the WHO, a decision that is being reversed by his successor, President Joe Biden. At the same time, the Bill and Melinda Gates Foundation announced a huge increase in its grants to the WHO. It raised the total to $531 million, or 12 per cent of the WHO's budget. The foundation granted an extra $1.6 billion to the Vaccine Alliance, which is a major donor to the WHO. 'No donor is interested in just replacing funds that have been taken away, and so I will certainly encourage the United States to stay as a member of WHO and continue the support they provide', Gates said. He added that one third of US support for the WHO is earmarked for polio eradication, which is also a major priority of the Gates foundation, and said he does not see how polio can be eradicated without the WHO.

President Macron told Morrison that now was not the time for an international investigation into the coronavirus pandemic, and that the urgency was to act in unison before looking for who was at fault. UK Prime Minister Boris Johnson pledged to give the WHO more money. Johnson told the UN General Assembly that Britain will increase funding by 30 per cent over four years, £340m spread across four years making it the third largest funder after America and the Gates Foundation. Officials said that the money is coming with strings attached, including reforms. The British leader will also present a five-point plan to improve the international response to future pandemics, including a global network of research hubs, more vaccine manufacturing capacity, and an agreement to reduce export tariffs imposed at the start of the COVID-19 pandemic. He committed an initial £71 million to the global vaccine partnership known as COVAX to secure purchase rights on 27 million doses, and £500 million to a separate COVAX initiative to help poorer countries access a vaccine.

In April 2020, the EU's European External Action Service issued a report which originally included the statement that China was conducting a 'global disinformation' campaign. The EEAS documents demonstrated that the PRC has been actively and widely spreading 'conspiracy narratives and disinformation both at public audiences in the EU and the wider neighbourhood'. It said there has been a 'coordinated influence campaign with ties to the Chinese government' on social media such as Twitter, through bots and fake accounts, to disseminate pro-PRC messages. In response to Chinese pressure, the references to China running a 'global disinformation' campaign and Chinese criticism of France's reaction to the pandemic were erased.

China also persuaded the EU to remove a reference to China as the virus's origin in an editorial celebrating forty-five years of EU-China diplomatic relations, which was published in China.

The EEAS subsequently published a statement expressing regret that the op-ed wasn't published in its original form.

Later in the year, the EU drew up a document on the reform of the UN agency, which outlines a series of sweeping changes needed to boost the WHO's powers and resources, enabling it to become faster in its reaction to health crises, while its member states should share more information in emergencies.

In response to the Australian leaders' temerity in criticising China and calling for more powers to forcibly investigate a future epidemic emergency emerging in China, Beijing started a vicious campaign of intimidation. It suspended some beef imports on a technicality and effectively blocked a $308.5 million trade in barley by slapping tariffs of 80.5 per cent on Australian imports. It also launched an anti-dumping probe into Australian wine imports, before adding a 212 per cent tariff on Australian wine. It stopped unloading Australian coal at its ports. A Chinese foreign ministry spokesman tweeted a mocked-up image of an Australian soldier threatening to kill an Afghan child after a report alleging that Australian troops had committed war crimes. It detained two Australian journalists working in China and forced them to flee. Beijing also cautioned students and tourists against going to Australia, citing racist incidents in light of COVID-19.

China is Australia's largest trading partner, but ties began to sour in 2017, after the Australian Security Intelligence Organisation (Asio) warned of growing Chinese attempts to influence decision making in Canberra. Donations from Chinese businessmen to local politicians came to light. Next, the Australians announced laws to curb foreign interference, and Beijing responded by freezing diplomatic visits. In 2018, Australia became the first country to publicly ban the Chinese tech giant Huawei from being involved in its 5G network, citing national security reasons.

The campaign to intimidate Australia warned other countries not to blame China for the virus, or they would face a barrage of threats and trade sanctions. The strategy worked. The international community has been loath to confront China or to challenge its version of events. It makes it unlikely that the WHO investigation into the origins of the virus will be very illuminating, since it excluded any investigation into the research carried out in various labs in Wuhan. Western scientists working in virology had early on united behind a conclusion that concurred with China's view that the research at the WIV had absolutely nothing to do with COVID-19. Anyone trying to publish articles linking the WIV experiments in gain-of-function research to COVID-19 found it nearly impossible to get them published in any well-known scientific publications. Arguments over the merits of or risks of gain-of-function research were conducted out of sight in obscure twitter feeds. A handful of individuals such as Yuri Deigin, Francisco de Asis, Alina Chan, Moreno Colaiacovo and Rossana Segreto continued to dig for evidence that would challenge the accepted view.

Part of the opposition to the lab theory rested on antipathy to the Trump administration, which earlier on had blamed the Chinese government and wanted to hold it to account. Since the Trump administration accused the Chinese of hiding the truth about the origins of the virus, and of misleading the world, there were feelings that the opposite must be true. Given a choice between supporting the Trump administration or the Chinese Communist Party, most scientists openly sided with the Chinese. They could claim that the Trump administration was telling lies, but the Chinese government had acted forcefully, effectively and responsibly to stop the outbreak. As a result, things had quickly returned to normal in China and it had experienced strong economic growth. By contrast, in the United States, Trump had allegedly ignored scientific advice, mismanaged the crisis and let the virus range out of control. It was America that saw anti-government riots, which allowed Twitter and Facebook to censor unscientific 'conspiracy theories' about the virus, and which saw its leader voted out of office. There were no public protests against the CCP either in America, Europe or China. Even though the CCP openly did other shocking things, such as imprisoning Uighurs and democracy activists in Hong Kong, the leading scientific journals never took a stance against China, although the *Lancet*, *Nature* and *Science* magazine would publish scathing editorials against Trump. The issue became the sort of left-versus-right controversy in which each side drew on the tribal loyalty of their respective followers.

Another way of looking at it is that the COVID-19 pandemic was the 'disease x' which for many years many people had predicted would arrive, with terrifying consequences. In a sense they were secretly gratified in being proved right. In a 2015 TED lecture called 'The Next Outbreak? We're Not Ready', Bill Gates explained that, while the greatest threat to humanity when he was growing up was nuclear war, the greatest threat now was a virus. 'If anything kills over ten million in the next few decades, it's most likely to be a highly infectious virus rather than a war', he said, explaining that, while we had invested a lot of money into nuclear deterrents, we had 'invested very little in a system to stop an epidemic'. He concluded the lecture by saying that we needed to deal with the prospect of an epidemic in the same way that we would prepare for war, by investing in a global health system, knowing that the cost of preparing would not only save lives, but also the trillions of dollars that a pandemic would cost. He also said doing so would make the world 'more just as well as more safe'. On 28 February 2020, Gates wrote a blog saying that 'COVID-19 has started to behave a lot like the once-in-a-century pathogen we've been worried about'. And he urged the government to take immediate action. 'Obviously, billions of dollars for anti-pandemic efforts is a lot of money', he wrote. 'But that's the scale of investment required to solve the problem. And given the economic pain that an epidemic can impose—just look at the way COVID-19 is disrupting supply chains and stock markets, not to mention people's lives—it will be a bargain...'

Gates has for a long time used his personal fortune to improve health care around the world, in particular in regards to infectious diseases. Whenever there was a new pathogen, such as swine flu in 2009, Ebola in 2014, Middle East respiratory syndrome (MERS) and Severe Acute Respiratory Syndrome (SARS), he became ever more convinced that the handling of it demonstrated that the world was underprepared. He spoke in favour of compulsory lockdowns, face masks and vaccinations, which, he said, had worked in Australia and South Korea.

The COVID-19 pandemic was also, therefore, a vindication of the beliefs of the EcoHealth Alliance. Its pitch for years had been that at any moment, an unknown virus could emerge from some remote jungle and wreak havoc. It was essential to find these first and then to discover how they could evolve in order to stop the next pandemic. Any narrative that suggested that the Chinese, with American money, had created the crisis by being careless or irresponsible was intolerable.

From the point of view of a politician seeking to do something that was achievable, attainable and relatively effortless, it was easier to promise more money for a global monitoring or vaccination programme than to get down in the mud and have a nasty public fight with China. Perhaps it was better to deal with China quietly behind closed doors, and to persuade it to act differently in the future. As China has been the origin of so many disease outbreaks in the past, its cooperation is essential. And if you pushed it too hard, it could just refuse to cooperate with the WHO, as some feared would happen in January 2020.

Besides, even if Western leaders did impose their will, China's ability to frustrate any investigation is limitless. Take the story about the researcher at the WIV, Huang Yanlin, who might have been the first to catch the virus and to die from it. The government simply deleted all records of her existence and that of two other students. It said she had left the institute in 2015, even though she was in a New Year photograph from 2018 that was posted on the WIV website. She simply disappeared. So how were you going to get to the bottom of that issue? Where would it get you to enter into a fight that you weren't going to win?

Consequently, even though the pandemic showed up the shortcomings of the WHO, the organisation stands to be a great beneficiary of the COVID-19 pandemic. It is unlikely to pay a penalty for its deference towards China, and the investigation into its handling of the crisis is not going to matter very much since countries such as Britain had already pledged more money. The WHO wants an extra $18 billion to deliver two billion doses of the vaccines, on top of the $5.8 billion it already has budgeted. So it will be a case of 'lessons learned' for the future.

The EcoHealth Alliance also benefited. It won the support of thirty-one scientific societies, comprising several hundred thousand scientists who signed a joint protest letter after its grant was axed, as did seventy-seven Nobel laureates. In August, the NIH restored its grant, although it is still demanding information about the laboratory work done in Wuhan. The NIH also went ahead with a project called CREID—Centers for Research in Emerging Infectious Diseases—worth $82 million over five years. It will fund eleven research nodes, mostly at US universities, who will build research partnerships in twenty-eight other countries—including China. EcoHealth will be given $7.5 million to run one of these nodes, focusing on South East Asia and the emergence of coronaviruses, filoviruses (the family responsible for Ebola) and paramyxoviruses (the family of viruses that includes measles and mumps).

Ralph Baric at the University of North Carolina found himself in high demand. 'UNC's Ralph Baric has long been a leader in virus research. Now, the world is listening', as a local paper put it in a headline. His laboratory became a recipient of a new $433,000 grant from the Chan Zuckerberg Initiative to purchase a 'liquid handler'—a robotic arm that can pipette fluids much more quickly and accurately than humans can—and supporting instruments, including another robot that detects active virus particles in samples, as well as a machine to sequence RNA. Together, these tools increase the rate of testing compounds twenty-fold.

Those involved in making the first test kits at the start of the pandemic also seem to have done quite well. In September 2020, Tan Wenjie, the CDC official who was put in charge of developing test kits, was appointed inaugural director of a new National Novel Coronavirus Centre. In a nationally televised ceremony, the parent company of one of the kit makers, GenevoDx, won plaudits from President Xi for 'outstanding contributions' in the struggle against COVID-19, including developing a test kit. Another maker of faulty kits, Huirui, expanded by selling commercial test kits, not in China but Latin America.

In his New Year address, Xi Jinping looked back at the year with an air of triumph. 'Facing the sudden coronavirus pandemic, we put people and their lives first to interpret the great love among humans. With solidarity and resilience, we wrote the epic of our fight against the pandemic.

'During the days when we addressed the hardships together, we saw the heroic spirit of marching straight to the frontlines, holding posts with tenacity, taking responsibility to get through thick and thin, sacrifices with bravery, and touching moments of helping each other.

'China is the first major economy worldwide to achieve positive growth, and its GDP in 2020 is expected to step up to a new level of 100 trillion yuan.

'We still have a long way to go in pandemic prevention and control. People from all over the world should join hands and support each other to early dispel the gloom of the pandemic and strive for a better "Earth home"', he said.

The year turned out far better than he might have expected, with a complete return to normality, a resurgent economy and strong exports. China showed Wuhan as a city packed with revellers on New Year's Eve, while cities like New York and London were empty. The first American president to take a tough line on China for a generation is gone and replaced by one who may return to past policies.

Yet the COVID-19 crisis may also usher in a new phase in China's relations with the outside world. The idea that as China grew richer it would become more open, tolerant and pluralistic has taken a severe blow. The row over Huawei had already shaken faith in China's good intentions. Now the heavy costs of dealing with the pandemic will seed a hardening in attitudes towards the Chinese government. It will be treated with far more suspicion, and in some quarters with outright hostility. There could be a slow sea change, as the public in many countries now distrust it and have personally suffered the consequences of its actions. Some will blame their leaders for getting too close to China and demand that it stops being treated as a friend.

As for the threat of future pandemics, the one great positive that will emerge is the new vaccine technology using mRNA, and the new low-cost testing techniques, which have transformed the odds in neutralising mankind's smallest but deadliest enemy. There might never be a pandemic like this again, and it may spell the end of the race to develop bioweapons.

NOTES

1. INTRODUCTION

1. Liwen Fang, Pei Gao, Heling Bao, Xun Tang, Baohua Wang, Yajing Feng, Shu Cong, Juan Juan, Jing Fan, Ke Lu, Ning Wang, Yonghua Hu, Linhong Wang: 'Chronic obstructive pulmonary disease in China: A nationwide prevalence study', *the Lancet Respiratory Medicine*, 2018; DOI: 10.1016/S2213-2600(18)30103-6.
2. https://www.reuters.com/article/us-health-coronavirus-italy-sewage-idUSKBN23Q1J9.
3. Ma, Josephine: 'Coronavirus: China's first confirmed Covid-19 case traced back to November 17', Hong Kong: *South China Morning Post*, 13 March 2020, https://www.scmp.com/news/china/society/article/3074991/coronavirus-chinas-first-confirmed-covid-19-case-traced-back (11 Feb. 2021).

2. BUBONIC PLAGUE

1. Mark R. Wilson: The Untold Origin Story of the N95 Mask, *The Fast Company*, 24 March 2020, https://www.fastcompany.com/90479846/the-untold-origin-story-of-the-n95-mask.

5. DOES CHINA HAVE A BIOWARFARE PROGRAMME?

1. US Department of State: 'Fact Sheet: Activity at the Wuhan Institute of Virology', https://2017-2021.state.gov/fact-sheet-activity-at-the-wuhan-institute-of-virology//index.html (11 Feb. 2021).
2. Smith, R. Jeffrey: 'China may have revived germ weapons program,

U.S. Officials say', *Washington Post*, 24 Feb. 1993, https://www.washingtonpost.com/archive/politics/1993/02/24/china-may-have-revived-germ-weapons-program-us-officials-say/67418b05-fab1-490b-b9b5-c280218d08dc/ (11 Feb. 2021).

3. US Department of State: '2005 Adherence to and Compliance With Arms Control, Nonproliferation, and Disarmament Agreements and Commitments', US Department of State, https://2009–2017.state.gov/t/avc/rls/rpt/51977.htm (11 Feb. 2021).

4. https://fas.org/man/eprint/dod-china-2013.pdf (12 Feb. 2021).

6. THE COMMERCIALISATION OF CHINA'S MILITARY ENTERPRISES

1. Eban, Katherine, and Sony Salzman: 'In generic drug plants in China and India, data falsification is still a problem', 19 Oct. 2019, https://www.statnews.com/2019/10/29/data-falsification-still-problematic-china-india-generic-drug-plants/ (11 Feb. 2021); Zhuang Pinghui, 'Rabies Vaccine maker to stop output in China's latest drug safety scandal', *South China Morning Post*, 17 July 2018, https://www.scmp.com/news/china/society/article/2155520/chinese-drug-watchdog-orders-rabies-vaccine-maker-stop-output (19 Feb. 2021).

2. Zhao Huanxin: 'Fake and shoddy drugs a threat to people, challenge for administrators', *China Daily*, 8 March 2017, https://www.chinadaily.com.cn/opinion/2017–12/08/content_35258859.htm (11 Feb. 2021).

7. MADE IN CHINA PLAN

1. Fialka, John: 'Why China Is Dominating the Solar Industry. Between 2008 and 2013, China's solar-electric panel industry dropped world prices by 80 percent', *Climate Wire*, 19. Dec. 2016, https://www.scientificamerican.com/article/why-china-is-dominating-the-solar-industry/ (11 Feb. 2021).

2. Obiko Pearson, Natalie: 'Did a Chinese Hack Kill Canada's Greatest Tech Company? Nortel was once a world leader in wireless technology. Then came a hack and the rise of Huawei', *Bloomberg*, 17 Jan. 2020, https://www.bnnbloomberg.ca/did-a-chinese-hack-kill-canada-s-greatest-tech-company-1.1459269 (11 Feb. 2021).

8. WUHAN AND THE PHARMA INDUSTRY

1. Bloomberg News: 'Chinese Investment Floods US Biotech Pharmaceutical Start-Ups are Raising Money at a Breakneck Pace', *The Gazette*, 21 Apr. 2018, https://www.thegazette.com/subject/news/nation-and-world/chinese-investment-floods-us-biotech-20180421; Hui Li and Jonathan Browning: 'China Inc. Goes on a Buying Spree for Global Health Assets', *Bloomberg*, 5 July, 2016, https://www.bloomberg.com/news/articles/2016-07-05/china-inc-goes-on-a-buying-spree-for-global-healthcare-assets (10 Feb. 2021).

2. 'Gryphon Scientific and Rhodium Group presented a report: China's Biotechnology Development: The Role of US and Other Foreign Engagement,' https://www.uscc.gov/sites/default/files/ResearchUS-China%20Biotech%20Report.pdf (10 Feb. 2021).

9. ILLUMINA AND CRISPR

1. Quick, Josh: 'Real-time gene sequencing can help control—and may someday prevent—pandemics', 11 Sept, 2020, https://www.statnews.com/2020/09/11/real-time-gene-sequencing-can-help-control-and-may-someday-prevent-pandemics/ (10 Feb. 2021).

10. CHINA'S BIOTECHNOLOGY RACE

1. Kania, Elsa B., and Wilson Vorndick: 'Weaponizing Biotech: How China's Military Is Preparing for a "New Domain of Warfare"'. Defense One website, 14 Aug. 2019. https://www.defenseone.com/ideas/2019/08/chinas-military-pursuing-biotech/159167/ (10 Feb. 2021).

12. THE VIRUS HUNTERS

1. Carlson, Colin J.: 'From PREDICT to prevention, one pandemic later', the *Lancet*, Vol. 1, Issue 1, E6–E7, 1 May 2020, doi: https://doi.org/10.1016/S2666-5247(20)30002-1.

2. Source: Newsweek. Fred Guterl, Naveed Jamarli, Tom O'Connor *The Controversial experiments and the Wuhan Lab Suspected of Starting the Coronavirus Pandemic*. April 27, 2020.

13. THE MYSTERIOUS SARS OUTBREAK 2002–03

1. Vijgen, Leen, Els Keyaerts, Elien Moës, Inge Thoelen, Elke Wollants, Philippe Lemey, Anne-Mieke Vandamme, Marc Van Ranst: 'Complete Genomic Sequence of Human Coronavirus OC43: Molecular Clock Analysis Suggests a Relatively Recent Zoonotic Coronavirus Transmission Event', *Journal of Virology*, DOI: 10.1128/JVI.79.3.1595–1604.2005; German Center for Infection Research: 'Common cold viruses originated in camels, just like MERS'; its summary states: 'there are four globally endemic human coronaviruses which, together with the better known rhinoviruses, are responsible for causing common colds. Usually, infections with these viruses are harmless to humans. Researchers have now found the source of 'HCoV-229E,' one of the four common cold coronaviruses, to have originated in camels, just like the dreaded MERS virus', *Science Daily*, 18 Aug. 2016, www.sciencedaily.com/releases/ 2016/08/160818093438.htm (10 Feb. 2021); Victor M. Corman, Isabella Eckerle, et al.: 'Link of a ubiquitous human coronavirus to dromedary camels', *Proceedings of the National Academy of Sciences*, 30 Aug. 2016; 201604472 DOI: 10.1073/pnas.1604472113.

14. GOING BATS IN CHINA

1. Lau, Susanna K. P., Patrick C. Y. Woo, Kenneth S. M. Li, Yi Huang, Hoi-Wah Tsoi, Beatrice H. L. Wong, Samson S. Y. Wong, Suet-Yi Leung, Kwok-Hung Chan, Kwok-Yung Yuen: 'Severe acute respiratory syndrome coronavirus-like virus in Chinese horseshoe bats', *Proceedings of the National Academy of Sciences*, 16 Sept. 2005, DOI: doi.org/10.1073/ pnas.0506735102.

2. Zhou, P., et al: 'Discovery of a novel coronavirus associated with the recent pneumonia outbreak in humans and its potential bat origin', *Nature*, 3. Feb. 2020, DOI: 10.1038/s41586-020-2012-7.

3. Hou, Y., Peng, C., Yu, M. et al.: 'Angiotensin-converting enzyme 2 (ACE2) proteins of different bat species confer variable susceptibility to SARS-CoV entry', *Archives of Virology* 155, 1563-1569, 22 June 2010, https://doi.org/10.1007/s00705-010-0729-6.

4. Ge, X. Y., Li, J. L. Yang, X. L. et al.: 'Isolation and characterization of

a bat SARS-like coronavirus that uses the ACE2 receptor', *Nature*, 30 Oct. 2013, doi.org/10.1038/nature12711.

5. Ning Wang et al: 'Serological Evidence of Bat SARS-Related Coronavirus Infection in Humans, China', *Virologica Sin.*, Feb. 2018, DOI: 10.1007/s12250-018-0012-7.

6. Hongying Li et al.: 'Human-animal interactions and bat coronavirus spillover potential among rural residents in Southern China', *Biosafety and Health*, Vol. 1 Issue 2, pp. 84–90, Sept. 2019, DOI: org/10.1016/j.bsheal.2019.10.004.

15. THE STRANGE STORY OF FRANCE AND WUHAN'S BS4-LAB

1. Liu, H., Zhang, H. and Chen, D.: '"I make efforts, people make comments": Prof. H. Zanyin Gaw—pioneering the world, the trailblazer and founder of China's virology research', *Protein Cell* 6, 859–861, 2015, https://doi.org/10.1007/s13238-015-0227-4.

2. Leitenberg, M., Zilinskas, R. A.: *The Soviet Biological Weapons Program: A history*. Cambridge, MA: Harvard University Press, 2012.

3. Bouey, Jennifer: 'China's Health System Reform and Global Health Strategy in the Context of COVID-19'. Testimony presented before the U.S.-China Economic and Security Review Commission on 7 May 2020. Published by the RAND Corporation, Santa Monica, CA.

4. Walgate R.: 'SARS escaped Beijing lab twice', *Genome Biol.* 2004; 4:spotlight-20040427–03. Published 27 Apr. 2004, doi:10.1186/gb-spotlight-20040427–03.

Additional sources:

https://www.francetvinfo.fr/sante/maladie/coronavirus/covid-19-enquete-sur-le-p4-de-wuhan-ce-laboratoire-en-partie-finance-par-la-france-ou-a-ete-identifie-le-virus_3920783.html.

https://www.esmagazine.com/articles/94287-biosafety-ventilation-systems.

http://www.indiandefencereview.com/spotlights/covid-19-the-chinese-military-and-maj-gen-chen-wei/.

http://lssf.cas.cn/en/facilities-view.jsp?id=ff8080814ff56599014ff59e677e003d.

Izambard, Antoine: 'L'histoire secrète du laboratoire P4 de Wuhan vendu par la France à la Chine...' *Le Figaro* https://www.challenges.fr/entreprise/sante-et-pharmacie/revelations-l-histoire-secrete-du-laboratoire-p4-de-wuhan-vendu-par-la-france-a-la-chine_707425 (11 Feb. 2021).

Lasserre, Isabelle: 'Les inquiétants transferts de technologies de la France vers la Chine,' 5 May 2020, *Le Figaro*, https://www.lefigaro.fr/international/france-chine-les-liaisons-dangereuses-20200503 (11 Feb. 2021).

Han, M., Gu, J., Gao, G.F., and Liu, W.J. (2017). 'China in action: national strategies to combat against emerging infectious diseases.' *Sci China Life Sci* 60, 1383–1385. https://doi.org/10.1007/s11427-017-9141-3.

Reltien, Philippe: 'Le laboratoire P4 de Wuhan: une histoire française,' France Culture, https://www.franceculture.fr/sciences/le-laboratoire-p4-de-wuhan-une-histoire-francaise (11 Feb. 2021).

Website of Engineered Systems, https://www.esmagazine.com/articles/94287-biosafety-ventilation-systems (11 Feb. 2021).

5. Wu, F. et al.: A new coronavirus associated with human respiratory disease in China. *Nature* 3 Feb. 2020, https://doi. org/10.1038/s41586–020–2008–3 (2020)].

6. https://doi.org/10.1016/j.envint.2020.105964 Available online 14 July 2020. Published by Elsevier Ltd.

7. 'The Institute of Model Animals of Wuhan University, China,' *European Heart Journal*, Volume 37, Issue 43, 14 November 2016, Pages 3257–3259, https://doi.org/10.1093/eurheartj/ehw445].

16. LOOKING FOR A GAS LEAK WITH A LIGHTED MATCH

1. Subbaraman, Nidhi: '"Heinous!": Coronavirus researcher shut down for Wuhan-lab link slams new funding restrictions', Nature 21 Aug. 2020, https://www.nature.com/articles/d41586–020–02473–4 (11 Feb. 2021).

2. Piplani, Sakshi, et al.: 'In silico comparison of spike protein-ACE2 binding affinities across species; significance for the possible origin of the SARS-CoV-2 virus', 21 Nov. 2020, https://arxiv.org/abs/2005.06199 (11 Feb, 2021).

3. Hu B., Zeng L. P., Yang X. L., et al.: 'Discovery of a rich gene pool of

bat SARS-related coronaviruses provides new insights into the origin of SARS coronavirus', *PLoS Pathog*, 2017;13(11):e1006698, 30 Nov. 2017, doi:10.1371/journal.ppat.1006698.

4. Ibid.

5. 'Using the reverse genetics technique we previously developed for WIV1 [23], we constructed a group of infectious bacterial artificial chromosome (BAC) clones with the backbone of WIV1 and variants of S genes from 8 different bat SARSr-CoVs. Only the infectious clones for Rs4231 and Rs7327 led to cytopathic effects in Vero E6 cells after transfection (S7 Fig). The other six strains with deletions in the RBD region, Rf4075, Rs4081, Rs4085, Rs4235, As6526 and Rp3 (S1 Fig) failed to be rescued, as no cytopathic effects was observed and viral replication cannot be detected by immunofluorescence assay in Vero E6 cells (S7 Fig). In contrast, when Vero E6 cells were respectively infected with the two successfully rescued chimeric SARSr-CoVs, WIV1-Rs4231S and WIV1-Rs7327S, and the newly isolated Rs4874, efficient virus replication was detected in all infections (Fig 7).'

6. Addendum to: *Nature* https://doi.org/10.1038/s41586-020-2012-7 published online 03 February 2020.

7. Liu P., Jiang J.-Z., Wan X.-F., Hua Y., Li L., Zhou J. et al.: 'Are pangolins the intermediate host of the 2019 novel coronavirus (SARS-CoV-2)?', 2020, *PLoS Pathog* 16(5): e1008421. https://doi.org/10.1371/journal.ppat.1008421.

8. 'This week in virology' no. 591, 15 March 2020, https://www.microbe.tv/twiv/twiv-591/.

9. Yount, Boyd, et al.: 'Reverse genetics with a full-length infectious cDNA of severe acute respiratory syndrome coronavirus', *PNAS*, 28 Oct. 2020, doi.org/10.1073/pnas.1735582100.

10. Hong Zhou et al.: 'A close relative of SARS-CoV-2 found in bats offers more evidence it evolved naturally', *Cell Press*, 11 May 2020, DOI: https://doi.org/10.1016/j.cub.2020.05.023.

11. Hu D., Zhu C., Ai L. et al.: 'Genomic characterization and infectivity of a novel SARS-like coronavirus in Chinese bats', *Emerging Microbes and Infections*, Vol. 7(1):154, pp. 1–10, 12 Sept. 2018, doi:10.1038/s41426-018-0155-5; Yan, Li-Meng, Kang, Shu; Guan, Jie; Hu,

Shanchang: 'Unusual Features of the SARS-CoV-2 Genome Suggesting Sophisticated Laboratory Modification Rather Than Natural Evolution and Delineation of Its Probable Synthetic Route', 14 Sept. 2020, DOI: 10.5281/zenodo.4028830; Hu, Dan et al: 'Genomic characterization and infectivity of a novel SARS-like coronavirus in Chinese bats', *Emerging Microbes and Infections* (2018) 7:154, DOI 10.1038/s41426-018-0155-5 www.nature.com/emi.

12. Yan, Li-Meng, Kang, Shu; Guan, Jie; Hu, Shanchang: 'Unusual Features of the SARS-CoV-2 Genome Suggesting Sophisticated Laboratory Modification Rather Than Natural Evolution and Delineation of Its Probable Synthetic Route', 14 Sept. 2020, DOI: 10.5281/ zenodo.4028830.

13. Qiu, Jane: 'How China's 'Bat Woman' Hunted Down Viruses from SARS to the New Coronavirus', *Scientific American*, 1 June 2020, https://www.scientificamerican.com/article/how-chinas-bat-woman-hunted-down-viruses-from-sars-to-the-new-coronavirus1/?fbclid= IwAR0ZFPmkgMfZEQPd3RPYTlaeAuQadQTTF8qbtvHXW1ogrt PJMa 1gAqYijEk (11 Feb. 2021).

17. SECRECY STOPPED CHINA'S DISEASE CONTROL CENTRE FROM DOING ITS JOB

1. Session 5 Part 2: Gao, 28 Aug. 2015, https://www.youtube.com/ watch?v=INrz0Eri5Ow.

2. Pages, Jeremy, Lingling Wei: 'China's CDC Stumbled When it Mattered Most', *Wall Street Journal*, 17 Aug. 2020, https://www.wsj.com/articles/chinas-cdc-built-to-stop-pandemics-stumbled-when-it-mattered-most-11597675108 (11 Feb. 2021).

3. Kang, Dake: 'China Testing Blunders stemmed from secret deals with firms', Associated Press, 3 Dec. 2020, https://apnews.com/article/china-virus-testing-secret-deals-firms-312f4a953e0264a3645219a08c62a0ad (11 Feb. 2021).

18. 'IT'S ALL FAKE': CONFUSION AND DECEPTION IN WUHAN

1. Ibid.

2. Nick Paton Walsh: 'The Wuhan Files: Leaked Documents reveal China's mishandling of the early stages of COVID-19', CNN.

3. Kinetz, Erika: 'Five million were able to flee Wuhan before it was put under quarantine', Associated Press, 9 Feb. 2020, https://apnews.com/article/c42eabe1b1e1ba9fcb2ce201cd3abb72 (11 Feb. 2021).
4. Su, Alice: 'Xi Jinping visits Wuhan As China declares success in battle against coronavirus'. *Los Angeles Times*, 10 March 2020, https://www.latimes.com/world-nation/story/2020-03-10/xi-jinping-visits-wuhan-china-declares-success-fight-against-coronavirus (11 Feb. 2021).
5. 'Wuhan virus patient numbers manipulated for Xi visit: Local doctor', *Kyodo News*, 19 March 2020, https://english.kyodonews.net/news/2020/03/b09b868ec468-breaking-news-wuhan-doctor-blows-whistle-on-manipulation-of-virus-patient-numbers.html (11 Feb. 2021).
6. Li, Li et al.: 'Influenza-associated excess respiratory mortality in China, 2010–15: a population-based study', *the Lancet Public Health*, Vol. 4, Issue 9, e473–e481, doi.org/10.1016/S2468-2667(19)30163-X.

19. CHINA AND THE WORLD HEALTH ORGANISATION

1. 'China delayed releasing coronavirus information, frustrating WHO', Associated Press, 2 June 2020, https://apnews.com/article/3c061794970661042b18d5aeaaed9fae (11 Feb. 2021).
2. Ibid.
3. 'China didn't warn public of likely pandemic for 6 key days', Associated Press, 15 Apr. 2020, https://apnews.com/article/68a9e1b91de4ffc166acd6012d82c2f9 (11 Feb. 2021).
4. 'China delayed releasing coronavirus information, frustrating WHO', Associated Press, 2 June 2020, https://apnews.com/article/3c061794970661042b18d5aeaaed9fae (11 Feb. 2021).
5. Relman, David A.: 'Opinion: To stop the next pandemic, we need to unravel the origins of COVID-19', *Proceedings of the National Academy of Sciences*, 24 Nov. 2020, 117(47) 29246-29248, DOI:10.1073/pnas.2021133117.

20. PANIC AND DISSENT IN WUHAN

1. Crete-Nishihata, Masashi, Jakub Dalek, Jeffrey Knockel, Nicola Lawford, Caroline Wesley, and Mari Zhou: 'Censored Contagion II: A Timeline of Information Control on Chinese Social Media During COVID-19',

The Citizen Lab, 25 Aug. 2020, https://citizenlab.ca/2020/08/censored-contagion-ii-a-timeline-of-information-control-on-chinese-social-media-during-covid-19/ (11 Feb. 2021).

2. Spectator magazine, 19 Oct. 2020, https://twitter.com/davidnabarro; #SpectatorTV https://youtu.be/x8oH7cBxgwE?t=915.

3. Newey, Sarah: 'Top WHO disease detective warns against return to national lock downs', *Daily Telegraph*, 1 August 2020, https://www.telegraph.co.uk/global-health/science-and-disease/exclusive-top-disease-detective-warns-against-return-national/ (11 Feb. 2021).

4. CNBC: 'Cuomo says it's shocking that most new coronavirus hospitalisations are people who have been staying at home', 6 May 2020, https://www.cnbc.com/2020/05/06/ny-gov-cuomo-says-its-shocking-most-new-coronavirus-hospitalizations-are-people-staying-home.html (11 Feb. 2021).

5. Nakazawa, Katsuji: 'Campaign to Thank Xi Jinping flatly rejected by Wuhan Citizens', *Nikkei Asia*, 12 March 2020, https://asia.nikkei.com/Editor-s-Picks/China-up-close/Campaign-to-thank-Xi-Jinping-flatly-rejected-by-Wuhan-citizens (11 Feb. 2021).

6. Denyer, Simon, and Joel Achenbach: 'Researchers ponder why COV-19 appears deadlier in the US and Europe than in Asia', *Washington Post*, 28 May 2020, https://www.washingtonpost.com/world/researchers-ponder-why-covid-appears-more-deadly-in-the-us-and-europe-than-in-asia/2020/05/26/81889d06–8a9f-11ea-9759–6d20ba0f2c0e_story.html (11 Feb. 2021).

7. Ibid.

8. Smith, Nicola: 'Vietnam Miracle Escape from COVID may be down to "natural immunity"', *Daily Telegraph*, 1 Aug. 2020, https://www.telegraph.co.uk/news/2020/08/01/vietnam-miracle-escape-covid-may-natural-immunity/ (11 Feb. 2021).

9. Graham-Harrison, Emma, and Robin McKie: 'A year after Wuhan Alarm, China seeks to change COVID origin story', *The Observer*, 29 Nov. 2020, theguardian.com/world/2020/nov/29/a-year-after-wuhan-alarm-china-seeks-to-change-covid-origin-story (11 Feb. 2021).

10. Dake Kang, Maria Cheng and Sam McNeil: 'China Clamps down in hidden hunt for corona virus origins,' Associated Press, 30 Dec. 2020, https://apnews.com/article/united-nations-coronavirus-pandemic-

china-only-on-ap-bats-24fbadc58cee3a40bca2ddf7a14d2955 (11 Feb. 2021).

21. CONCLUSIONS

1. Rozo, M., Gronvall, G. K.: 'The Reemergent 1977 H1N1 Strain and the Gain-of-Function Debate,' *mBio*, 6(4):e01013-15, 18 Aug 2005, doi:10.1128/mBio.01013-15.

INDEX

INDEX

INDEX

INDEX

INDEX

INDEX

INDEX

INDEX

INDEX

INDEX

INDEX

INDEX

INDEX

INDEX

INDEX

INDEX

INDEX

INDEX

INDEX

INDEX

INDEX

INDEX

INDEX

.